CONFUSING REALITIES

Bernardine J. Ensink

CONFUSING REALITIES

A study on child sexual abuse and psychiatric symptoms

VU University Press
Amsterdam 1992

The Nederlandse organisatie voor
wetenschappelijk onderzoek (NWO)
has made a financial contribution to
the publication of this book.

VU University Press is an imprint of:
VU Boekhandel/Uitgeverij bv
De Boelelaan 1105
1081 HV Amsterdam
The Netherlands
Tel. (020) - 644 43 55
Fax (020) - 646 27 19

Cover illustration: Bernardine J. Ensink
Printed by: Wilco bv, Amersfoort

Isbn   90-5383-085-5
Nugi   662

Opgedragen aan mijn moeder, wier
raadselachtig functioneren mij een
lange reis langs verschillende
onderwerpen in de psychologie heeft
doen maken en aan Jan en Berik.

Acknowledgments

This study has been performed at the Department of Psychology of the University of Amsterdam, in cooperation with Francine Albach, and was made possible by a special allocation for women studies. Professor Nico H. Frijda gave me the possibility to work in an inspiring, sometimes exciting, intellectual environment. I want to thank him for all the discussions we had and for close reading of the manuscript. Professor Walter Everaerd's support has been growing during the progress of the research. His encouragement and enthusiasm were a great help to me. After the fieldwork of the study, Francine Albach elaborated our findings about post-traumatic stress disorders and 'hysterical complaints', while I focussed on dissociative disturbances and self-destructive behaviour.

In our study 100 women participated who, as a child, were sexually abused. Above all, I want to thank these anonymous women, who voluntarily cooperated in the project.

At the start phase, we discussed our research questions with 'Stichting Tegen Haar Wil', especially Bernardette and Gonnie, and 'Stichting De Maan', especially Ingrid Foeken. These discussions have influenced the direction the study has taken.

Our project, as it has been performed, would not have been possible without the help of Judith Rothen, Ineke Jonkers, Nelleke Nicolai, Ineke Fabery-de Jonge, Margot van der Linden, Ingrid Foeken, Joke Groenenweg, and Stichting Tegen Haar Wil. They brought our study to the attention of women with a history of child sexual abuse.

Jaap van Heerden, Marius Romme, Onno van der Hart, Suzette Boon, Marjan van Egmond, Nicole Muller, Beulah MacNab, and Simone De Vries indicated to me major publications. These publications constitute the building blocks of this book. Our questionnaire was commented by Suzette Boon, Nelleke Nicolai, Willeke Beezemer, Ingrid Foeken, Frits Bruinsma and Herwig Schacht. By their contributions the interviews were improved and more reliable data were obtained. Methodological advice on specific areas was given by Harry Vorst and Peter Molenaar.

Greta Noordenbos, Rie van Rijswijk, Hetty Rombouts and Bob Bermond were always willing to support me in complicated matters concerning the general project. And at the time of the fieldwork of this study, I could rely on my friends Madeleine van Drunen and Faridah Zwanikken.

Initial versions of the chapters were commented by Lydia Vorrink, Greta Noordenbos, Rie van Rijswijk, Hetty Rombouts, Faridah Zwanikken, and Frank van Balen.

I am very glad, that Beulah MacNab was willing to help me in formulating my texts in proper English. Her corrections gave the text in some chapters a more fluent character. The final correction of the English text was performed by Hans Rothuizen.

The interviews were typed out, amongst others, by Monique van Drunen, Ursela, Peter and Jan Visschers, and Francine Visser.

Last, but not least, I want to mention the support of Jan Visschers, who sometimes in the middle of the night, would go to his Institute to print an initial version of a chapter. He informed me about matters concerning the computer and always detected too many imperfections in my texts.

Contents

Chapter 1

Frame of reference

1.1 Introduction

In our study almost one hundred women participated who as a child experienced sexual abuse at the hands of elder family-members or family-friends. Five case histories, more or less exemplary of all those reported, will be presented below.

Nelly (F12)[1] comes from a religious and stable working class family. Her mother used to clean the house of a catholic priest and she would often help her mother. On Sundays he used to visit their home. At the age of ten the priest started to kiss her in a passionate way. When she grew older they lay down and he masturbated. They never had intercourse. Until she was eighteen years old these sexual activities took place at least once a week. Nelly told: 'The sexual acts I found disgusting, but I was pleased with the attention and affection I got from him, he made me feel very special. He paid for my school books and for my musical education'. However, the secret became a big burden, it made her feel alone and isolated. Nelly often went to church to pray to God. She never dared to tell her parents nor anybody else what happened. She was afraid they would blame her, because priests could not have any sexual feelings, she thought. By isolating herself and by praying to God the secret lost somewhat of its danger. When she grew older, she entered a convent where the priest came to visit her. After she left the nunnery the secret was broken. Then she found out that this priest had sexually abused her sister too.

Betty (B7) grew up in a well to do family. Her father owned an apartment in the city where he was working, and only spent weekends in the small town where his family lived. The family had a nurse to take care of the children. When father came home, mother preferably dined alone with him. Betty couldn't get on with her mother. Her seven year older brother regularly approached her sexually from seven to nine years and once more when she was thirteen years of

---

[1] All names are fictitious. To guarantee anonymity in our study the women were given case-numbers. The numbers (B7 or F12) refer to these case-numbers.

age. In general, this brother caused much trouble in the family. She said: 'my mother could not handle the children. My older brother (the one who abused her sexually) used to tease me and fight with me. Once he locked me up in the ward-robe and another time he locked me out of the house, while it was snowing and I was bare footed. He held me out of the window on the second stock only grasping my ankles. He used to put his hands around my throat or held my head under water. At night when I felt afraid I used to lie down with the dog, but I also went to my brother. It is strange, but in spite of his teasing he was the only one who paid attention to me. When I came to him at night he was very protecting and this is how it started. Sexual contact was not bad and I agreed it did not hurt me. He never was aggressive during sexual contact. In a way I was glad, because those activities gave me some binding, a secret, with somebody. On the other hand morals regarding sexuality made me feel bad. You are considered to be a slut when you are not a virgin. At least this is what they said at primary school and my brothers and sisters also commented on girls in this way. I thought everybody could see I was not a virgin any more. I felt a pariah, because my menses didn't come, I knew this was the punishment from God for my sins. Once when I was thirteen, my brother came home, grasped me and really screwed me, afterwards he said to me 'good girl'. Much later he tried to restore our relation by paying my studies at an academy, which my parents refused to pay. He also paid my journeys and introduced me in a friendly way to his wife and friends. I still do not feel like telling it to my parents. I know what their reaction will be: they will either blame him or me. I do not blame him. I think it is my parents' fault, my brother had such an awful youth himself and now he is trying to make the best out of it'.

Janny's (B40) father and her mother both had high-qualified jobs and they arranged many educative activities with their four children. To an outsider her family looked like a 'model-family'. When she was a small child her father used to touch her between her legs in a special way. At the age of seven her father came to her in the middle of the night and asked her to help him with masturbation. He did not come often, because usually he went to her three year older sister. When she was thirteen years her father came to her more frequently, because her sister had got a boyfriend. From that moment on her father had intercourse with her. Neither he nor she used any anti-conception, but she never gave a thought to the possibility of becoming pregnant. It seemed to her that the father who came during the night was different from the father during the day-time, they never talked at night. When she resisted he did not dare to protest, but the days after her resistance he used to be bad-tempered and really provoking to everybody in the family. Her mother and sisters would ask Janny to make it up with daddy. They never asked her the reason for daddy's bad temper and how she could make it up. She couldn't stand these pressures exerted on her. At the age of 17, she left home for further education. Her parents gave her everything she needed like her own car, but they insisted on her coming home every week-end. Sometimes Janny refused to go to her parents and went to the place of a girl-friend. If so, her parents came to take her away from that place, made a big quarrel and brought her home again. She did not find ways of escaping this situation, she tried hard not to think about it and studied all the time. The incest ended when she met her current husband at the age of 27. She had to break all contacts with her parents in order to escape from the situation. After a while, a younger sister who was still living with her parents, ran away and came to her home. Her sister stayed in her place for one week, and then their parents came, while Janny was working. Her sister let them into the apartment, and when Janny came home that day, everything had been ruined or taken away.

Fien (B25) was the oldest of five children in a working class family. The marriage between her father and mother was bad. Her father used to assault her mother. As a small child she often could not sleep, because she was afraid that father would kill mother. She always felt she had to protect mother and mother confided all her problems to her. Father used to beat Fien too and she was frightened of him. When she was ten years old father started the sexual abuse. This abuse was sadistic of character. For instance, he often held a hot poker to her naked buttocks and if she screamed he laughed and got sexually excited. He used to put his hands around her throat in such a way that she would feel suffocated. At the age of fifteen years she became pregnant at the same time that her mother expected a baby. Her father hated pregnant women and treated her as dirt. She saw her mother busy with soap-suds to provoke an abortion and she also tried to provoke an abortion in such a way. Nonetheless at a certain moment a child was born in the presence of her father and mother. She saw the child only for a short moment and felt confounded the baby already was that big. She did and still does not know what happened to the baby. She never dared to ask her mother, although they still have a regular and close contact. When she got a boy-friend at sixteen years of age, she threatened her father with disclosure if the raping would not stop. She married at the age of 17 and lived with her family-in-law for another seven years.

Wendy (F38) was born in a refuge for one-parent families. When she was 6 months old her mother started living with her stepfather. This man did seasonal work and regularly had no job. She got a sister, when she was twelve. Her mother was frequently ill, so Wendy had to take care of the baby. She was often absent from school. Her stepfather regularly assaulted her mother and she tried to protect her mother against him. Sexual abuse started, as far as she can remember, when she was five and it lasted until she was thirteen years old. Initially he abused her sexually when they were alone. When she grew older he 'invited' his friends. These 'friends', sometimes three of them, raped her, used to strap her and afterwards gave a bottle of genever to her stepfather. Sometimes she was raped in the shed, sometimes her stepfather put his hands around her throat and she was afraid to be killed. He allowed his 'friends' to rape her as a punishment, because she regularly avoided to come home from school. He hit her with a carpet-beater, and warned her not to disclose it to any-body. He and 'his friends' raped her once more when she was 24. Her younger sister, twelve years old at that time, told Wendy that father had threatened to rape her. Wendy became very angry and went to visit her stepfather. She said 'I thought he would be at home alone, but he was there with three of his friends. They strapped me and the four men raped me'. Together with her mother and her sister she fled to a refuge shelter for women, to hide from the stepfather. They got a new house together and mother still lives with her and her children together in one home. From the gang-rape Wendy got pregnant and she takes care of this child now.

Most women who told us about their childhood have been severely traumatized. If the five case histories would have been reported in a study on a sample of the general population, they would all have been considered to be of a severe character. But, in our study these histories represent a continuum of severity of traumatization.

Similar histories of severe traumatization can be found in psycho-therapeutic and psychiatric communities, (Herman, Russell, & Trocki, 1986). Certain (American and Canadian) studies indicate that in those communities more than half of the female patients experienced physical or sexual or both types of abuses as a child, (Carmen, Rieker, & Mills, 1984; Brière and Runtz, 1986; Bryer, Nelson, Miller, & Krol, 1987; Chu and Dill, 1990; Brière and Zaidi, 1989).

1.2 Developments in research on child sexual abuse

Many discussions have been devoted to the question of how to define child sexual abuse, (Finkelhor, 1979; Draijer, 1985; Wyatt and Peters, 1986; Finkelhor, 1986). Several criteria are considered to be important in this respect. The debate centres around topics as the child's age at the start of the incidents, the type of sexual events involved, the coercion applied, or the age difference between child and perpetrator, (Finkelhor, 1986, p.22-27). At present all relevant considerations seem to have been put forward. Although the dispute may continue for some time we do not expect new criteria to be formulated. In our study child sexual abuse is defined by the following criteria: (a) sexual events include bodily contact with primary or secondary genital zones, (b) they are experienced by girls of fifteen years or younger, (c) sexual acts are committed by family-members or family-friends who are at least five years older than the girl.

The central question of our study concerns the connection between child sexual abuse and psychiatric symptoms. Over the last fifteen years many studies have been published on the psychological impact of child sexual abuse. The early studies have the character of personal documents, like the study 'Kiss Daddy Goodnight' by Louise Armstrong (1978) and 'Conspiracy of Silence' by Sandra Butler (1978) and in the Netherlands 'The penalty for silence lasts a life-time' by the Incest-Survival Groups (1983)[2], and Imbens and Jonker's study 'Religion and Incest' (1985)[3]. Soon these publications were followed by influential articles and books written by therapists treating women with histories of child sexual abuse: Herman (1981), Gelinas (1981, 1983), Goodwin (1982), Summit (1983), and in the Netherlands Lichtenburcht, Bezemer & Gianotten (1986), Albach (1986), Rijnaarts (1987), and Foeken (1987). In these publications, theories, deduced from systematic observations, are presented about the impact of child sexual abuse.

Although these studies had an enormous emotional impact, they were also criticised. Personal documents and clinical observations do not fulfil scientific requirements well enough to allow reliable statements on the impact of child sexual abuse. Many authors stressed the importance of a rigid and sound research methodology in searching questions as 'do women with a history of child sexual abuse have more symptoms than women without such a history?' or 'do women with a history of child sexual abuse show special symptoms?', (Meiselman, 1980; Mrazek and Mrazek, 1981; Conte, 1985; Finkelhor, 1986; Haugaard, 1988).

In the next stage the design of research projects met the requirements of a strict and sound methodology. These projects were performed with samples drawn from the general population or control-groups were used. Besides, most projects incorporated standardized instruments for measuring psychological symptoms. Within ten years after the publication of the first personal document, in 1986, Browne and Finkelhor could already review results of 14 research projects on psychological impact of child sexual abuse, all using a sound research methodology. Since then almost an equal number of studies has been performed.

The speed at which the impact of child sexual abuse has been examined is incredibly high. However, it also shows that not much time has been devoted yet to the more fundamental questions. One of the main problems researchers always have to tackle concerns the way of reducing information, because a study can not be reported by merely giving all the case histories. This means that from all characteristics of child abuse and all possible psychological impacts, researchers have to choose the relevant ones. One may select control-groups and standard instruments in an adequate way, but did one choose the relevant characteristics? Ignoring these fundamental questions has sometimes given rise to remarkable speculations. One example in this respect concerns the categorisation of child sexual abuse. As described above, Browne and Finkelhor (1986) made an

---

[2] Vereniging Tegen Sexuele Kindermishandeling: De straf op zwijgen is levenslang.

[3] Godsdienst en Incest.

extensive review of all studies on impacts of child sexual abuse with a sound research methodology. In this review, they evaluated the relations found among differential characteristics of child sexual abuse and psychological impacts. At the same time they proposed, in order to get a better understanding of the psychological impacts, to categorise the histories of child sexual abuse in a different way than usual[4], (Finkelhor and Browne, 1986; Finkelhor, 1987). In our opinion not only a sound methodology, and a good categorisation, but also theories are needed when the connections among characteristics of child sexual abuse and psychological symptoms are to be understood.

Typically most authors review previous studies on the subject, before designing a new project. In the early eighties one finds lists with a variety of psychological symptoms that were found to be associated with child sexual abuse, (Justice and Justice, 1976; Mrazek and Mrazek, 1981). These lists gave the impression that the impact of child sexual abuse is rather 'unspecific'. In general, child sexual abuse was thought to induce stress, and the diversity of personal coping strategies with stress was thought to result in a spectrum of complaints[5]. Another conceptualization proposed by Summit (1983) and Brière and Runtz (1986) specifies respectively a 'child sexual abuse accommodation syndrome' and a 'child sexual abuse syndrome'. In an elegantly designed study Brière and Runtz demonstrated that women with a history of child sexual abuse tend to report specific clusters of symptoms. Their 'child sexual abuse syndrome' consist of symptoms as dissociation, sleep disturbance, alienation, sexual difficulties, tension, anger and self-destruction.

The debate on impacts of child sexual abuse changed direction again after the consistent findings that within psychiatric communities more than half of the female patients as a child have experienced physical or sexual or both types of abuses, (Carmen, Rieker, & Mills, 1984; Bryer, Nelson, Miller, & Krol, 1987; Chu and Dill, 1990: Brière and Zaidi, 1989). Nowadays the debate centres on the spectrum of psychiatric syndromes associated with child sexual abuse. Several kinds of psychiatric diagnoses are thought to be important in this respect: the post-traumatic stress disorders, the dissociative disorders, the panic disorders, and somatoform disorders (diagnosis on Axis I in D.S.M.-III-R) and the borderline personality disorder (diagnosis on Axis II in D.S.M.-III-R). Extreme dissociative disorders are thought to represent an adaptation to very severe

---

[4] Finkelhor and Browne (1986) propose a model for a better understanding of the psychological impact of child sexual abuse. In this model they specify four traumagenic dynamics: sexualization, stigmatization, betrayal and powerlessness. They suggest that a categorisation of the abuse history according to these dynamics will offer a better understanding of the psychological impact. Unfortunately, most of these categories are formulated in unclear terms.

[5] Draijer's study implicitly departs from this conceptualization (Draijer 1988, 1990). In the research design of Draijer (1988) all psychological symptoms measured, such as the symptoms list of SCL-90, self-injury, suicidality, sexual alienation etc, are simply added and no differentiation is made between different kinds of psycho-pathology.

childhood abuse, borderline character disorder is thought to be an 'intermediate' adaptation and panic and somatoform disorders are thought to represent an adaptation to more circumscribed traumatic events, (van der Kolk and van der Hart 1989). For an extensive review of this debate we refer to Courtois (1988, p.142-162).

We have chosen to concentrate on psychiatric symptoms and not on psychiatric diagnostic categories. Typically, diagnostic categories are based on observations of psychiatrists that a particular cluster of symptoms can often be found. But, many studies have shown that questions about reliability, construct validity and predictor validity of psychiatric syndromes are rarely met in a satisfactory way, (Bentall 1991).

1.3 The aim of the study

Our study departs from the viewpoint that connections between child (sexual) abuse and particular psychiatric symptoms have already been rather well established. For instance, several studies have shown that women who were sexually abused as a child are more inclined to attempt suicide than women without such a history. Such findings however do not immediately provide insight in why this relation exists. Does a history of child sexual abuse in general increase the vulnerability of women for suicidal behaviour? Does child sexual abuse with particular characteristics increase the risk of suicidal behaviour? Which theory or combination of theories contributes most to the understanding of suicidality in women who were sexually abused as a child? The aim of our research is to investigate such questions in more detail.

The central question of this study is: are different characteristics of child (sexual) abuse associated with different psychiatric symptoms in adult life? The primary practical aim of this study is to gather information useful for therapists treating women who experienced sexual abuse as a child. Women with such a history who ask therapy or are admitted to medical or psychiatric hospitals, may indirectly profit from these insights.

Only women participated in our study. This limitation had a practical reason. According to certain studies boys experience sexual abuse less frequently and predominantly outside the family context, (Finkelhor 1979). Men are also less inclined to admit or openly discuss these experiences. Moreover, if men and women have experienced similar types of sexual abuse as a child, they still tend to differ with respect to certain typical psychological problems in adult life, (Carmen, Rieker, & Mills, 1984).

In studying the impact of child (sexual) abuse one touches the core of many psychological theories, that will be attended to in more detail, in the following chapters of this report. Findings of our study may be useful in further development of several psychological concepts, notions and models of the human mind.

The central question of our study implies selection of the psychological impacts relevant to be examined. It seems to be of little use to select psychological problems many people have or women who were sexually abused as a child all may have, like sexual problems or problems in relationships. For this reason it was decided to focus on problems that generally are considered to be psychiatric symptoms. From all symptoms ascribed to child sexual abuse, those belonging to four problem areas have been chosen: *dissociative disturbances in consciousness, hallucinations, self-injury and suicidality.*

In some of these problem areas the connections with child sexual abuse are rather well established. Several studies report connections between child (sexual) abuse and dissociative disturbances, self-injury or suicidality. In appendices 5-1, 7-1 and 8-1, recent studies on child (sexual) abuse and these symptoms are summarised. Hardly any systematic studies have been performed on child sexual abuse and hallucinatory phenomena, but studies on dissociative disturbances do report auditory hallucinations in relation to childhood traumatization, see appendix 6-1.

1.4 General considerations on the impact of child sexual abuse

Some individuals are able to express very lucidly what has happened when they were a child and how it influenced their psychological functioning. Such information should be regarded with care. In psychology, self report is almost always a starting-point for systematic compilation of information. Self-report may have an important heuristic value, but it can not be considered as providing sufficient information by itself. If connections exist between (characteristics of) child (sexual) abuse and psychiatric symptoms in adult life, nobody will assume that these always have to be conscious. On the contrary, most psychological theories suggest that if such psychological connections exist, they tend to be unconscious. This suggests that guesses and wrong inferences about connections between child sexual abuse and symptoms are to be expected. In the life of one individual two experiences, like child sexual abuse and psychological symptoms in adult life, may be accidentally and not causally related. Systematic exploration and statistical analysis of information gathered about the lives of many women is necessary to elucidate the (lack of) experienced connection between a history of child sexual abuse and psychological functioning.

If such relations are found, this does not necessarily imply that childhood history has caused these problems. One might also assume that the psychological functioning in adult life influences recall processes. For instance, in a depressive mood state parental attitudes are recalled as being more rejecting and unloving than in a non-depressive mood state. We tried to decrease the risk of such mood distortions in recall processes by inquiring as much as possible after facts characterising child sexual abuse.

The childhood incidents are presented as seen through the eyes of adult women. This choice limits the scope of our study. We did not obtain records from perpetrators, mothers or other members of the family. Of course an individual reports his or her own point of view. When such abuses are reported to the police and brought to court, the viewpoints of all parties involved must be examined to assess the 'truth', to come to a final conclusion. But, even to the court the task to assess the 'truth' for a single case is very complicated, because all witness have their own concerns. In this investigation the concern of the child, as seen through the eyes of adult women, is taken as the most important point of departure.

1.5 The design of the book

A selection of all the results obtained during our investigation is reported in this book. This publication contains four chapters concerning the four selected psychiatric symptoms introduced above. In general these chapters are constructed in the following way: a summary is given of research findings about the connection between child sexual abuse and a particular psychiatric symptom; a synopsis describes the most important theories concerning the connection between child sexual abuse and that symptom; assumptions are deduced from these theories; the validity of the research inquiries is evaluated; a description is given of the phenomenology of the psychiatric symptom; statistical analyses are performed in order to investigate the assumptions formulated. Finally theoretical and practical implications of the findings are summarised and discussed.

We have chosen to present relevant theories in close connection with the information obtained, because these theories have been our guide in investigating and selecting the data. An exception has been made for the theories on dissociation. Dissociation theories are rather complex, have often been discussed and are progressing rapidly. So, a separate chapter has been devoted to dissociation theories.

Most chapters are written in a such a way, that they can be read on their own, but for a better understanding of the data presented we refer to the chapters 'Research design' and 'Family dynamics and characteristics of child sexual abuse'.

In Chapter 2 the research design is presented. The chapter contains information on the methodological issues, such as the reliability of childhood memories; the research strategy, such as the construction of the questionnaire; the gathering and coding of information, such as the coding of interviews; detailed information of certain significant measures used, such as the construction of a cumulative trauma-score. Finally demographic and child sexual abuse characteristics of women participating in this research are compared with those in other relevant studies.

Chapter 3 deals with the fluctuating interests in dissociative disorders; our choice of dissociative disorders as 'disturbances in consciousness' is elucidated; it presents certain historical notions on the concept of consciousness; it discusses modern insights in the unity and continuity of consciousness; a distinction is made between dissociative disturbances in consciousness and other unconscious mental processes; the dissociative disturbances in modern psychiatry are presented; and insights from cognitive psychology are applied to redefine certain dissociative concepts used in psychiatry. This chapter forms the theoretical background for information presented in chapter 5 about childhood trauma and dissociation and chapter 6 about childhood trauma and hallucinatory experiences.

In Chapter 4 the family context and relevant characteristics of child sexual abuse are described. Information is given about the family context in which child sexual abuse occurred, such as the relation between perpetrator and child preceding sexual abuse. Several characteristics of child sexual abuse are presented, such as age of onset of sexual abuse, type of perpetrator, intrusiveness of sexual acts and pregnancy resulting from child sexual abuse. Special attention is given to means of coercion applied by the perpetrator and the factors associated with severe aggression. Child sexual abuse is mostly supposed to be something between one perpetrator and one child, but sexual networks were found to be rather common.

Chapter 5 starts with a presentation of theories and findings about 'severe' trauma (during childhood) and dissociative reactions. Theories and observations led to several assumptions on characteristics of childhood trauma and level of dissociation. Difficulties confronted when inquiring about 'unconscious' experiences are explained. Statements about severe disturbances in consciousness are presented, because we think they may have a heuristic value. Statistical analyses are performed in order to investigate the formulated assumptions. Finally the implications of the findings are discussed.

Chapter 6 begins with the confusion around the diagnosis of schizophrenia and of multiple personality disorder and this problem is evaluated against the general difficulties in distinguishing meaningful psychiatric syndromes. Hallucinations are conceived as symptoms to be studied on their own. A synopsis is given of several theories about the relation between trauma and hallucinations. These theories have led to assumptions that are investigated and discussed. Moreover, a description is given of the hallucinatory experiences, as some of those reports may have a heuristic value.

In Chapter 7 the relation between self-injury and psychiatric diagnoses is presented. Theories about the psychological mechanism linking childhood trauma to self-injury are discussed and assumptions are formulated. The phenomenology of self-injurious behaviour gets ample attention. The formulated assumptions are investigated by statistical analyses. The chapter concludes with a discussion about the implications of the findings.

Chapter 8 deals with childhood trauma and suicidality. Although self-injury and suicidality are both considered to be expressions of self-destruction that can be explained by similar psycho-dynamics, different theoretical models also exist. From these theoretical models assumptions are deduced and investigated. At the end of the chapter findings are summarised, evaluated and discussed.

Albach (in press) will present data on post-traumatic stress and 'hysteria'.

Chapter 2

Research design

2.1 Introduction

In this chapter several methodological issues are considered. Section 2-2 starts with a discussion of problems concerning the reliability of childhood memories (2-2-1), and the selection of relevant psychological symptoms in adult life (2-2-2). Research strategies, like the recruitment of women with a history of child sexual abuse (2-3-1, 2-3-2) and the construction of the questionnaire (2-3-3), were based on an analysis of the reliability of childhood memory. The course of the actual interview and how women were recruited is described in sections (2-4-1) and (2-4-2). Information on coding procedures of the interview is given in section (2-4-3). An inter-judge agreement concerning statements of dissociation has been calculated (2-4-4). Certain parts of the questionnaire needed some additional elaboration. The construction of a cumulative trauma-score is presented (2-5-1). A structured questionnaire on dissociative symptoms - the Dissociative Experience Scale (D.E.S.)- is discussed in detail (2-5-2). We performed a small validation study with the D.E.S. in the Netherlands (2-6-1). In order to obtain information regarding the generalizability of our results, demographic characteristics and characteristics of child sexual abuse of our respondents are compared with those reported by relevant other studies (2-6-2 and 2-6-3). The chapter ends with a summary (2-7).

2.2 Methodological issues

Several methodological issues have greatly influenced the chosen research strategy. The most important issue, extensively discussed before the actual research design was fixed, deals with the reliability of childhood memories.

2.2.1 Reliability of childhood memories

The central question of our study concerns the connection between a history of child (sexual) abuse and psychological problems in adult life. Such a research goal implies gathering information about childhood incidents.

Usually, a distinction is made between studies with a prospective character and those with a retrospective character. In studies on connections between child sexual abuse and psychological symptoms in adult life, data on childhood incidents usually have a retrospective character. Studies on child sexual abuse with a prospective character have never been performed. In the future such studies might be designed, especially because several retrospective studies have predicted which children are at risk. But, a study with a prospective design, in which researchers know a child is (severely) assaulted, but do not intervene for research purposes, is objectionable for ethical reasons. So, retrospective study seems the only possible way. One of the main methodological problems in our study concerns this retrospective character of data on childhood incidents.

A study with a retrospective character necessarily struggles with the question of reliability of information on childhood incidents. Different psychological processes may influence the reliability of reports on such incidents. Textbooks on the function of memory present a certain model for memory processes, (Wolters and van der Heijden, 1989; Parker, 1987). During rehearsal of memory some cognitive restructuring always takes place: rehearsal of memory is not a static, but a dynamic process. Forgetting is a normal psychological process and amnesia for early childhood incidents can be found in most human beings. Forgetting and remembering are influenced by interference of new similar experiences. Remembering of original events is thought to be possible, as a result of the 'schemata' of original events person retains. Although the person is thought to reconstruct original events on the basis of these schemata, certain details may be remembered rather well, too.

The fact that the childhood incidents under study may have a traumatic character complicates the matter of memory. Two different kinds of memory distortions have been observed after traumatic experiences: amnesia and hypermnesia, (Albach 1986). Many authors describe that memories of traumatic incidents will be repressed; thoughts about stressful events are warded off, (Breuer and Freud, 1895; Horowitz, 1986; Kleber, 1986; van der Kolk, 1987; Pennebaker, 1987). Not only thoughts about trauma are repressed, certain studies (see chapter 5) indicate that when a person experiences overwhelming trauma 'encoding' as well as 'retrieval' processes are disturbed. This means that during the trauma a person has excluded several incidents accompanying the trauma from consciousness and besides has difficulties in remembering details of the incidents not excluded from consciousness.

Gelinas (1983) observes that during initial therapy assessments, many women with a history of child sexual abuse do not confirm such a history. They tend to have a 'disguised presentation' of their childhood history. Only when therapy progresses do they start talking about these incidents. Women may not trust the therapist, may deny the incidents or may have completely forgotten them.

Amnesia for child sexual abuse is found to be associated with the severity of childhood traumata by Brière and Conte (1989). Their findings show that the more severe coercion was exerted during child sexual abuse, the more likely women report periods in which they had forgotten these incidents. In women with a history of severe child sexual abuse, denial and repression may decrease the reliability of retrospective reports.

Another 'distortion' of memory after traumatic incidents concerns hypermnesia; memories about the traumatic incident involuntarily intrude upon a person's consciousness. Involuntary intrusions of traumatic memories are called flashbacks when they occur during the wakened state and post-traumatic nightmares when they occur during the sleep. During flashbacks and nightmares, specific frightening events are played back repetitively, almost unchanged. Persons with a post-traumatic stress disorder repeatedly relive certain particularly traumatic incidents. Researchers studying 'post-traumatic stress disorders' and therapists treating such patients have been struck by the absence of memory rehearsal processes during flashbacks, (Hartmann 1984). These relivings usually start shortly after the occurrence of traumatic incidents, but a considerable time delay has often been observed. Memories are said to integrate into the 'mental system' when rehearsal processes -cognitive restructuring- occur and repression of these memories lessens. Cognitive restructuring primarily concerns the process of giving a meaning to traumatic incidents. If cognitive restructuring occurs, the frequency of the intrusions diminishes.

Several authors find women with a history of child sexual abuse to experience vivid flashbacks and nightmares concerning childhood incidents, (Silver, Boons & Stones, 1983; Gelinas, 1983; Lindstad and Distad, 1985; Goodwin, 1985; Albach, 1991). In a from a theoretical point of view well-founded study, Silver, Boons & Stones (1983) discovered that 20 years after the termination of child sexual abuse, 3/4 of the women experienced relivings of childhood traumata. In half of these women no signs existed that cognitive restructuring of those memories had taken place: these women were unable to give a meaning to these traumatic incidents. These findings that, in general, flashbacks after trauma and, more particularly, after child sexual abuse are hardly integrated into the mental system may account for the fact that certain memories of traumatic incidents are quite accurate. Problems with regard to the retrospective character of our study appear to be non-existing when retrospective information is obtained by inquiring about flashbacks. Retrospective information gathered on flashbacks is supposed to be more valid than retrospective information of 'non-traumatic' memories.

Studies on the reliability of retrospective data do not take into account the special memory processes observed after traumatic incidents. Such studies deal with normal forgetting and rehearsal processes. In the Netherlands, Sandfort, while planning a study on sexual contacts in early youth, reviewed studies on the reliability of retrospective data, (Sandfort, 1982). He concluded that: (1) no studies are found indicating that retrospection as a method of gathering data is completely untrustworthy, (2) the trustworthiness of retrospective data can be enhanced by different interview techniques, e.g. offering cues that facilitate retrieval processes, and (3) the trustworthiness of retrospective data is less when used at an individual level than when used to calculate relations among sets of data, (Sandfort, 1988, p.60).

Parker (1987) and Noordenbos (1987) reviewed several studies on the relation between the mood at the time of the interview and the recall of childhood situations. The mood during the interview does influence the kind of events recalled. In a depressive mood one tends to recall bad incidents, in a happy mood one recalls happy incidents. A depressive mood does not permanently impair recall-processes. For instance, Lewinsohn and Rosenbaum (1986) find that somebody in a depressive mood recalls parental attitudes as being more rejecting and unloving than others who are not in a depressive mood state. Those others included persons who had been (repeatedly) depressive and persons who became depressive after their participation in the study. Lewinsohn and Rosenbaum concluded that 'recalling one's parents as having been rejecting is not a stable personality characteristic'. The depressive mood colours the memory of the childhood situation, negative aspects are stressed more during a depression than before a period of depressive mood. But, when the depression is over, the predominance in recalling negative incidents is also gone.

The considerations presented above show a rather complicated picture of the memory processes in women with a history of child sexual abuse. First of all, memories of childhood incidents may simply be forgotten. Secondly, memories of traumatic childhood incidents may be repressed or denied. Thirdly, it seems plausible that a large proportion of the women experience flashbacks of traumatic childhood situations in which memories are very detailed and almost unchanged. Finally childhood circumstances are perhaps rated more negatively when women are in a depressed mood during an interview, than when they are not in a depressive mood.

The discussion presented above had several implications for the design of our project:

- To obtain adequate information one should first of all recruit women who are or have already been willing to lift up this repression. In a randomly selected sample of women with a history of child sexual abuse, one will find women who hardly remember child sexual abuse incidents. Women who hardly remember anything about child abuse can not be expected to function as adequate informants.
- In stimulating retrieval processes one overcomes processes of normal forgetting (e.g. by offering cues).
- To decrease problems with memory rehearsal, one should inquire about flashbacks of child sexual abuse.
- A way to prevent the recruitment of predominantly depressed women is, to incorporate a selection procedure for this purpose.
- The investigation of intercorrelations among several kinds of 'data sets' may reduce problems inherently associated with retrospection. The effects of

retrospection important at an individual level are less prominent when at a general level retrospective reports are correlated with other data sets (like psychiatric problems), because the distortions will lower the statistical relations among data-sets.

2.2.2 Psychological and behavioural symptoms selected for study

The central aim of our study implies a selection of psychological and behavioural symptoms relevant to be studied. But which problems can be considered to be relevant in this respect? Several considerations have influenced our choice to concentrate on four psychological or behavioural problems: *dissociative disturbances in consciousness, hallucinations, self-injury and suicidality.*

The first consideration concerns the question of control-groups. Psychological symptoms in women with a history of child sexual abuse may be compared in a global way with psychological problems found in samples of the 'normal' population. For this purpose, one may select psychological problems already studied in samples of a normal population. For several problems, such studies are available. Suicidality is adequately measured in other Dutch studies, Kerkhof and Diekstra (1982), Draijer (1988, 1990). These other Dutch studies may function as 'global control-data' for our respondents. The level of dissociation in 'normals' is measured in the United States by Bernstein and Putnam (1986), Ross, Heber, Norton and Anderson (1989). Level of dissociation in a sample of a normal Dutch population is measured by van Otterloo (1987). Self-injury is notoriously difficult to measure in samples of a normal population. Frequently self-injury is hidden and seen as socially undesirable. However, certain writers, like Walsh and Rosen (1987) estimate a prevalence range of self-injury in normal populations. Other authors, like Slade and Bentall (1988) discuss a prevalence range of hallucinations in samples of normal populations.

We selected psychological problems generally considered to be psychiatric symptoms. Psychiatric symptoms are thought to indicate serious psychological problems. Findings of studies about the impact on severe child sexual abuse indicate that it is more suitable to select psychiatric problems than more common psychological complaints, like sexual problems or problems with relationships.

For some of the symptoms chosen, a connection with a history of child sexual abuse is already rather well established, (for instance, for suicidality). One of the aims of the present study is to investigate different theoretical models of these connections, in order to gain a better understanding of psychological processes. In the selection of symptoms, the existence of such models has formed an important consideration. Models are needed when the research aim is to gain a better understanding in psychological processes associated with different kinds of child sexual abuse. Theoretical models give rise to assumptions that can be verified or falsified.

We have chosen to investigate symptoms reported by a considerable part but not all of the women under study: It is impossible to investigate relations between characteristics of child sexual abuse and particular symptoms, when almost all or almost none of the respondents report that symptom.

2.3 Research strategy

The methodological issues have implications for the research strategy actually adopted.

2.3.1 Recruiting women with a history of child sexual abuse

Child sexual abuse may be forgotten, repressed or dissociated. Women who are aware of a history of sexual abuse are often not willing to share such personal information with others, (Gelinas, 1983). As one of the consequences of their history, women , as a child are sexually abused, may develop a general distrust towards other people, (Summit, 1983; Jonker, 1986; Finkelhor and Browne, 1986). One can expect adequate information on child sexual abuse or socially undesirable symptoms, like severe dissociation or self-injury, only when women do trust the investigator. If they do, they are perhaps willing to disclose their experiences. Women who repress or deny child sexual abuse or have no confidence in the research project will not share personal, intimate and socially undesirable information with an interviewer. These considerations influenced our choice to recruit women in an indirect way. We chose to approach contact persons specialized in emotional support or therapeutic care of women with a history of child sexual abuse, and asked them to help us with recruitment. This choice was based on ethical considerations too. As researchers we couldnot guarantee long-lasting psychological support. We couldn't predict whether questions on child sexual abuse and symptoms elicit intolerable intense emotions. This reason restricted the kind of women we could approach: women who already had some kind of psychological support.

The choice we made reflects our attempts to obtain valid information and to take ethical questions into account. This choice had certain obvious disadvantages. The most important disadvantage concerns a lack of detailed advance information on the characteristics of the women recruited. This might bias the sample and might hamper the generalizability of our findings. However, the way of recruiting was not considered to be a total jump in the dark. We recruited women who had certain supportive contacts. Earlier studies of women with a child sexual abuse history in therapy had shown these women to have a history of predominantly severe child sexual abuse, (Herman, Russell & Trocki, 1986). We could predict our respondents to have a more severe history of child sexual abuse than on average reported in a community sample. In order to check this prediction a comparison has been made between characteristics of our respondents and respondents of other studies on child abuse, (see section 2-6-2).

Another disadvantage of the present recruitment strategy concerns the question of memory rehearsal. When women with therapeutic contacts are recruited, one tends to expect the history of child sexual abuse to be an important focus of attention in therapy. The therapy may be aimed at cognitive restructuring of memories and emotions evoked by childhood incidents, (Jehu, Klassen & Gazan, 1986; Cole and Barney, 1987). Memories may change by rehearsal during therapy. In the reconstruction processes of childhood incidents the interpretations of therapists may play an important role.

This disadvantage of the chosen recruitment strategy would be very important, if histories of child sexual abuse were a main subject in therapy, if therapy was in progress and repeated flashbacks were being integrated into the 'mental system'. In our study, however, this disadvantage is not likely to have played an important role, because the actual therapeutic situation at the time of our study was generally like this: the majority of women had hardly talked about child sexual abuse during therapy, many therapist were not able to provide enough support to establish a relation of trust, women frequently contacted several different therapist before they found one they trusted enough to disclose their childhood incidents, (Frenken and van Stolk, 1987). Most of our respondents received their best emotional support from volunteers offering individual help or guiding incest-survivor-groups, (see section 2-4-1). Fortunately, some of our respondents had found a therapist they trusted.

In general, however, the actual therapeutic situation of women with a history of child sexual abuse is (was?) rather bad. In such a bad situation one can't expect restructuring processes due to therapeutic interpretations to play a major role in reporting of memories. The possibility can however not be excluded that in a few women changes in memories have occurred due to memory rehearsal processes in therapy.

An important value of incest-survivor groups is that one woman telling about her childhood provides cues for other women who participate in such a group. These cues may trigger memories and flashbacks and lift repression. The recruitment of women from incest-survivor-groups may have as a disadvantage that particular psychological symptoms have been thoroughly discussed in those groups. If so, reports of particular symptoms may be influenced by processes going on in those groups. We checked beforehand whether dissociative phenomena, hallucinatory phenomena, self-injury and suicidality are subjects of discussion in incest-survival groups. The contact persons of the incest-groups assured us that dissociation, hallucination and self-injury are not considered to be topics for group-therapy[6]. In general, volunteers and professional therapists

---

[6] The discussions on impact of child sexual abuse focussed on emotions elicited by telling about the own life history and centres around the body. Bodily complaints and lack of esteem for ones own body were subjects discussed in incest-survivor groups at the time of the field work of our study.

suppose that those psychological symptoms are too severe to be dealt with in (poli-clinical) groups of relatively unselected women. Only suicidal ideation was sometimes discussed.

Proto-professionalism constitutes another problem. Women may report psychological symptoms that they have read to be associated with child sexual abuse. Especially reports of dissociative symptoms have been thought to result from proto-professionalism and suggestibility, (Fahy, 1988; Aldridge-Morris, 1989; Bennebroek Evertsz, 1989). As already described above, dissociative phenomena were not discussed in incest-survivor groups at the time of the interviews. In order to prevent the possibility of suggestion, only one oblique remark concerning dissociative symptoms was made in our brochure. At the period of the field work -in 1987- dissociative phenomena were not yet publicly discussed in the Netherlands, (Boon and van der Hart, 1988). The knowledge on dissociative disorders came only from the book and the movie 'Sybil', Schreiber (1973). Publications about dissociative disorders in Dutch professional Journals preceding our fieldwork period are rarely found, (Megens, 1985 and Hof, 1985 in: van der Hart and Boon 1990). However, during the last months of the fieldwork period, a workshop on Dissociative Disorders was given for therapists, (van der Hart, 1987)[7].

We can not exclude the possibility that some women report dissociative symptoms because their therapists suggested these symptoms to them. It seems unlikely that this plays a major role in the reports of dissociative symptoms.

The advantages of recruiting women willing to talk about child sexual abuse seem to us of more importance than the disadvantages. The disadvantages can partly be met by comparing our data to other relevant studies and by particular interview techniques.

2.3.2 Way of recruitment

We approached contact persons of self-help incest-survival groups, professionally guided incest-groups and individual persons specialized in emotional support or therapeutic care. Before we approached contact persons, we asked permission of the N.V.A.G.G.[8] (Union of Ambulant Mental Health Care), the official organization of psycho-therapist participating in R.I.A.G.G.'s[9] (Regional Institutes of Ambulant Mental Health Care). Most contact persons forwarded a brochure with information about our study to women they knew have a history of child sexual abuse. Cooperation was given by 'De Maan', 'Tegen Haar Wil', 'Verenigingen Tegen Sexuele Kindermishandeling', 'Stichting tegen seksuele kindermishandeling Rotterdam' and therapists affiliated

---

7 Therapist may have participated in the workshop on dissociative disorders. In case of one respondent we know that her therapist participated in this workshop.

8 Nederlandse Vereniging voor Ambulante Geestelijke Gezondheidszorg

9 Regionaal Instituut voor Ambulante Geestelijke Gezondheid

to RIAGG's, specialized in guiding incest-survival groups, (see appendix 2-1). Together with the brochure, some contact-persons (of unofficial organizations) sent a letter in which they recommended our study. Therapists put up the brochure of our study in a well visible place.

A good brochure has to meet two contradictory requirements. On the one hand the brochure should give adequate information in such a way that women can give an informed consent, but on the other hand we should avoid problems of suggestion and of recruiting women with particular 'symptom characteristics'. To meet both requirements, the information in the brochure had a rather general character. When a woman got a brochure and wanted to participate in our study, she had to phone us herself. By this procedure a threshold was created. Women had to be rather well motivated and active to surpass this threshold. We expected this threshold to exclude women who did not feel capable of managing the interview situation. This threshold may have decreased the possibility that women in an acute depressive mood participated in the study. A depressive mood is characterized by symptoms as lack of energy and loss of interest, (Klerman and Weissman 1980).

2.3.3 Construction of the questionnaire

The considerations presented above specify several requirements for the interview and the questionnaire.

*   The questionnaire should provide cues to stimulate retrieval processes. To stimulate retrieval processes, a questionnaire may contain several questions on the same subject and the interviewer should take time to allow for retrieval processes, (Sandfort, 1988; Steinberg, Rounsaville & Cicchetti, 1990).

*   The best way to avoid problems of memory rehearsal is to ask about flashbacks. Such questions should have an open character, because questions reflecting formal categories specified by researchers may interfere with important incidents experienced during flashbacks.

*   The interview situation should allow the development of a personal contact between respondent and interviewer. It is assumed that in an open and respectful relationship, women will feel more at ease when disclosing painful intimate details or socially undesirable complaints.

*   The questionnaire should avoid problems of suggestibility. A certain tension exists between the requirement of stimulating retrieval processes and the problems of suggestibility. In this study emphasis was laid on retrieval problems. Many questions were introduced by a made-up fragment of a case history. The problem of suggestibility was compensated by the neutral formulation of the questions we posed after this fragment. Moreover, when a woman confirmed a question, she was asked to illustrate her answer by giving experiences that made her answer positive. The interview incorporated

no questions allowing an abstract interpretation of the childhood incidents or complaints. Most questions concerned 'facts' or experiences of 'facts'. Only a minority of the questions concerned 'feelings' or 'attitudes'.

- The questionnaire should allow comparison with other studies on child sexual abuse as well as with other studies on selected psychological and behavioural problems.

These considerations have led to the construction of a rather complicated questionnaire. In collecting information three different ways of data acquisition have been applied. The general structure of the interview was:

1. In a semi-structured inquiry questions can be divided into main questions and questions called 'points of attention'. Main questions have a closed character, possible answers are yes or no. When a woman confirmed a question she was asked to illustrate her answer with examples from her own history.
2. Points of attention had the function to explore in more detail the topics of the main questions. In general, points of attention concerned age periods in which something occurred, the frequency, the antecedents, triggers for the experience etc.
3. In a structured part of the interview women could indicate intensity and frequency of their psychological problems. The structured part consisted of a self-report scale in a visual analog form, (see appendix 2-2 and section 5-2).

The design of the interview schedule is presented in scheme 2-1.

Scheme 2-1: Design of the interview schedule [a].

I	Demographic variables, social back-ground, family of origin, household duties, emotional parentification, relationships within the family.
II	Characteristics of child sexual abuse.
III [b]	Flashbacks, nightmares, repression, latention, external validation of memories.
IV	Depersonalization, derealization, body awareness and anaesthesia
V	Self-injury, suicidality, spouse-beatings, eating problems, alcohol and drugs-addiction.
VI	Dissociation, hallucinations
VII	D.E.S. and P.T.S.D. (structured questionnaire)

[a] The questionnaire also contains questions about emotions during child sexual abuse, hysterical complaints, gynaecological complaints. Albach (in press) will report findings on those questions. [b] Findings of this part will be discussed in detail by Albach (in press).

ad I: The questions in the initial phase of the interview had a general character. These questions served several purposes. First, general information was acquired such as, characteristics of current living situation, and characteristics of family of origin. Inquiry on the family-origin preceded inquiry on incidents of child sexual abuse, because information about the family constellation would otherwise interrupt the questions about child sexual abuse. The questions in the first part of the interview were scheduled in a flexible way, to permit the development of a confidential relationship between respondent and interviewer. The questions about emotional and household parentification are based on the work of Kroon (1986).

ad II: Questions about characteristics of child sexual abuse are in most aspects similar to questions in the studies of Frenken and van Stolk (1987) and Draijer (1988). One main difference between this study and the projects of Draijer, and Frenken and van Stolk concerns the more detailed elaboration in our study of 'coercion' in different phases of child sexual abuse. Most questions could be answered with a simple yes, no, don't know. When a woman confirmed a question we asked her to give an illustration. If a woman said she could not, she was asked to explain this answer in more detail. When a woman had been sexually abused by different perpetrators, the same questions were repeated for each perpetrator.

ad III: Questions about flashbacks had a relatively open character. By the descriptions detailed information is obtained on reliving of traumatic childhood incidents. We expected that questions on flashbacks may confuse women or may evoke intense emotions. Questions about flashbacks were alternated with relatively formal questions, (How long did it last? When did it start etc.?). Formal questions provided a structure and had as a purpose to reduce intense relivings at the moment of interview. If nevertheless intense emotions were evoked, the interviewer stopped the interview for a while ('Let us have some tea').

ad IV: Questions about depersonalization and derealization are derived (a limited version) from a questionnaire of Cappon (1969). Questions about special depersonalization feelings concerning one's own body preceded general questions about depersonalization. Questions on awareness of the body were derived from 'The body awareness questionnaire' by Shields (1986).

ad V: Questions about suicidality were based on a study by van Egmond (1988), questions about anorexia and bulimia nervosa were derived from a study by Noordenbos (1987), questions about self-injury were based on the description of self-injurious behaviour given by de Young (1982), questions about spouse-beatings were based on descriptions by van Rappard (1988). When a woman stated that she had injured or was still injuring herself, we inquired about: the frequency of self-injury, the part of the body injured, feelings of pain associated with self-injury, emotional feelings surrounding self-injury, age at with it started, and time that it lasted. When a woman stated she had attempted suicide, we inquired about: suicidal ideation, frequency of suicide attempts, age at which suicidality started, purpose of the attempts, and emotional feelings surrounding suicidality.

ad VI: The questions in the semi-structured questionnaire on dissociative symptoms were initially based on descriptions in the literature of dissociative phenomena, (Janet, 1911; M.Prince, 1911; Ellenberger, 1970; Bliss, 1980; Kluft, 1985). Such dissociative phenomena consist of acting automatically, being in a daze, trance, extensive daydreaming, extreme forgetfulness, sleepwalking, fugues, and pseudo-epileptical attacks. Almost at the moment the field work started, the Dissociative Experience Scale of Bernstein and Putnam (1986) came to our attention. We decided to further investigate the impact of the dissociative features with the Dissociative Experience Scale, when a woman confirmed she experienced dissociative phenomena as described above. Boon and van der Hart (1988) and Putnam (1989) suggest ways of exploring the extent of dissociation with the help of questions contained in the Dissociative Experience Scale. We did not inquire in a direct way about hallucinatory experiences, but certain points of attention concerned hallucinatory experiences. For instance, we asked women about auditory hallucinations if they mentioned 'time-gaps'. When asking about emotional states surrounding self-injury and suicidality, hallucinatory experiences could be mentioned. When asking about dissociative phenomena as a point of attention we would enquire about the 'as if' character of these experiences.

ad VII: The structured part of the questionnaire contains self-report questionnaires on features described in part III, part IV, and part VI. A Post-traumatic Stress List was created; most existing Post-Traumatic Stress lists do not take into account the possibility of a delayed post-traumatic stress disorder. The Dissociative Experience Scale (D.E.S.) was incorporated to measure level of dissociation. The contents of the D.E.S. items predominantly concern disturbances in consciousness. Our items of the D.E.S. have two versions: one variant concerns the recent past and the other the remote past. Only the version about the recent past has been scored. For contents of the Post-Traumatic Stress Disorder List, see appendix 2-2, for contents of the D.E.S. items, see appendix 5-2. The D.E.S. includes one item about hearing voices inside the head, that are commenting or arguing.

In its preliminary state the questionnaire was discussed with contact-persons of 'Tegen Haar Wil Amsterdam'. We consulted them about formulating questions on child sexual abuse; they considered whether the questions were formulated in an understandable way and regarded the ethical side of the questions. The questionnaire in a more elaborated form was discussed with several therapists and researchers specialized in different subareas. Ten trial interviews were held to test the wording of the questions and the duration of the interview. Based on these trials an interviewing protocol was designed. This protocol was extensively discussed with a therapist specialized in the treatment of women with a child sexual abuse history. She advised us on how to prevent arousing too intense emotions and if so, how to manage these emotions. Moreover, she suggested when to incorporate breaks within the interview[10].

2.4 Gathering and coding information

2.4.1 The interview

When a woman got a brochure and felt like participating, she had to phone the therapy-secretariat of the department of clinical psychology of the University of Amsterdam. She was called back by one of the researchers. In this initial telephone call, some preliminary information was given on the interview. We assured anonymity and asked whether she had objections against a tape-recorder. We warned that the interview might elicit intense emotions, we advised to plan something for the evening after the interview, relaxing or distracting activities. When a woman had a regular therapeutic contact, we recommended to inform the therapist and to plan a therapeutic contact shortly after the interview. The actual interview could be held on one or two occasions, according to the preference of the woman.

At the start of the interview the assurance was given that if a woman did not want to answer a question, she should say so, it would be no problem. During the interview the interviewer tried to note down the answers to the questions and to monitor the emotions activated by these questions. When intense emotions were elicited the interviewer should be able to manage this situation. The first five interviews were supervised by a therapist specialized in treating women with a history of child sexual abuse.

During 1987 one hundred interviews were held. The actual interview started with an introductory phase of about half an hour. And after the interview half an hour was reserved for talking about relaxing things. According to the needs of the respondent or the interviewer, breaks were introduced. The actual interview lasted three to four hours on the average. The interviews were recorded with a tape-recorder.

2.4.2 The women recruited

A considerable proportion of our respondents (44%) came from recruitment in incest-survival groups guided by volunteers; 28% came from incest-groups guided by professional therapists; 13% came from individual therapists; and 14% got the information via other respondents.

During the introduction phase we inquired after the motivation to participate. The answers to this question were not tape-recorded or coded. Our impression is that most women wanted to testify about what happened during childhood. The

---

[10] The name of this therapist is mentioned in appendix 2-1a.

study offered the opportunity to disclose and tie down the history of child sexual abuse under safe and anonymous circumstances[11] . These women didn't want to go to a court-room for several reasons. For instance, because they still had feelings of loyalty towards the perpetrator; wanted to protect family-members; the perpetrator had died; it happened too long ago, or they were the only witness and the perpetrator denied. Some women were very glad, that at least once they were able to tell their history to somebody prepared to listen to it. For one woman the interview evoked too intense emotions. After the interview she experienced auditory hallucinations involving commands to commit suicide. She had no satisfying contact with a therapist and an attempt was made to rearrange her therapeutic contacts in a more satisfying way.

2.4.3 Coding the interviews

The interviews were screened as to whether they met the specified criteria of child sexual abuse. Three interviews proved not to be valid. Two women had been sexually abused by brothers who were older but the age difference between girl and brother was less than five years[12]. One woman had no memories of child sexual abuse. She had particular dreams and her therapist had suggested that these dreams indicated child sexual abuse. These dreams had a symbolic character (crossing a river etc.) and had no features in common with most dreams reported by the other women in our study (most dreams of women in this study had the character of post-traumatic nightmares, nightmares with monsters or night terrors).

Valid interviews were literally typed-out. The scoring of characteristics of child sexual abuse was a time-consuming and rather difficult job, but it had to be done by the researchers[13]. In a previous study on sexual offences (Ensink and Albach, 1983), we found that women themselves have difficulties in rating their histories in the rather formal categories used by researchers[14]; very dissimilar experiences were reported in the same category. Moreover, memories of later traumata, like assaults by spouses, interfered with child sexual abuse experiences. Difficulties in scoring existed, because answers given to questions about characteristics of child sexual abuse sometimes differed from the contents of flashbacks. A few (circa four) women gave rather inconsistent information about the history of child sexual abuse. For instance, when asked about intercourse some women said they had been able to prevent it, but ten minutes later

---

[11] Amnesty International offers a similar possibility to political refugees.

[12] If a women was sexually abused by her father and brothers, or by several brothers, the age difference between the youngest perpetrator and the girl was not taken into account.

[13] Some other researchers studying severe psychological symptoms and childhood incidents, like Noordenbos and Egmond decided to follow the same procedure.

[14] Other studies, like the one by Frenken and van Stolk (1987) have struggled with the same problems (personal communication Vorrink, who cooperated in that study).

implicitly assumed that you knew intercourse had taken place. Inconsistencies in reporting memories can be expected in case of severe dissociation (see chapter 3 and 5). In scoring the interviews on child sexual abuse several rules were applied. The contents of flashbacks are considered to reflect childhood incidents in a better way than answers to more formal questions. Images accepted by women as memories were scored as such. Images or contents of voices not recognised by women as concerning memories were not coded (see chapter 6). If a woman gave inconsistent answers these were scored in the category 'don't know'. However, a few women reported inconsistent information as well as severe dissociation, like 'repeated time-gaps'. In these cases the most severe incidents reported were scored.

Scoring self-injury and suicidality was a relatively easy job. In cooperation with a student these ratings were performed.

The scoring of psychological problems as specified in part IV and VI (depersonalization etc., dissociation, and hallucinations) contains more pitfalls. Hallucinatory experiences mentioned during the semi-structured interview were coded as such, when these experiences met the definition of Slade and Bentall, (see 6-2-4). Hallucinatory images occurring just before falling asleep or just after waking up and vivid daydreams a person said to have under voluntary control were not coded as hallucinatory experiences. Neither did we score hallucinations associated with sensory deprivation, fever, alcohol or drugs consumption as hallucinatory experiences. Hallucinations were coded as present or absent. Different forms of visual hallucinations were summed in order to construct a sum-score of visual hallucinations.

Dissociative symptoms reported in combination with an excessive use of alcohol, drugs, medicaments or evoked by meditation are not coded as such. One of the biggest problems consists of the inextricable clew of concepts related to depersonalization and dissociation[15]. It is very difficult to define differences between: being in a daze, extensive daydreaming, derealization, depersonalization, extreme forgetfulness, fugues, twilight states, trance, and 'time-gaps'. Not to mention concepts concerning disturbances in identity, like: alienation from self; being ruled by impulses experienced as ego-dystonic; not recognising one's own thoughts or visual memories, but attributing these to external sources; feeling two persons; feeling possessed; regression to child-like states with corresponding perceptions and attitudes; or attributing memories, thoughts and behaviour to other personalities sharing the same body.

In a scientific research concepts have to be defined in an unambiguous way and preferably should be mutually exclusive or hierarchical organized, (De Groot 1961). One strategy to disentangle the jungle of concepts is to collect material in

---

[15] The Frankel's remark is clarifying in this respect. He states: 'In reviewing the history of the use of the term dissociation, it is apparent that clarity is conspicuous by its absence', (Frankel 1990, p.827).

a systematic way and categorize it, (Glaser and Strauss, 1971). In order to try to define several concepts in a mutually exclusive way, 25 interviews were closely examined, statements were selected and arranged under different concepts. A prototypical statement was selected for each concept. Theoretical reflections together with the properties of prototypical statements formed the basis for the specification of attributes defining different concepts. Appendix 2-3 contains the list of criteria defining the different but related concepts.

2.4.4 Inter-judge agreement

Inter-judge agreement has been calculated[16] in order to investigate the unambiguity of various 'disturbances in consciousness'[17]. A graduated, but relatively uninformed, student functioned as an independent judge. This student got written information on criteria of dissociative concepts. No oral information was given, neither did the student receive information about the central question of our study. This procedure was followed in order to guarantee an independent judgement of the student. The student could ask information about particular concepts and criteria if she did not understand. An aselect sample of ten interviews was drawn out of the 97 interviews. The first five interviews were scored independently by student and researcher. The next step consisted of student and researcher together discussing the ratings of three of those interviews. After these discussions these three interviews were scored again. Then five interviews were scored independently and two of those were discussed and scored again. As a measure of inter-judge agreement kappa was chosen. The kappa was .53 for the interviews judged before discussing the ratings and .91 for the interviews after discussing the independent ratings. A kappa of .53 is considered fair, but not really convincing [18]. Moreover, inter-judge agreement differed considerably for each dissociative concept. For instance, the kappa of the disturbance 'time-gaps' was .80, the kappa of 'amnesia for childhood incidents' was lower than .20, (De Vries, 1990)[19].

---

[16] Advice for the procedure of the calculation of the inter-judge agreement was given by the department of methodology of the University of Amsterdam (H. Vorst).

[17] The following disturbances are differentiated: extensive amnesia for childhood incidents in general, reports of depersonalization or time-gaps during traumatic incidents as child, feelings of depersonalization (recently), derealization (recently), decreased awareness of bodily pain or sensations (recently), somnambulism, daze-states (recently), twilight states (recently), fugues (recently), time-gaps (recently) and amazing verbal inconsistencies in the report of childhood incidents.

[18] Kappa below .40 = poor; .40-.59=fair; .60-.74=good; and .75-1.00=excellent, Fliess, Cohen and Everitt (1969).

[19] A detailed analysis of the discrepancies in initial scoring and discussed interviews shows some concepts to be difficult to distinguish. For instance faulty categorisation of statements under the concepts derealization and depersonalization contributed to a low kappa.

The somewhat disappointing outcomes of the inter-judge agreement testing constituted one of the considerations[20] for our preference of the self-reported disturbances in consciousness on the D.E.S.[21]. Statements about disturbances in consciousness made during the semi-structured interview are only presented when they have a heuristic value or when they concern dissociative concepts that showed to have a reasonable inter-judge agreement.

2.5 Detailed information on certain significant measures used

Certain topics discussed in previous sections need further elaboration. Two issues, the construction of a cumulative trauma-score and the Dissociative Experience Scale, are discussed in more detail.

2.5.1 Constructing a cumulative trauma-score

Many characteristics of child sexual abuse can be distinguished. It would be practical to find some way of reducing the possible information coded in the different characteristics of child sexual abuse, (see chapter 4). The common practice is to find a way of measuring 'severity of child sexual abuse'. There are several methods to tackle this problem. Russell (1986), Frenken and van Stolk (1987), Ribberink and Slurink (1988), and Draijer (1988) tried to create a 'score of severity of child sexual abuse' by reducing the history of child sexual abuse to one of its characteristics: the intrusiveness of sexual acts. Sandfort (1988) characterizes sexual abuse by severity of coercion applied. In this way one gains a reduction of information, but in our opinion one also loses too much information. Other researchers, like Conte, Brière and Sexton (1989) reduce the information on the history of child sexual abuse by means of a factor analysis, (see chapter 4).

The most sophisticated measure of severity of childhood traumatization has, in our opinion, been constructed by Herman, Perry and van der Kolk (1989). They composed a cumulative trauma-score in which all forms of abuses are taken into account as well as the age at which these abuses took place. They calculated their cumulative trauma score as follows:

---

[20] Another consideration concerns the question of standardisation. The use of the D.E.S. makes it possible to compare our data with those obtained in other studies.

[21] Although at the individual level of the statements there was a disappointing inter-judge-agreement, at the level of the sum-scores, no big differences existed between the sum-score on the D.E.S. and the sum-score of dissociative statements obtained the semi-structured interview, (see appendix 2-4).

The interviews were scored for positive indices of trauma in three areas: physical abuse, sexual abuse and witnessing domestic violence. Instances of culturally accepted corporal punishment and fighting or consensual sexual exploration between peers were not included as abusive. Protocols were scored for occurrence of each type of trauma at each of three developmental stages: early childhood (0-6 years), latency (7-12 years), and adolescence (13-18 years). Within each developmental stage, no distinction in scoring was made between single and repeated instances of abuse by the same perpetrator. However, additional positive score in each category was given for abuse by different perpetrators. A rough composite measure of trauma was constructed by adding the positive scores for each trauma at each developmental stage. Thus a range of scores was generated from 0 (no trauma at any developmental stage) to 9 or higher (all three forms of trauma at all three stages or multiple perpetrators at one or more stages), (Herman, Perry and van der Kolk, p. 491).

In our study a cumulative trauma-score has been constructed in a similar way as reported above[22]. The cumulative trauma score was constructed by dividing childhood into three age periods, young child (0-6 years), child (7-12 years), and adolescent (13 years and older). Each woman got a score for having experienced sexual abuse; for physical abuse by perpetrator; and for abuses by other persons in the family. The way of calculating is similar as described above. This procedure resulted in one general cumulative trauma-score and 9 sub trauma-scores, namely (1) child sexual abuse before the age of 7, (2) physical child abuse by the perpetrator before the age of 7, (3) emotional neglect or physical abuse by other family-members (predominantly the mother), or witnessing severe domestic violence, (4) child sexual abuse from 7 years to 13 years of age, (5) physical abuse by the perpetrator from 7 years to 13 years of age, (6) emotional neglect or physical abuse by other family-members (predominantly the mother), or witnessing severe domestic violence from 7 years to 13 years of age, (7) child sexual abuse from 13 to 18 years of age, (8) physical abuse by the perpetrator from 13 to 18 years of age, and (9) emotional neglect or physical abuse by other family-members (predominantly the mother), or witnessing severe domestic violence from 13 to 18 years of age.

2.5.2 Information on the D.E.S.

The D.E.S. has been developed by Bernstein and Putnam (1986) to offer a means of reliably measuring dissociation in normal and clinical populations. Dissociation phenomena are considered to lie on a continuum, mild dissociative phenomena being normal, extreme phenomena being rare. The D.E.S. is a 28-item self-report questionnaire. The scale has a visual analog form. Subject's scores on individual items are coded as actual distances in millimetres from the

---

[22] In our study an accumulation of characteristics of child sexual abuse is permitted, because factor analysis shows the important characteristics load at unrelated factors, (see appendix 4-1).

left hand anchor point of a 100 mm line. The scores given in this research refer to this actual distance in millimetres to the anchor point. The questionnaire has a good internal consistency and a good criterion validity in English-speaking countries.

The Dissociative Experience Scale is a recently developed scale (1986). When a person frequently experiences dissociative symptoms incorporated in the D.E.S., therapists in the United States are inclined to give the diagnosis 'multiple personality disorder'. In order to specify the sensitivity and specificity of the D.E.S. for the diagnosis of multiple personality disorder, a large scale discriminant validity study with 800 patients has been performed, Carlson, Putnam et al., (personal communication Putnam, 1990). In this study it is found that a cut-off score of 30 correctly classifies 84% of patients receiving the diagnosis multiple personality disorder. If a cut-off score of 30 would be conceived to indicate a multiple personality disorder, 12% would receive this diagnosis, while the therapists would indicate another diagnosis (false positives) and 4% would not receive this diagnosis, while therapists would diagnose a multiple personality disorder (false negatives). The sensitivity is 74%, and the specificity is 86%. Of the patients incorrectly classified by the D.E.S. as having a multiple personality disorder by the cut-off score of 30 (false positives), 43% were diagnosed by their therapists as having another dissociative disorder, such as a post-traumatic stress disorder or a dissociative disorder not otherwise specified.

2.6 Studies permitting a comparison

2.6.1 A Dutch validation study with the D.E.S.

In the United States therapists are more than in Europe inclined to give the diagnosis multiple personality disorder. In order to investigate whether dissociative symptoms can be found in comparable situations in the Netherlands, we undertook a validation study with the D.E.S., (Van Otterloo, 1987; Ensink and Van Otterloo, 1990). The D.E.S. has been translated into Dutch. The D.E.S. was administered in two versions, with and without dummy questions[23], to 80 psychology students (40 students in each condition), and in one version to 20 patients with a clinically diagnosed dissociative disorder. The findings of the validation study show that the D.E.S. has a good internal consistency and construct validity. Persons who received the diagnosis 'multiple personality disorder' in the Netherlands have scores on the D.E.S. comparable to the scores of patients receiving this diagnosis in the United States. Therapists in the United States and the Netherlands consider similar symptoms to be formative of the diagnosis multiple personality disorder. The Dutch 'normals' score higher on the

---

[23] Dummies consisted of questions about common dissociative phenomena, but they did not count in statistics.

D.E.S. than the American ones. This difference in scores can be mainly attributed to the high levels of attention deficits and daydream activities reported by the Dutch students. The differences probably reflect differences in groups of 'normals' studied.

The level of dissociation in normals as measured by Van Otterloo will function as control-data for the level of dissociation measured in women with a history of child sexual abuse participating in our study.

2.6.2 Demographic characteristics of our respondents, a comparison

As already mentioned in the section on recruitment, our respondents are not randomly sampled. A question is whether the demographic characteristics of our respondents differ from those found in other samples. Samples important in this respect are: women with a history of child sexual abuse, women in therapy in general, and women with the same age in the general population. In order to investigate our question, figures were collected about demographic characteristics in these samples. Those figures are presented in scheme 2-2.

Two other Dutch studies on child sexual abuse exist. One study presents characteristics of women with a history of child sexual abuse as reported in a large sample of the general community, (Draijer, 1988, 1990). In another study, therapists reported characteristics of women with a history of child sexual abuse being in therapy, (Frenken and van Stolk, 1987). Certain registration of the general characteristics of patients soliciting for mental care is done by a general organisation for ambulant mental health care, (the N.V.A.G.G.). Registration of characteristics of the population is done by the C.B.S. One of the organisations that have sent the brochure about our study to women with a history of child sexual abuse is called 'De Maan'. This organisation has published certain figures about women soliciting for their help.

Scheme 2-2: Demographic characteristics of our respondents.

		Ensink 1992 sample women with C.S.A.[a]	Frenken 1991 sample women in therapy C.S.A.	Draijer 1988 sample general female populat. C.S.A. 20-40 yrs	C.B.S. 1986 [b] sample general female populat. 20-40 yrs	NVAGG 1990 Mental Health Care, female 20-40 yrs	De Maan '86-'88 contact-persons for our study
		%	%	%	%	%	%
educatio nal	low	54	60	62	57	-	-
level	middle	29	32	21	22	-	-
father	high	17	8	17	21	-	-
work	househ	59	80			-	-
mother [c]	low	26	14	79	79	-	-
	middle	10	4	18	18	-	-
	high	5	2	3	4	-	-
number	1	4	6	14	22	-	-
of	2/3	36	26	43	41	-	-
children	4/5	29	32	23	19	-	-
	6 ≥	31	33	21	16	-	-
Age [d]	20-24 y	14	22	-	25	20	38
	25-29 y	26	22	-	24	26	-
	30-34 y	37	36	-	23	27	40
	35-40 y	22	19	-	28	26	-
education	low	34	-	-	36	-	-
resp.	middle	33	-	-	29	-	-
	high	33	-	-	24	-	-
relation	alone	33	20	-	34	-	54
ships [e]	hetero sex relat.	52	66	-	66	-	-
	homo sex relat.	13	8	-	-	-	14
	other	2	6	-	-	-	19

a) C.S.A. means child sexual abuse. b) Most socio demographic figures for the group of women between 20-40 years were especially calculated by CBS for Draijer's research. Certain figures of the family of origin are not presented by CBS for the group of females between the 20 and 40 years. As the best approach, the general findings about activities presented by Draijer are taken. c) In our research we made the differentiation between mothers who did the household during childhood of the respondents and mothers who have been working some or all of the time. The figures presented in other studies give the impression that performing household duties and taking care of the children are evaluated as a low educational job, no explanations are given in this respect. [d] Not all the studies present figures about the same age-groups. E.g. some researchers incorporated women of the age of 40 in the figures, others or did not, etc. NVAGG, give figures about all age categories. A recalculation has been performed on women between 20 and 40 years of age. [e] Relationships are very differently registered in the various groups. Some give figures about being married, divorced (CBS, NVAGG) etc. Others give figures about the actual relationships, this makes it difficult to compare the figures.

In scheme 2-2 socio-economic characteristics of the family of origin of our respondents are compared with those in relevant other Dutch studies. Such a comparison meets many difficulties. For instance, general population data about the occupational level of the father (usually taken as an indication for the socio-economic level of the family) are not easily available. Currently available data on child sexual abuse suggest that socio-economic class and child sexual abuse are unrelated, (Russell, 1986; Draijer, 1988). The figures presented in scheme 2-2 indicate that the socio-economic background of our respondents does not differ from this back-ground of women with a history of child sexual abuse in general, (Draijer, 1988) or from the socio-economic background of women of the same age in a representative sample of Dutch women, (CBS, 1986).

An advanced professional education or a university study is or has been followed by 32% of our respondents, whereas 24% of all Dutch women between 20-40 years report such an education, (CBS, 1986). The educational level of our respondents shows to be somewhat higher than that of the average Dutch women. In general, respondents volunteering to participate in studies have a higher than average level of education, (Nederhof, 1981). The relatively high level of education of our respondents is probably due to our way of recruitment. The median age of the women participating in this study is comparable to the median age of women in therapy, whether they have or do not have a history of child sexual abuse. Scheme 2-2 shows that a considerable proportion of women with a history of child sexual abuse comes from families with a large number of children, (Frenken and van Stolk, 1987; Draijer, 1988; Ensink, 1991). In chapter 4 this finding will be discussed.

2.6.3 Child sexual abuse characteristics of our respondents, a comparison

We expected to recruit women with rather severe histories of child sexual abuse. This expectation was investigated by comparing characteristics of child sexual abuse of our respondents with those reported in relevant other studies. As mentioned in the previous section two other Dutch studies on child sexual abuse exist. One study has been performed in a large sample of the general Dutch population, (Draijer, 1988, 1990), and the other concerns characteristics of women with a history of child sexual abuse known to therapists, (Frenken and van Stolk, 1987). In the United States Russell (1986) has performed a study about child sexual abuse in a sample of a community and Herman (1986) reports characteristics of women with a history of child sexual abuse in therapy. Scheme 2-3 presents characteristics of child sexual abuse reported in five different studies.

Scheme 2-3: Characteristics of child sexual abuse in three Dutch and two American studies.

	Ensink N= 97 1992 Dutch	Frenken N=118 1987 sample women in therapy Dutch	Herman N=53 1986 sample women in therapy U.S.A.	Draijer N=181 1988 sample general population Dutch	Russell N=152 1986 sample community U.S.A.
	%	%	%	%	%
Father (step-, foster-)	67	69 b)	75	19	28
Sexual penetration (positive)	67	78 c)	-	27	-
Start C.S.A.a) before 10 years of age	69	48	32	22	46
C.S.A. lasting 4 years or more	74	54	-	18	-
Physical aggression first perpetrator	43 d)	37	11	9	5
More than one perpetrator	40	25		35	

a) C.S.A. means child sexual abuse. b) This number concerns 1114 cases, the other figures concern 118 or less. c) In this number masturbation is included, in the other studies it is not. d) This concerns the physical aggression of the main perpetrator during sexual abuse. For a detailed account of all physical aggression associated with child sexual abuse, see 4-4-4.

The comparison learns that women in our study have similar characteristics of child sexual abuse to those reported in the study of Frenken and van Stolk (1987). The histories of child sexual abuse of our respondents are best comparable to the histories of women known to Dutch therapists. In certain respects the characteristics of child sexual abuse reported in our study are even more severe. These findings are in agreement with our research strategy. Besides, the majority of our respondents (80%) (had) received some form of therapy for mental problems[24] and 24% had ever been admitted into a psychiatric institution.

---

[24] 80% of our respondents had received some form of therapy, but 44% were recruited from incest-survivor groups. Women who came from self-help groups did not have a history of child sexual abuse with a less severe character. The opposite tendency exists, for instance all women sexually abused by five or more perpetrators came from these self-help groups. Women with a

2.7 Summary and conclusions

Several methodological issues have been considered. A main methodological problem in our study relates to the retrospective character of data on child sexual abuse. Respondents participating in our study report incidents that on the average had stopped 12 years before the interview took place, (Albach, 1991). Analysis of memory processes of (traumatic) childhood incidents gives a rather complicated picture. First of all, memories of childhood incidents may simply be forgotten. Secondly, memories of traumatic childhood incidents may be repressed or denied. Thirdly, relivings of traumatic childhood situations are expected in many women with such a history. During these relivings, memories on specific incidents are very detailed and almost unchanged. Finally, childhood circumstances tend to be rated as more negative when women are in a depressive mood during an interview than when they are not in a depressive mood. The reliability of memories on traumatic childhood incidents will be high when flashbacks are concerned. Retrospective information on flashbacks is probably more valid than retrospective information about 'non-traumatic' memories. On the other hand women tend to have a 'disguised presentation' of their childhood history. Denial and repression seem to hamper questions on the reliability of retrospective reports in women with a history of traumatic child sexual abuse. In the evaluation of the role of retrospection, one important finding is that one fifth of the women were still sexually abused after the age of eighteen, (see chapter 4). Not all the memories on sexual abuse concern remote childhood incidents!

One can only expect adequate information on child sexual abuse and socially undesirable complaints, when women do trust the study, are willing to disclose their problems and the interview allows personal contact. Women who repress or deny child sexual abuse and do not trust the research project will not share personal, intimate and socially undesirable information with an interviewer. These considerations influenced our choice to recruit women in an indirect way. We made the choice to approach contact persons specialized in emotional support or therapeutic care of women with a history of child sexual abuse and asked them to help us with contacting. This approach had certain disadvantages. One disadvantage concerns the lack of information on the characteristics of the group of women recruited. This lack will be especially important when questions are considered as 'do women with a history of child sexual abuse have more symptoms than other women'. Our main research question concerns the connections between characteristics of child sexual abuse and several psychological and behavioural symptoms. With such a research question the way

---

history of severe abuse have difficulties in finding a satisfying relation with the therapist. They often go from one therapist to the other therapist, (Frenken and van Stolk, 1987). For some of these women participating in this study, the volunteer incest survival groups gave them the best emotional support they ever got.

of recruitment becomes less important. Anyway, we also investigated the characteristics of women recruited. Our respondents have a relatively high level of education and their histories of child sexual abuse can best be compared to those of women receiving poli-clinical or psychiatric help. The data obtained in this study are partly generalizable to women in such populations who have a history of child sexual abuse.

Our way of recruiting respondents implies that our respondents have some form of emotional support or had psychotherapy. A question is whether these contacts have influenced memory rehearsal processes or reports of psychological and behavioural symptoms. Before we started recruitment we checked whether symptoms, like dissociative symptoms, hallucinations, self-injury or suicidality were 'topics' during sessions of incest-groups. Of the symptoms mentioned, only suicidality had sometimes been discussed. In the Netherlands the actual situation of (individual) therapy for women with a history of child sexual abuse was (is?) rather bad. Most therapist did (do) not know how to cope with reports of child sexual abuse. It seems unlikely that restructuring of memories and symptom formation due to therapeutic processes plays a major role in the reports of most our respondents. Moreover, particular interview techniques may compensate for the problem of memory rehearsal.

Chapter 3

The Concept of Dissociation

3.1 Introduction

As a clinical entity dissociative disturbances have a rather long history. The attention to the role of severe childhood trauma in the etiology of dissociative disorders is of recent date. Dissociative disorders are frequently described and discussed without reference to severe childhood trauma. This chapter deals with certain conceptual problems inherently associated with the description of dissociative disorders. Causes of decline and renewal of interest in dissociative disorders are discussed, (3-2). Section (3-3) contains a discussion of the concepts that are used to define 'dissociative disturbances'. 'Disturbance in consciousness' is chosen as being the most important component of dissociative disorders. Historical speculations on the concept 'consciousness' are given, (3-4). Developments in thinking on two properties of 'consciousness' -unity of consciousness and continuity of consciousness- are presented, see (3-5) and (3-6). Section (3-7) deals with differences between 'dissociative unconsciousness' and other forms of unconscious processing. The role of extreme disturbances in consciousness in extreme dissociative disorders as defined by the D.S.M.-III is elucidated (3-8). An attempt is made to define the most extreme disturbance in consciousness: the time-gap (synonyms are: time-loss, blackout, subconsciousness, co-consciousness), see (3-9). The chapter concludes with summary and discussion, (3-10).

3.2 Fluctuating interests in dissociative disorders

Different groups of scientists are currently paying much attention to the concept of dissociation: psychiatrists or clinical psychologists, who describe dissociative disorders in patients seeking help for treatment, and cognitive psychologists who consider dissociation in the light of what is known today about information processing. Both groups build on concepts introduced by Janet (1889, 1907), Breuer and Freud (1893-1895), James (1890), Morton Prince (1905) and others.

One definition of dissociation, which combines the ideas of clinical psychiatry and cognitive psychology, is Ludwig's:

(dissociation is) a process whereby certain mental functions, which are ordinarily integrated with other functions, presumably operate in a more compartmentalized or automatic way, usually outside the sphere of consciousness or memory recall, (Ludwig, 1983, p.93).

This definition of dissociation implies that certain agreement exists on the nature of 'consciousness', the integration processes of mental functions and on 'normal and abnormal integration processes'. But, matter is not so simple. Debates have frequently been devoted to the concept of dissociation and disputes about the diagnosis of 'dissociative disorders' continue.

At the turn of the century, Janet (1889, 1907) introduced the term 'desagregations psychologiques' into psychology. By this concept a common denominator is given to several symptoms Janet observed in his patients. Morton Prince (1905) used the concept multiple personality disorder in the detailed description of his patient Ms. Beauchamp. Reviewing the history of dissociative disorders Putnam notes that until 1920 many books and articles were published on dissociative disorders. A decline of interest in dissociative disorders occurred after 1920, (Putnam, 1989, p.27-36). The book 'The discovery of the unconsciousness' written by Ellenberger (1970) initiated again an upsurge in interest in dissociative disturbances.

Putnam attributes the temporary decline in interest in dissociative disturbances to several synchronous developments. He mentions that psycho-analysis emerged shortly after the introduction of the concept dissociation and introduced the concept of repression. These two concepts competed with each other; similar symptoms initially interpreted as manifestations of dissociation were later conceived as indications of repression. Besides, psycho-analysts, like Breuer and Freud, severely criticised the use of hypnosis. It was stated that therapists not using hypnosis will not find cases of dual or multiple personality. Dissociative disorders were thought to be an artifact of hypnotic induction. These thoughts were illustrated by M. Prince's description of Ms. Beauchamp, (Putnam, 1989, p.5).

Another additional cause for the decline of interest in dissociation is thought to be the introduction of the diagnostic category schizophrenia. Bleuler published in 1908 a book called 'Dementia praecox or the group of schizophrenias'. In this book Bleuler includes the multiple personality disorder under the category of schizophrenic disorders[25]. Acceptance of Bleuler's schizophrenic disorder (around 1930) is accompanied by a sharp decline in publications on patients with a diagnosis of multiple personality disorder. Rosenbaum (1980) made this decline visible by counting articles on multiple personality disorder as published in the United States in the Index Medicus.

---

[25] The incorporation of the diagnosis multiple personality disorder in the group of schizophrenias only occurred in the American Diagnostic System. The European Diagnostic System has always differentiated hysterical psychosis from schizophrenic disorders.

Bleuler defines the group of schizophrenias as:

In every case we are confronted with a more or less clear-cut splitting of the psychic functions. If the disease is marked, the personality loses its unity: at different times different psychic complexes seem to represent the personality. Integration of different complexes and striving appears insufficient or even lacking. The psychic complexes do not combine in a conglomeration of striving with a unified resultant as they do in a healthy person, rather, one set of complexes dominates the person for a time, while other groups of ideas or drives are 'split off' and either partly or completely incompetent. Often ideas are only partially worked out, and fragments of ideas are connected in a illogical way to constitute a new idea, (Bleuler in Monograph series on schizophrenia no.1, reprinted in 1950, p.9).

In this definition of schizophrenia Bleuler definitely incorporates the concept of 'desagregations psychologiques' of Janet. In Bleuler's view the fundamental symptoms of schizophrenias consist of disturbances of association and affectivity, the predilection for fantasy as against reality, and the inclination to divorce oneself from reality (autism), (Bleuler, p.14). Bleuler's description of 'disturbances in association' concerns thought disorders, illogical and bizarre associations of ideas. The form of schizophrenia dominated by incoherent and illogical associations is still called schizophrenia, dissociative type, in France, (Robert, Ellul, Vernet, Desportes, Lecleire, Mollo & Darcourt, 1989). Another fundamental symptom Bleuler describes, relates to 'an inclination to divorce oneself from reality'. Such a detachment of reality is associated with a predominance of inner life and this predominance may result in difficulties in reality discrimination. A clouded consciousness and a deterioration of attention can often be observed in persons preoccupied with inner reality. In later years detachment of reality and clouding of consciousness are denoted by the concept dissociation. West (1962, 1975) uses the concept of dissociation in this way, when he presents theories on the etiology of hallucinations. These examples show that, although the diagnosis multiple personality disorder is only infrequently given after 1920, the concept of dissociation survived in the descriptions of fundamental symptoms of 'schizophrenic disorders'.

Even today a large overlap in phenomenological experiences exists between patients receiving a diagnosis 'multiple personality disorder' and patients receiving a diagnosis 'schizophrenia'. For instance, persons receiving a diagnosis 'multiple personality disorder' frequently have auditory hallucinations meeting Schneiderian criteria, (Bliss, 1980; Coons and Milstein, 1986; Kluft, 1987; Ross, Norton, & Wozney, 1989; see chapter 6 and appendix 6-1). Auditory hallucinations meeting the Schneiderian criteria are considered to be core symptoms for the diagnosis of schizophrenia. Ross et al. (1989) report that 41% of the patients who received a diagnosis of multiple personality disorder, have previously been diagnosed as schizophrenic. When considering the historical developments these findings are hardly surprising.

3.3 Dissociative disturbances as disturbances in consciousness

As we saw in the previous section, Bleuler included 'multiple personality disorder' in the group of schizophrenic disorders. Previously Janet and M. Prince, using the concept of dissociation, described 'disturbances in consciousness' in 'hysterical patients'. Symptoms of patients constituent of these psychiatric diagnoses did not change, (Ellenberger, 1970). But, nowadays a similar cluster of psychological symptoms are described as disturbances in 'identity' in patients with a 'multiple personality disorder', especially when the patient has a history with severe childhood traumata.

Let's look more closely at the description of dissociative disorders as current today. A dissociative disturbance is defined as 'a disturbance or alteration in the normal integrated functions of identity, memory or consciousness', (DSM-III-R, American Psychiatric Association, 1987). The most extreme form of dissociative disorders is multiple personality disorder. Other dissociative disorders specified in the D.S.M.-III-R are: psychogenic fugue; psychogenic amnesia; depersonalization disorder; and dissociative disorders not otherwise specified. A diagnosis 'dissociative disorder' indicates disturbances in three psychic functions: identity, memory, and consciousness. Kluft, Steinberg and Spitzer (1988), giving a rationale for the definition of dissociative disorders in the D.S.M.-III-R, emphasize the 'disturbances in identity'.

Although the connection among disturbances in the three psychic functions constituent of dissociative disorders seems rather evident, a conceptual analysis of interrelation between these functions has not yet been made. In the next section we will attempt to make such a conceptual analysis.

Extreme disturbances in consciousness and disturbances in memory (especially amnesia), are allied in an obvious way. For instance, when a person has not been conscious of the fact that certain events are taking place, it is very unlikely that this person will in a later period recall those events. When a person did not notice an event this will most likely result in amnesia for that event. On the other hand amnesia need not be the result of an extreme disturbance in consciousness. For instance, amnesia may be traced back to retrieval problems as well as to disturbances in consciousness.

How do these disturbances relate to disturbances in identity? Before we can reflect upon this question, the concept 'identity' has to be considered. This concept is used in at least two different ways; the first way concerns immediate 'self-reference' processes and the second way concerns a complex, higher-order concept of 'identity'.

William James noted that the most important aspect of consciousness is 'self reference'.

*The universal conscious fact is not 'feelings and thoughts exist', but 'I feel' and
'I think', (James, 1890, p.225-229)*[26].

The two functions, consciousness, and self-reference, are obviously
interrelated. From this point of view disturbances in self-reference are epi-
phenomena of disturbances in consciousness. A person with moderate
disturbances in consciousness will experience ego-dystonic feelings, thoughts
and attitudes. For instance, depersonalization feelings are characterized by
changes in consciousness as well as by feelings of ego-alienation. In more severe
disturbances a person may ascribe these ego-dystonic feelings to 'somebody or
something else'. It is likely that disturbances in self-reference have a rather
irreflective character. For instance, auditory hallucinations are thought to concern
thoughts a person does not mark with self-reference. These auditory
hallucinations have the form of immediate perceptions.

The concept of 'identity', by contrast, refers to higher-order, conscious,
reflections on 'the self', (Gergen, 1971; Burns, 1979; Edelman, 1989). Many
processes are involved in 'the sense of identity'. One of these processes may
consist of reflections on one's own disturbances in consciousness or problems
with recall.

In the work of Janet, James, and contemporaries, dissociative disturbances are
primarily conceived as 'disturbances in consciousness'. The importance of these
disturbances for the diagnosis of multiple personality is subject of debate. In the
D.S.M.-III-R 'amnesia' (read: time-gaps in the stream of consciousness) is no
longer a diagnostic criterion, (Kluft, Steinberg and Spitzer, 1988). However, this
will be changed again in D.S.M.-IV, (personal communication Frischholz,
October 1989). The analysis presented above seems to favour disturbances in
consciousness above the problematic concept 'disturbances in identity'. At
present the concept 'disturbances in identity' is given most emphasis. In our
study we conceive dissociation as a 'disturbance of consciousness'. Although
'disturbances of consciousness' deserve to be preferred to disturbances in
memory or identity, this does not mean that the concept 'consciousness' is free
from problems. On the contrary, consciousness has been banished from
psychology for decades, because it was considered to have too fuzzy a meaning.
However, certain developments in cognitive psychology and neurology have led
to a renewed interest for this concept. In the next section these problems and new
developments concerning the concept of consciousness are discussed.

3.4 Some historical notions on the concept 'consciousness'

As stated earlier, consciousness is an important concept in the definition of
dissociative phenomena. Wilkes (1988) recently discussed the implications of

---

[26] James's remarks have recently gained independent support from developments in the field of
artificial intelligence. See for instance Hofstadter and Dennett (1981).

definitions of identity and consciousness from a philosophical viewpoint. We paraphrase from her book the following passages on the history of these concepts.

The term 'conscious' and its cognates are, in their present range of meanings in West-European languages, scarcely three centuries old. These terms are notoriously difficult to translate into certain other (non-European) languages. Initially, the concept referred to the sharing of knowledge with other persons. Descartes was the first to introduce the concept of 'conscious mind', or at least is primarily responsible for making it the central and dominating theme in the philosopher's notion of what it is to be a person, (Wilkes, p. 214-217). The concept of the human mind became an inner space in which both sensations and clear and distinct ideas passed in review before a single 'inner eye'. Descartes could 'see clearly that there is nothing which is easier for me than to know my mind'. Locke based his conception on Cartesian ideas when he described a person as 'a continuity and unity of consciousness', (see Wilkes, p. 219).

Two centuries later Janet and Freud treated 'hysterical' and Bleuler and others observed 'schizophrenic patients'. They described the problems of these patients in terms of experienced disunity and discontinuity of the self, (Ellenberger, 1970). Freud grounded his general theory of psychological functioning on the problems of these patients. The fundamental premise became the division of the mind into conscious and unconscious parts, (Freud, 1923 [1960], p.3). He stressed the importance of unconscious processes for the definition of a person and assumed a 'tripartite structure of being' (ego, superego and id). In his description disunity and discontinuity processes became 'normal' in persons. 'Being conscious' is in the first place a purely descriptive term resting on perception of most immediate and certain character', (Freud, 1923 [1960], p.3-4)

> What is meant by consciousness we need not discuss; it is beyond all doubt, (Freud, 1933 [1969], p.508).

Freud's theories are mainly concerned with the nature of unconscious processes. From the sixties on, the interest has again been growing in the 'mystery of consciousness', (see Hilgard, 1986, p.2-3). The great debate today is on the nature of consciousness. Consciousness is now considered to be an obscure and perplexing notion, (Wilkes, p. 163). What was obvious to Descartes and Freud is not so obvious any more. But, probably all contemporary writers on the subject will agree with Freud that it is dangerous and misleading to identify the mind with the *conscious* mind. The problems around the concept 'consciousness' are partly caused by its fuzzy meaning. Wilkes suggests that there are at least four interestingly distinguishable kinds of ascriptions of consciousness, (Wilkes, p.174- 191):

- Consciousness means roughly awake, as opposed to being asleep or in a coma.

- Consciousness might be ascribed to the set of sensations, that are private to their possessors. Sensations are private, but can be communicated to others (I have pain). Consciousness may concern sensations, but not all the sets of sensations need to be conscious.
- Consciousness might be ascribed to perceptions. Perceptions, like vision and hearing, can be distinguished from sensations. Perceptions may reach consciousness, but are not by definition conscious, as subliminal perceptions illustrate.
- Consciousness of one's own attitudes and self-consciousness. Consciousness may concern reflections on a meta-level about one's own identity.

The first three forms of consciousness are considered to be primary forms of consciousness. Only the last is considered to be a higher order-form of consciousness, (Edelman, 1989).

3.5 Unity of consciousness

From a *philosophical point of view,* Wilkes argues that in all persons, in essence two different forms of unity and continuity exist. Research with patients suffering from commissurotomy constitutes this conclusion. Experimental study shows that, in these patients, information that is received by one hemisphere cannot be used by the other hemisphere. In itself, each hemisphere of these patients has its own consciousness, (Wilkes, p.142-143). Each hemisphere can sustain complex, conscious, and organized cognitive activity. In an individual with commissurotomy each hemisphere has an unity of consciousness. If then two minds exists in post-operative patients with a bisected brain, two minds must have existed in the pre-operative situation. She therefore concludes that we all may be really dual persons. However, commissurotomy patients are not aware of two different forms of consciousness. Researchers observed that in these patients a drive exists strongly to assert unity, a need to confabulate a unity. The psychological effects of the commissurotomy are not dramatic and only 'apparent' in laboratory situations.

The cognitive psychologist, Hilgard (1986) begins his book on 'divided consciousness' with the following passage:

The unity of consciousness is illusory. Man does more than one thing at a time - all the time- and the conscious representation of these actions is never complete. His awareness can shift from one aspect of whatever is currently happening inside his body or impinging on him from without, or events that are remembered or imagined. Furthermore, as an active agent, he is always making decisions and formulating or implementing plans, and he likes to believe that he exerts control over what he is doing; often, however, he may be deceived about the causes of his behaviour, (Hilgard, 1986, p.1).

Divided attention (awareness, consciousness) is an on-going process, and considered to be 'normal'. In all situations no unity of consciousness exists. As Hilgard has shown, human psychological functioning is best understood as the outflow of a general system, in which several sub-systems exist. These sub-systems consist of complex psychological functions that operate relatively autonomously. All these relatively autonomous systems send information to a centre, this centre may be called the 'ego'. This 'centre' does long term-planning and decides to which information attention should be (selectively) given. The 'decisions' of this centre are constrained by the information it receives from the relatively autonomous systems. For instance, one can plan to finish a job, but this planning may be achieved only if the several sub-systems are functioning normally. If strong sensations of pain reach consciousness, one will tend to change the direction of one's attention, change one's planning, or ignore these sensations.

With this general theory of psychological functioning, Hilgard tries to arrive at a deeper understanding of certain special forms of 'disunity of consciousness', which he calls dissociation. Hilgard speaks of dissociation when 'the attentive effort and planning continues without any awareness of it at all'. When attention and planning are present in a person, and at the same time she or he is not conscious of these processes, dissociation has taken place. Hilgard mentions two extreme forms of this dissociation of consciousness. In some persons with an excellent capacity to be hypnotised, a 'hidden observer' phenomenon can be demonstrated. Under hypnosis, certain persons seem to be capable of being aware and unaware of feelings of pain at the same time. The other example of 'dissociated consciousness' can be found in persons with a diagnosis of multiple personality disorder or related states, such as 'hysteria', extreme depersonalization and certain forms of schizophrenia, (van Heerden, 1982). In these conditions, more than one layer of consciousness seems to exist. In general, dissociated states of consciousness under hypnosis are not irrevocable, whereas these states in patients with a psychiatric disorder are not easy to reverse.

3.6 Continuity of consciousness

Janet began by considering the elementary parts of the mental system. He assumed that the elementary structures of the mind are psychological automatisms: complex acts, tuned to environmental and intra-psychic circumstances, preceded by an idea and accompanied by an emotion. Each of these psychological automatisms, by combining cognition, connotation and emotion with action, represent a rudimentary consciousness. All these elementary automatisms are bound together into a single, united stream of consciousness, and normally operate both in awareness and under voluntary control, (Janet, 1889,1907, as interpreted by Kihlstrom, 1984, p.158). During somnambulism a person is not aware of this 'stream of consciousness'.

James (1890) stated that psychologists have to study the fact that in each person, when awake, some kind of consciousness is always going on. There is a stream of feelings, of desire, of deliberation etc., that constantly passes and repasses and that constitutes our inner life. The fundamental quality of consciousness is that it has continuity. There may be interruptions, -time-gaps- during which consciousness disappears altogether, to come into existence again at a later moment; or there may be breaks in the quality or contents of thought, so abrupt that the following segment has no connection with the preceding one. However, time-gaps might be more numerous than is usually supposed. Consciousness itself may not have the quality of being aware of time-gaps, nor feel these time-gaps as interruptions.

If the consciousness is not aware of 'time-gaps', it cannot feel them as interruptions, (James, 1890 [1950],vol. I, p. 237-239).

For James the occurrence of time-gaps in the stream of consciousness is a subject for discussion. James can't answer the question whether or not time-gaps are a 'normal' condition. He specifies certain examples, in which time-gaps are definitely present. He notices that such time-gaps exist in somnambulism, naturally or induced. Other examples concern dreams which often are only remembered for a few minutes and then become irretrievably lost. When awake and absent-minded, we are visited by thoughts and images, that the next instant we cannot recall.

Only a few psychologists or psychiatrists after Janet and James have studied the phenomena of 'gaps in consciousness'. Recently Bowers (1984) has considered time-gaps, (although he does not use this word). His examples concern a special kind of dissociative time-gaps, the daze states and the reveries. Mental processes that occur during daze states or reveries are *not selectively attended* to, they are experienced as 'time-gaps'. That these processes are not selectively attended (are not noticed, have not reached consciousness) does not imply that they are not influential. All kinds of things may be perceived without being noticed. Bowers illustrates the importance of the distinction between perceiving and noticing, by investigations on subliminal perception and memory. Important determinants of thought and action can be unconscious by virtue of being perceived without being noticed. Thoughts passing through the mind during time-gaps may have great influence on the behaviour. Unattended and unnoticed facts, fantasies or daydreams may have an impact extending well beyond the person's ability to recall. Mental processes, such as daze states and reveries which take place during time-gaps, are examples of unconscious mental processes[27].

---

[27] These unconscious processes should not be equated with the psychoanalytic notion of 'the unconscious'.

Bowers states that there are several stages in mental processing that take place before a perception is noticed. One stage involves *selectively attending to* a perceived stimulus. It is the selective attention that transforms a perception into consciousness of what has been perceived (into noticing). If events, thoughts, images are not selectively attended to, it is unlikely that they will be processed in long-term memory. First, there is the occurrence of an event to be remembered, and then there is the memory of the event's occurrence. Dissociation is an illustration of the distinction between perceiving and noticing. Repression is about motivated forgetting. It is about emotional material that has been selectively attended to, processed in short-term and long-term memory, but is subsequently excluded from consciousness.

Kihlstrom (1984) mentions another example of 'time-gaps' in the stream of consciousness, in terms of James 'natural or induced somnambulism'. For Kihlstrom, dissociation refers to a lack of awareness of adequately registered inputs or adequately encoded memories, and perceived involuntariness, (Kihlstrom, 1984, p.186). The events, thoughts and images, during hypnosis and related mental states are *selectively attended and still remain unconscious*. During hypnosis, mechanisms which ordinarily occur when a person is selectively attending can be demonstrated; yet a person may still report being unconscious about what is going on.

According to Kihlstrom the phenomena of hypnosis and related states (read: 'time-gaps') deal with:

> *Mental representations, fully activated by perceptual inputs or acts of thought,*
> *above the threshold ordinarily required for representation in working memory,*
> *and available to introspection under some circumstances, seem nevertheless to*
> *be inaccessible to phenomenal awareness, (Kihlstrom, 1987, p.1451).*

Time-gaps, like those mentioned by James, Janet, Kihlstrom and Bowers, do not necessarily break 'the feeling of continuity' of a person. But, when there are breaks that are produced by sudden contrasts in the quality of the successive segments of the stream of thought, these may interrupt the feeling of continuity, (James, 1890, p. 239).

3.7 Unconscious mental states versus dissociative unconsciousness

Time-gaps are a special class of unconscious processes. There are also other forms of unconscious processes. First, two ways in which the word unconsciousness is used have to be considered. The concept unconscious may concern fainting, coma, being asleep as opposed to being awake, and being conscious, (Kihlstrom, 1984). In an alert state of mind different unconscious processes may be going on, (Kihlstrom, 1987):

- There are unconscious, automatic processes. One form of these processes is automatic by nature, for example, a listener is aware of the meanings of words but not of the linguistic principles by which the meaning of it is decoded. Another form concerns simple and complex skills, which are not innate, but may become unconscious by practising these skills until they become unconscious. These automatic processes consume little or no attentional resources. For instance, expert typists may carry on a conversation while transcribing complicated material.

- Preconscious processes. Empirical evidence exists that stimuli can be analyzed for emotional significance, as well as for certain physical features and patterns, before they reach awareness. It has, for instance, been demonstrated that stimuli too weak to be consciously detected may nonetheless have an impact on perceptual and cognitive functioning. Kihlstrom gives examples of subliminal perception and implicit memory.

- Subconscious processes. Examples are hypnotic alterations of consciousness and related states. For instance, in hypnotic analgesia subjects may be unaware of stimuli that have been thoroughly processed by the sensory-perceptual system. These hypnotic processes consume attention but are still taking place out of consciousness.

Virtually all psychological functions may operate without consciousness. The question nowadays is not which processes are unconscious but which mental processes are associated with consciousness. Kihlstrom formulates an answer to this question. Generally, persons are consciously aware of facts, thoughts, images which are *selectively attended to and thoroughly processed* (by the sensory-perceptual system). Moreover, 'declarative knowledge structures' are in principle available to phenomenal awareness. Declarative knowledge structures are a person's funds of general and specific factual information. The specific fund refers to personal experiences and is marked by self-reference, (Kihlstrom, 1987).

Kihlstrom states that consciousness has two functions: (1) Monitoring ourselves and our environment so that percepts, memories, and thoughts come to be accurately represented in phenomenal awareness. (2) Controlling ourselves and our environment, so that we are able to voluntarily initiate and terminate behavioural and cognitive activities, (Kihlstrom, 1984, p.150-151). Consciousness seems necessary for voluntary control, as well as for communicating one's mental states to others.

3.8 Dissociative disturbances in modern psychiatry

Nowadays most attention is given to multiple personality disorder. Psychiatrists involved with patients who receive a diagnosis of multiple personality disorder do report these patients to have 'disturbances in consciousness'.

Two different conceptualizations exist on 'disturbances in consciousness' in patients with a diagnosis multiple personality disorder. In one conceptualization persons with an extreme dissociative disorder suffer more frequently and more intensely from disturbances in consciousness. Disturbances in consciousness are thought to vary among persons in extensity, frequency and intensity. Minor and major or pathological forms of dissociation are conceptualized as lying along a continuum from the minor dissociations of everyday life to major forms of psychopathology, such as multiple personality disorder, (Putnam, 1986). All patients with an extreme dissociative disorder suffer from a variety of dissociative symptoms, like amnesia (read: time-gaps), daze states, depersonalization, derealization and fugue states, (Putnam, 1989). Such conceptualization of 'dissociation' allows the development of research instruments. One such research instrument -the Dissociative Experience Scale-has been used in our study.

The other conceptualization emphasises the most extreme disturbances in consciousness. Many articles and handbooks have recently been published on dissociative disorders, (Kluft, 1985; Bliss, 1986; Braun, 1986; Putnam, 1989; Ross, 1989; the Journal 'Dissociation'- since March 1988). Putnam's book, 'Diagnosis and Treatment of Multiple Personality Disorder' is used as a main source to elucidate the most extreme disturbance in consciousness. Putnam (1989) writes that 'amnesia' or 'time loss' is the single most common dissociative symptom in patients receiving the diagnosis multiple personality disorder. Amnesia or 'time loss' is defined by Putnam by an example:

> An example of what I mean by 'time-loss' would be the experience of looking at a clock and seeing that it was, say, 9:00 in the morning and the next thing that you are aware of is that it is, say, 3:00 in the afternoon, and you have absolutely no recollection of what has happened between 9:00 a.m. and 3:00 p.m., (Putnam 1989, p.75).

A patient who acknowledges periods of 'time-loss' can provide examples of performing complex tasks for which she or he has no memory. For instance, one patient, a certified public accountant, would report that he often lost three or four hours, only to find completed work sheets on his desk at the end of the day.

How do periods with extensive 'time-loss' relate to the diagnosis of multiple personality disorder? The essential phenomenological experience of a patient with such a disorder is, that there are patterns of behaviour about which 'a personality' says he or she has no consciousness, nor has voluntarily initiated these patterns of behaviours. Another 'personality' claims consciousness of, voluntary control over, and continuity of memories about, these patterns of behaviour. The lack of consciousness of behaviour patterns and environment may be experienced as a time-gap by one personality but not by the other. Under strict definition, one is not allowed to draw any 'diagnostic' conclusion from experiences of extensive time-gaps alone. One speaks of a multiple personality only if at least two distinct streams of consciousness are personified. This has to be stated by the patient her or himself. Only if a patient acknowledges at least two different streams of consciousness each with a 'unity and continuity of consciousness', behavioural control, and 'separate self-references' one speaks of a multiple personality, (Bliss, 1986, p. 123).

Can others, such as therapists, observe that a person is experiencing time-gaps? This is not an obvious question. When somebody is in a daze, other people are able to notice that something is going on. But, somebody experiencing a time-gap still acts in a normal way and nobody may notice a change. However, certain behavioural signs associated with changes in personalities can be observed. Observable behaviour during switches of personality are described by Putnam as:

> *The initiation of the switch is signaled by a blink or upward roll of the eyes. There may be a rapid fluttering of the eyelids. Transient facial twitching or grimacing often accompanies a switch. In addition, there may be bodily twitches, shudders, or abrupt changes in posture. If the switch takes several minutes to complete, the individual may go into an unresponsive, trance-like state with blank, unseeing eyes. A few multiples have convulsion-like switches that have, on occasion, been mistaken for epileptic seizures, (Putnam, 1989, p.120-121).*

3.9 Redefinitions and evaluations of dissociative disturbances

Cognitive psychologists describe the conditions under which sub- or unconscious processes (time-gaps) are called 'dissociative'. These conditions are not yet fully incorporated into the description of dissociative disturbances as used in psychiatry. Time-gaps are here defined as: discontinuities in the stream of consciousness while awake, during which a demonstrable selective attention exists to facts, and acts usually monitored, initiated and controlled by complex mental activities, are performed, while there is no consciousness of these facts or acts.

In this definition, dissociative disturbances of consciousness are conceived as disturbances of perception and not of memory; the disturbances are 'located' in the 'attentional strategies'. Attentional strategies are thought to play a crucial role in psychological processes between perceiving and noticing (consciousness). During dissociative disturbances of consciousness, attentional strategies are involved, but do not seem to result in consciousness. Disturbances of consciousness are experienced as time-gaps, as discontinuities in the stream of consciousness. During periods of 'time-loss' the person appears to function in a normal way.

The definition of time-gaps as specified above includes theoretical speculations of cognitive psychologists. We saw that experiences of time-gaps can be conceived as the most extreme disturbance in consciousness. Persons who report extensive time-gaps usually report other disturbances in consciousness too, like being in a daze state, depersonalization, derealization, acting automatically etc. In order to distinguish extreme time-gaps from other disturbances in consciousness several criteria are specified. Reports can only be called time-gaps if they meet these criteria:

1. The person reports to have had no consciousness of the environment or her/his own behaviour.

2. The person can not describe any focus of attention. This differentiates experience of time-gaps from daydreaming, being absorbed in thoughts, or events excluded from awareness because the focus of attention was on another event.

3. The person has no consciousness nor voluntary control over complex behaviour (like speaking, reading, writing), normally guided by consciousness. This criterion differentiates extensive time-gaps from passive behaviour, such as staring or sitting down and from complex but skilled acts normally not selectively attended, such as driving a car.

4. Other people tend not to notice any difference in functioning of the person: This criterion differentiates extensive time-gaps from immediate evident disturbances in consciousness, such as coma, fainting, pseudo-epileptical attacks or more subtle changes in consciousness, such as staring, daydreaming, sleep-walking etc.

The insights gained by cognitive psychologist can also be used to redefine the disorder 'multiple personality'. A multiple personality disorder is here defined as: 'several streams of consciousness co-existing in the same person, each stream of consciousness having its own self-reference, its personal declarative knowledge structure, and its own planning and control mechanism to direct behaviour and attention selectively to facts, thoughts and images. When one personality is exerting (voluntary) control over the behaviour, the other personalities may not monitor themselves. The environmental facts are not or not completely available to the stream of consciousness for the other personalities, nor do they exert substantial control over the behaviour'[28].

In this chapter much time and energy has been devoted to define experiences of time-gaps. The importance of time-gaps is situated in its logical implications. Time-gaps create a paradoxical situation in that a person seems to be at the same time aware and not aware of the environment, has initiated voluntary and involuntary behaviour. The logical conclusion from such descriptions would be that there exist several 'streams of consciousness'. Such a far reaching conclusion needs a firm base.

Until now we have not found a systematic study describing extensive time-gaps. Time-gaps are purely introspective phenomena. Other phenomena in psychology and psychiatry, like hallucinations, emotions or cognitions involve

---

[28] The matter is a complicated one, the DSM-III-R states that not only multiple personalities but also multiple personality states can exist. We will leave aside this further complication.

introspection too. However, introspection is considered to be a rather weak base of information. Generally, several sources of information are used to study psychological phenomena. For instance, data on self-reports, behaviour correlates, physiological measures and neurological processes are systematically gathered in order to study emotions. Experiments are designed to test theoretical models, (Frijda, 1988).

Certain attempts have been made to specify observable behaviour changes when 'switches between different streams of consciousness' are taking place, (Putnam, 1989). No independent studies have confirmed these observations.

Several studies have been undertaken to observe physiological differences associated with different streams of consciousness, for a review see Putnam (1984). When different personalities are exerting control, this is associated with differences in neurophysiological functioning such as visually evoked potentials, or frequency bands measured by topographical spectral electroencephalography. Such neurophysiological studies are still in their infancy.

Phenomena observed during experiments with hypnosis have been compared with dissociative features of patients, (Hilgard, 1986). Studies with hypnosis discuss the possibility of multiple streams of consciousness, because certain observed phenomena, like the hidden observer phenomenon and source amnesia, contain similar paradoxal situations. Persons with a high hypnotic capacity seem to be at the same time aware and not aware of their surroundings, (Hilgard, 1986; Kihlstrom, 1985).

3.10 Summary and discussion

Consciousness is considered to be a complex and obscure notion. Unity and continuity of consciousness are not fundamental properties of consciousness. Consciousness can not be attributed to specific mental functions. However, certain agreement exists on the function of consciousness. Consciousness has two functions: (1) Monitoring ourselves and our environment, so that sensations, percepts, memories, and thoughts come to be accurately represented in phenomenal awareness. (2) Controlling ourselves and our environment, so that we are able to voluntarily initiate and terminate behavioural and cognitive activities. Consciousness seems necessary for voluntary control and long-term planning as well as for communicating one's mental states to others.

Consciousness has certain properties: (a) It is usually marked by a self-reference. (b) In general, events that are not consciously identified are not likely to be consciously recalled later on. (c) Attentional strategies play a mediating role between perception of information and consciously identification of that information.

Normally, persons are only conscious of facts, thoughts, images that are selectively attended to. When selectively attended facts or declarative knowledge structures are (temporarily or permanently) not available to consciousness, this is considered to be a special, dissociative state. When such a state is spontaneously reported and frequently experienced it is considered to indicate multiple streams of consciousness. Such a state is conceived to be a pathological condition, indicating a severe dissociative disturbance. The most extreme form of dissociative disturbance in consciousness concerns thoughts, feelings, attitudes and actions which occur outside phenomenological awareness and voluntary control. In this study such a state is called a time-gap, on the analogy of the concept used by William James to denote a similar phenomenon. Time-gaps are defined as: discontinuities in the stream of consciousness while awake, during which there is a demonstrable selective attention to facts, and acts, usually monitored, initiated and controlled by complex mental activities, are performed, while there is no consciousness of these facts or acts. At the operational level this means: (a) The person reports that s/he has no awareness of the environment. (b) S/he can not describe any focus of attention. (c) S/he finds out that complex patterns of behaviour are performed, that are normally guided by decision making and voluntary control. (d) Others in the direct environment do not notice the person to be 'absent minded'.

One should make a distinction between time-gaps and repression. Repression concerns motivated forgetting. It is about emotional incidents that had been selectively attended to, and processed in short-term and long-term memory, but were subsequently excluded from consciousness. In retrospect, it may be difficult to differentiate between time-gaps and repression, (Kuiper, 1973). Amnesia as a concept includes both time-gaps and repressions.

Conceptual analysis of the properties of consciousness predicts that a disturbance in consciousness will be associated with a lack of self-reference, a lack of voluntary control, difficulties with long-term planning and difficulties in communicating one's mental state to others. As far as we know, no systematic investigation exists concerning the question whether a lack of self-reference or a lack of voluntary control is also associated with disturbance in consciousness.

Attentional strategies play a crucial role in processes that occur between perception of stimuli and becoming aware of stimuli. But, which attentional processes are associated with disturbances in consciousness? Not much has yet been published on this topic.

When recent developments in psychiatry about dissociative disorders are considered against the background of history, certain points of interest emerge:

• The recent fascination of psychiatrists and psychologists for dissociative states has resulted in a renewed interest in theories of psychologists and psychiatrists at the start of this century. Symptoms of patients with a dissociative disorder have remained the same over many years, but accents and concepts describing these symptoms have changed somewhat, (Ellenberger, 1970). Nowadays in the description of dissociative disturbances, the emphasis is on 'identity disturbances' in multiple personalities, whereas Janet and James stressed the 'disturbances of consciousness' in 'hysterical patients' and Bleuler included similar disturbances in the category of schizophrenic disorders.

- The most important change with regard to 'dissociative disorders' consists of the insight in the role of severe childhood traumata in the etiology dissociative symptoms. Although Janet (1911) acknowledges the role of trauma ('idées-fixes') in the etiology of 'hysteria', he stresses that the 'weak mentality' of the patient determines whether he or she will experience re-occurrences of the 'idées-fixes'. These trauma are defined by Janet as 'response-based', they had no 'stimulus-based' character. In his early works, Freud (1896) discovered the role of 'child sexual abuse' in the etiology of hysterical complaints. Within a decade he rejected these insights again.

In chapter 6 several current notions on the role of childhood trauma in the etiology of dissociative symptoms will be elaborated.

Chapter 4

Family dynamics and characteristics of child sexual abuse

4.1 Introduction

The family background of child sexual abuse has already been the subject of intensive study. Theoretical notions have been developed with regard to the dynamics of child sexual abuse. These notions serve as a frame of reference against which our findings will be evaluated and discussed. Relevant literature on this subject is presented in section (4-2). Findings of our study concerning the family background of child sexual abuse are offered in section (4-3). These findings concern the constellation of the family (4-3-1), parentification processes (4-3-2), emotional neglect by mother (4-3-3) and the relationship between girl and perpetrator preceding sexual abuse (4-3-4). Findings on characteristics of child (sexual) abuse are given in section (4-4). Age characteristics of the child being sexually abused, types of perpetrators and age difference between perpetrator and girl are examined (4-4-1) and (4-4-2). Data on intrusiveness of sexual acts and pregnancies resulting from intercourse are given (4-4-3). Extra attention is paid to means of coercion, ambivalences and relations with duration of sexual abuse (4-4-4). For data on multiple perpetrators and knowledge the respondents have about other sexually abused girls in their direct surroundings, see (4-4-5). Hiding of sexual abuse from mother and the factors contributing to this behaviour will be presented in (4-4-6). Ways of resistance and their relation with the coercion exerted by the perpetrator are examined in (4-4-7). Implications of the various characteristics for the psychological impact will be discussed in (4-5). The chapter ends with a summary and an evaluation of the findings (4-6).

4.2 Dynamics of child sexual abuse and family characteristics

Child sexual abuse has been found to follow a rather predictable pattern. According to Sgroi, Blick and Porter (1982) sexual abuse usually consists of five separate phases. These phases are fully described by Courtois (1988). In the following passage we summarize these five phases:

- The engagement phase. Child sexual abuse is usually perpetrated by somebody who has access and is known to the child either through kinship ties or by being placed in a position of caretaking or authority (baby-sitter, neighbour, friend, clergy, day-care worker etc.). The adult's position of authority communicates to the child that sexual abuse is acceptable. Most perpetrators do not need to resort to violence or coercion. Instead, they engage the child by suggesting that the activity is a game, something special, a way to gain exclusive attention or particular favours. This initial phase in child sexual abuse is often difficult to distinguish from hugging and expressions of warmth and affection.

- The sexual interaction phase. The next phase typically includes an escalation of sexual activities. Initially bodily contacts may have expressed warmth or affection, but the character of these contacts changes. Sexual misuse and abuse occur when boundaries are crossed, when bodily contact is not controlled or limited, but rather used to satisfy the 'dependency' or 'gratification needs' of the involved parent or 'authority'. When the purpose of the perpetrator is to satisfy such needs, often the intrusiveness of sexual activities progresses. Bodily contacts may extend to genital zones and start to be explicitly directed to these zones. Masturbation activities find their expression in presence of the child. Ejaculation by a male perpetrator, sometimes against the body of the child, may occur at any time in this progress. Oral sex, mutual masturbation, anal and vaginal penetration mark the escalation of sexual activities. Although this pattern of escalation is frequently found, it need not always be present.

- The secrecy phase. When sexual activities escalate, concealment is used to eliminate accountability and to allow repetition and continuation of the activities:

    Child sexual abuse has been described as an addiction/compulsion for the perpetrator due to the powerful reinforcement accompanying the behaviour, including sexual pleasure and orgasm, enhanced self-esteem due to feeling wanted and cared for, and a sense of power, dominance, and competence in a relation where few demands are made for mutuality and reciprocity. To continue this pleasurable activity the perpetrator must pressure the child to maintain the secret, (Courtois 1988, p.29-30).

    Different forms of blackmail and coercion are used to enforce the child's silence. For many children caught in intra-familial abuse, secrecy often seems to be the only option.

- The disclosure phase. Some children disclose the secret, by accident or on purpose. Whether the disclosure is accidental or planned, the family typically responds with anxiety and alarm. The perpetrator's role in the family and the family-loyalty are among the factors that determine how the family reacts. It is an unfortunate reality that parents of a child that has been sexually abused by someone other than a close family member are more likely to react in a protective fashion towards the child than when the child is sexually abused by somebody they know well. The degree of protectiveness will depend in part on the identity of the perpetrator. Many mothers of sexually abused children react in a protective fashion, although for some it is common to deny the abuse or to attack or to blame the child for its occurrence. Some may have known about the abuse all along or encouraged it or participated in it. These knowing or participant mothers are likely to join the perpetrator in denial, with self-protection as the primary goal.

- The phase of suppression. Family members frequently attempt to suppress the child's report and to minimize the severity of the abuse or the child's response to it. They want to rid themselves of the aggravation and discomfort of the situation and to avoid adverse publicity as well as intervention by the police or social services.

In literature family dynamics of child sexual abuse have been discussed from different perspectives. The family perspective gets support from different studies and is also elaborated in our study. The typical family in which sexual abuse occurs has rigid boundaries with regard to outsiders. Family members are mutually dependent on each other to meet their needs and are said to be enmeshed. Appropriate boundaries are lacking between individual family members and between generations. Children are involved in role-reversal with their parents, the most extreme example occurring, of course, when the child becomes sexually involved with a parent.

Another common manifestation is the child that becomes the one who takes care for one or both parents in the family, (Gelinas, 1981; Kroon, 1986; Courtois, 1988). Despite the enmeshment found in these families, emotional deprivation predominates. Children may starve for affection, with the emotional contact surrounding the abuse being their only source of nurturing.

Two types of families in which child abuse occurs are distinguished, (Kempe and Kempe 1984) the 'normal appearing family' and the 'chaotic family'. The 'normal appearing' family appears to be solid and well-functioning for outsiders, in that the parents have a stable long-term marriage, are socially and often financially stable and seem well-integrated in the community. These parents often lack the energy to nurture each other emotionally in an adequate way, much less their children. Both are affectionally needy as a result of their own emotional impoverished upbringings. The emotional impoverishment has as a consequence that the mother turns to the daughter for emotional and household support and that the father turns to the daughter for sexual and emotional sustenance. Children often turn to each other to meet emotional and other needs, and, not infrequently, their relation becomes sexual. The other type of family-the chaotic family- has been studied most, because welfare workers most frequently have contact with those families. The problems in chaotic families span generations, have a relatively low socio-economic standing, with a marginal functioning of individual members and the family as a whole (such as alcohol and drug abuse, instability of intimate relationships, and brushes with the law). Children in chaotic families are basically left to raise themselves and, without adult supervision, are vulnerable to all forms of abuse inside and outside the family.

4.3 Family-context of child sexual abuse

In the previous section a synopsis was given of investigations about child sexual abuse and family dynamics. Most studies pay attention to the family-context in which sexual abuse manifested itself, (Finkelhor, 1979; Herman, 1981; Summit, 1983; Gelinas, 1983; Russell, 1986; Fromuth, 1986; Draijer, 1988, 1990; Courtois, 1988 to name just a few). In section 2-6-2 we compared certain demographic characteristics of our respondents with such characteristics found in other relevant studies. For instance, we concluded that the socio-economic background of our respondents did not differ from such a background of women in general with a history of child sexual abuse or from the background of women in a representative sample of the population. The next section presents our findings on particular other characteristics of the family of origin.

4.3.1 Number of children in family of origin

In most studies little attention is devoted to the number of children in family of origin and child sexual abuse. In our study we found that 31% of the women came from families with six or more children, (see scheme 2-2). One possible interpretation for this finding is that children in large families get less individual attention or supervision. Courtois (1988) states that in case of emotional deprivation, children may turn to each other to meet emotional and other needs, and their relation easily becomes sexual. This interpretation predicts brothers to be the main perpetrators in families with a large number of children. An analysis of variance was performed to investigate this prediction.

When in our sample we select the women with siblings (N=93), an analysis of variance (one-way ANOVA) shows that women who were sexually abused by a brother come from larger families (mean number of children $M=3.71$, s.d.=1.08) than women who were not sexually abused by a brother (mean number of children $M=2.9$, s.d.=1.01), (F=13.29, p<.001).

4.3.2 Parentification

Mothers of women with a history of child sexual abuse are found to be frequently ill, depressed, or absent, (Finkelhor, 1979; Herman and Hirschman, 1981; Gelinas, 1983; Draijer, 1988). When mothers are absent, fathers do not take over female parental roles, but expect their daughters to run the household and to take care of younger children. A daughter, who functions as a 'mother substitute', runs a higher risk of being involved by her father in an incestuous relation than a daughter who is not a 'mother substitute'. To the father the sexual activities appear a 'logical extension of the mature female responsibilities' this daughter already has. We distinguished two forms of parentification, household parentification and emotional parentification, (see Kroon, 1986). A child is said to be emotionally parentified when the parents confide emotional problems to her and expect the child to give help and advise.

Of the women participating in our study, 27% told that as a child they were responsible for the household during more than half a year, 26% did support their mother emotionally and 15% supported their father emotionally. A girl responsible for the household is more frequently found to be sexually abused by her father than by other perpetrators, (χ^2=7.66, df=2, p<.05). Sexual abuse by father (-figures) prevails in girls involved in emotional parentification, (χ^2=9.6, df=2, p<.01). Moreover, oldest or only daughters are more often sexually abused by father (-figures) than by other perpetrators, (χ^2=12.04, df=3, p<.01). These findings show that parentification processes increase the risk of or are associated with sexual abuse by father(-figures), but not with abuses by other types of perpetrators.

4.3.3 Emotional neglect by mother

Sexual abuse has been found to occur mainly in family constellations in which the daughter has a poor relation with her mother, (Landis, 1956; Herman, 1981; Finkelhor, 1984; Draijer, 1988, 1990). Girls having a poor relation with mother turn to others for affection. Some men may respond with sexual feelings when children turn to them with needs for affection. When these men have no inhibitions or restrictions, sexual feelings are translated into sexual acts. A bad relationship with mother may not only precede but may also be the effect of sexual abuse: sexual abuse is mostly hidden from the mother and in the long run the girl feels isolated from her. In most studies no distinction is made between poor relationships preceding sexual abuse and poor relationships being caused by child sexual abuse.

In our study 38% of the women reported that before the age of seven they had either a neglectful relation with their mother or lived in children's refuge centres. Before the age of thirteen, 43% had such (non-) relationship with their mother. An early neglectful relationship between mother and daughter (before seven years of age) is associated with sexual abuse by natural fathers, (χ^2 = 7.9, df=2, p<.05), and not with abuses by any other type of perpetrator.

A note should be made on these findings: normally people do not remember much from before the age of five years. Memories from these early age periods can't be trusted. But, even then an important aspect of these findings remains that a considerable proportion of the women in our sample can't remember ever having had a warm and emotional relation with mother.

4.3.4 Type of relation preceding child sexual abuse

Perpetrator-girl relations preceding child sexual abuse are extremely diverse: these relations vary from intense emotional contact to brute denigration of the girl by the perpetrator, (Herman and Hirschman, 1977; Summit and Kryso, 1978). No studies are known to us explicitly reporting the relationship between perpetrator and girl preceding sexual abuse. In table 4-1 such data are presented.

Table 4-1: Relation between perpetrator and girl preceding sexual abuse, (percentages)

N=92	relation preceding sexual abuse
	%
He was the only nice one	14
Normal	36
Neglecting	12
Psychological aggression	4
Physical aggression	10
Don't know	24

A fourth part of the women in our sample (24%) can't remember anything about the relation with the (main) perpetrator before the onset of sexual abuse, mainly because this abuse started before the age of seven. A quarter (26%) reported that the (main) perpetrator has always been neglecting and denigrating or physically aggressive. A third of the women (36%) said that the relationship with the perpetrator was just normal, they did nice things together and sometimes made a quarrel. Some women (14%) had a special relation with the perpetrator, he was the only one paying attention to her.

Women reporting physical aggression preceding sexual abuse have all been sexually abused by their fathers. Most women sexually abused by a family-friend as main perpetrator reported the relation to be either normal or very special before sexual abuse began.

4.4 Characteristics of child sexual abuse

Histories of child sexual abuse can be categorized in different ways. Since abuses have many characteristics, different categories may be highly interdependent. In appendix 4-1 we present a principal component analysis of a number of these characteristics[29].

---

[29] In fact, the presentation of data in this chapter is based on the results of the principal component analysis.

4.4.1 Age characteristics of child sexual abuse

For many women it is difficult to exactly remember the onset of sexual abuse. Sexual abuse may have started early in life or may have evolved gradually. The start of sexual activities is difficult to establish in relations where hugging is common, like in normal parent-child relations. For most women the sexual abuse started at the moment they were persistently touched at genital zones or were asked to help the perpetrator with masturbation. An exact age at which these activities started is often difficult to determine: the best answer may be an estimate. The age at which sexual abuse started is reconstructed with the help of memories about synchronous events, such as activities with girl-friends, teachers in school-classes, family-members dying in certain periods, removals to other cities or countries, and changes in family-constellation. However, for some women situations triggering sexual abuse are well traceable in time. For instance, sexual abuse may have started when a sibling was born, when mother was in hospital, when moving to a house near grandfather etc. Moreover, for some women medical observations, placement in a children refuge centre, or a confinement by court of the perpetrator, clearly mark the period of sexual abuse. Data on the age at which sexual abuse started are presented in table 4-2.

Table 4-2: Age at onset of sexual abuse, (percentages)

N=97	age onset sexual abuse
	%
Before the age of 7 years	32
Between 7 and 9 years	38
10 years and older	30

A third of the women (32%) estimated or knew that sexual abuse started when they were six years or younger. One woman mentioned that sexual abuse also ended before the age of seven, for the others sexual abuse continued after the age of six. A third of the women (30%) reported the onset of sexual abuse to be at age of ten or older. For 5% of the women sexual abuse began at, or after, the age of 13 and one woman reported the onset to be at fifteen years of age.

Table 4-3 presents data on the age at which sexual abuse ended.

Table 4-3: Age at which child sexual abuse ended, (percentages)

N=97	age end sexual abuse
	%
Until 9 years	5
10-12 years	21
13-15 years	26
16-18 years	20
Older than 18 years	20
Don't know	8

For a quarter of the women child sexual abuse stopped before the age of thirteen. The finding that child sexual abuse continues into adulthood in a fifth of the women is quite surprising. This finding is exceptional, compared with data obtained in other studies, (see 2-6-3).

Table 4-4: Duration of child sexual abuse, (percentages)

N=97	duration
	%
< 1 year	5
1-3 years	10
4-6 years	27
7-9 years	23
10 years or longer	26
Don't know	8

In table 4-4 findings on duration of sexual abuse are presented. Data on duration of child sexual abuse include the best possible estimates of the start-age of sexual abuse. A fourth part of the respondents have experienced child sexual abuse for more than ten years. And only 5% of the women has been sexually abused for a time period less than one year or only a few times over several years. When women really did not know when sexual abuse ended, duration was coded as don't know.

4.4.2 Types of perpetrators

Table 4-5 presents data on the types of perpetrators by whom the girls have been sexually abused. Most women in our study have been sexually abused by their natural fathers (58%). In total, 67% of the women were abused by father (-figures) (two women were sexually abused by both their natural, and their stepfather).

Table 4-5: Types of perpetrators sexually abusing the girl, (percentages)

N=97	types of perpetrators
	% a)
Father	58
Stepfather, friend of mother	11
Mother	2
Brother	29
Grandfather	7
Uncle	8
Cousins, brother in law	8
Family friends	18
Unknown perpetrators	8

a) The percentages exceed 100%, because 41% of the women experienced sexual abuse at the hands of multiple perpetrators.

Sexual abuse by mother was reported by two women being abused by father and brothers too. If all sexual abuse experiences are taken into account, 9% of the women have been sexually abused by a perpetrator being at least five years older, but not yet adult at the onset of sexual abuse. The other women were sexually abused by adult perpetrators (over eighteen years).

In rather exceptional cases girls have been sexually abuse by mother. For instance, Dieuwertje told:

Dieuwertje (B14) was ordered into bed by her mother while her mother was laying naked. Then she had to kiss her mother all over the body. This started at an early age and lasted until Dieuwertje was fifteen years of age. Generally her mother had rather strict moral codes, so she felt frightened by these commands. Her father and her three brothers sexually abused her too.

4.4.3 Intrusiveness of sexual acts and pregnancies

In literature it is reported that sexual activities often gradually progress in intrusiveness, (Gelinas, 1981). Until the age of eleven or twelve, sexual activity is usually limited to fondling or oral-genital contact, due to the difficulty of vaginal intromission. After that age difficulties of vaginal intromission do not seem to restrain perpetrator from sexual penetration.

We distinguished a variety of sexual activities, such as touching breasts or genital zones, masturbation, oral, anal or vaginal penetration, and perversions. Frequently sexual abuse consists of a variety of sexual acts. We have chosen the most intrusive sexual act ever experienced, to characterize the sexual aspect in a child abuse. Table 4-6 presents data on the most intrusive sexual act ever experienced as a child.

Table 4-6: Most intrusive sexual act ever experienced as a child,
(percentages)

N=97	intrusiveness sexual acts
	%
Touching primary or secondary genital zones	9
Masturbatory activities/ attempted intercourse	13
Any form of penetration (oral, anal, vaginal)	67
Perverse sexual activities	10

For some women (9%) touching primary or secondary genital zones was the most intrusive sexual act they experienced as a child. For instance Hansje told,

Hansje's (B30) father used to pinch her breasts so hard, that tears often welled to her eyes. This happened over a period of many years and she tried to avoid being alone with her father whenever possible.

Another small proportion of the women (13%) were involved in masturbatory activities, and no sexual penetration took place. The majority of the women (67%) experienced a form of penetration, including oral or anal sex. Anal or oral sex was reported by 19% of the women and some women (10%) have been subjected to perverse sexual activities, such as objects inserted in vagina or anus, or being forced to have sex with an animal.

In our study, an analysis of variance (one-way ANOVA) shows an association between the most intrusive sexual acts ever experienced as a child (intrusiveness of sexual acts) and age at which sexual abuse ended, $(F=3.01, p<.05)$[30]. This association, although reaching a level of significance, is not really strong; this may be due to the fact, that for only five women sexual abuse stopped before the age of ten, (see table 4-3).

When girls grow older and vaginal penetration is involved, a real danger exists that sexual abuse results in a pregnancy. Sixty percent of the women in our study were exposed to such a risk, (N=94, 5 women couldn't remember if there was an actual risk of pregnancy). Often neither the perpetrator nor the girl used any contraceptives, when vaginal penetration was involved. Sometimes the perpetrator practiced dangerous methods to prevent conception, like coitus interruptus. Forty percent of the women were not exposed to dangers of childhood pregnancies, because sexual activities did not include vaginal penetration, contraceptives were used, or sexual abuse stopped before the menses

---

[30] Oral and anal penetration are included in the 'general concept' of penetration. At an early age sexual abuse predominantly consists of oral or anal sex. Women who experienced oral or anal penetration as the most intrusive sexual acts were excluded from analysis. If they were included the correlation between intrusiveness of sexual activities and end of sexual abuse disappears, $(F=2.58, p=.06)$.

began. Fear of becoming pregnant does not need to correspond with the actual danger of becoming pregnant, six percent of the girls not endangered, feared conception. They had inadequate information about sexuality. Eight percent of the women never felt afraid although actually running a risk of becoming pregnant. These women just never thought about this possibility or simply were convinced that such a thing would never happen to them. Of the women running the risk of pregnancy almost a quarter reported a conception. Nine women got an abortion after a pregnancy resulting from child sexual abuse, three women actually got a child and two women were doubting the paternity of their child: either their (step-) father or their husband could be the biological parent.

> Floor (B23) grew up in a family in which father frequently assaulted mother. She went to live with the family of her ten year older sister and brother in law. This escape from the situation with her father and mother brought no improvement, her brother in law soon started to abuse her sexually and at the age of ten years, father abused her too. As she grew older, sexual abuse by her brother in law involved intercourse and she permanently feared to become pregnant. Several times when her menses did not come, her brother in law tried to evoke an abortion by illegal means. One day after illegal abortion practices, she had to go to hospital, because things went wrong. She felt that she ran a risk to die if this situation were to continue, and that nobody would care. After this experience she found the power to escape from the family situation.

4.4.4 Means of coercion and ambivalent attitudes

Several authors state that a perpetrator does not need physical aggression as a means of coercion to establish sexual contacts with children, (Justice and Justice, 1979; Gordon and O'Kleefe, 1984). The preponderance associated with the age difference between girl and perpetrator is enough to establish sexual contact. An older perpetrator may use other means than physical aggression, such as seducing or misleading a child. Frequently, a child is sexually abused by an adult who has a responsibility for the child. Such an adult may have so much power that a child must obey.

Certain studies performed with representative samples of a general community indeed show physical aggression to be hardly used as a means of obtaining 'compliance'. In the study of Russell (1986), women hardly reported physical aggression. Moreover, such studies predominantly include sexual abuses occurring only once or a few times. As described in previous sections, physical aggression most often occurs in long-lasting sexual abuse when a situation escalates. For instance, Gelinas (1981) states: As children grow older, actual force is increasingly used by the offender. Older children are more frequently physically hurt by a perpetrator than younger children. Studies on samples of women soliciting for therapy find that long-lasting father-daughter incest dominates. In such studies, physical aggression in the perpetrator-girl relation is frequently present, (Jones, 1986). In long-lasting child sexual abuse, the situation may escalate in such a way that physical aggression is often used by the perpetrator.

Analogous to the questions asked in samples of general populations, our study included a question on 'means of establishing sexual contact' applied by the perpetrator to gain compliance of the girl. The answers to this question soon appeared to concern long-lasting and complex situations: Means of gaining compliance at the onset of sexual contacts frequently were non-aggressive. The answers of the women often appeared not to concern *means of establishing sexual contact*. So, the answers of 25 women on this question were analysed in more detail. This shows that some coercion and physical aggression mentioned by women concerned perverse acts. The experience of Lieneke is illustrative:

> Lieneke (B50): 'I got a lot of attention from my father. He gave me golden jewels. My brothers were jealous of me. They say I was my father's darling. But, in the night he came to me. My father was a tailor and he had a pressing-board. I was strained between it and I got blindfolded. He also used a heavy weight. He used to penetrate me with all kinds of tools, that I could not see'.

Other forms of aggression had the aim to denigrate the girl or to prevent disclosure. Such forms of aggression were performed after the perpetrator reached an orgasm. For instance, some perpetrators seduced the girl in sexual activities by promising nice things, but afterwards said 'you are very ugly, a whore, a bad girl'.

Table 4-7: Coercion used by main perpetrator during sexual abuse, (percentages)

N=95	coercion used by main perpetrator
	%
Seduced, misled	27
Obeyed, psych. coercion	28
Gripping, holding	14
Physical aggression	13
Life threats, verbal	4
Life threats, physical	12
Don't know	3

In most studies the means of coercion exerted by one perpetrator during child sexual abuse has been recorded. To compare our data with findings obtained in other studies, a similar categorisation has been applied. The most severe form of aggression ever experienced in such circumstances is taken to characterize the means of coercion. When a girl initially was seduced and violence started only after resistance, escalating in a verbal threat of murder, it is scored by us in the category, 'verbal threat of murder'. If the girl was seduced at the beginning and the sexual abuse ended when she started to resist, the means of coercion is coded as 'being seduced'. Findings about the most severe means of coercion used by the main perpetrator during child sexual abuse are presented in table 4-7. As is shown in this table more than half of the girls (55%) are seduced, misled or they just obeyed, a quarter (27%) experienced at least once physical force or physical aggression, and 16% experienced a verbal threat or actual attempt of murder. Threats of murder reflect an escalation of the situation. The history of Conny gives some insight in situations in which an actual threat of murder is experienced.

> Conny (B45): 'When I got older (fourteen years), I started to resist the sexual abuses by my father. He smothered my resistance by pressing cushions on my face. I felt these cushions as life threatening. It was life threatening, you did not know what he planned to do. Real assaults or fingers around your throat, very suffocating. Afraid to be killed'.

Descriptions of escalating relationships show that when child sexual abuse lasts for a long time, the abuse may dominate the entire relation. In these cases, coercion is not only applied during sexual contacts, but intrudes larger parts of the living situation. For 39% of the women, sexual abuse didn't intervene with normal life, 4% of the women told that the perpetrator was aggressive (psychologically or physically) in every day life, but these aggressive acts were unrelated to the sexual abuse and 24% of the women mentioned that from their viewpoint psychological aggression, physical aggression or threats of murder by the perpetrator in normal living situations were related to their resistance against sexual abuse.

Moreover, for a certain proportion of the women, aggression did not stop when the sexual abuse ended. Some women experienced the most severe coercion after they had successfully resisted sexual abuse. For instance, Hanna told:

> Hanna (B31): 'My father had always been beating me, but it got worse when I successfully resisted sexual abuse (at the age of twelve). When I got a boyfriend, my father and I really had big fights. Once it escalated and my father threatened me with murder. I believed he was really capable of doing so. When I started to resist, my father urged me to earn some money by cleaning a house. He said he needed the money for going to prostitutes, because I refused sexual contact'.

After the sexual abuse ended, 46% of the women had no intensive contact with the perpetrator any more, 17% of the women said that their relation with the perpetrator remained normal to good, and 23% reported that aggression started or continued after termination of sexual abuse.

One of the logical implications of the analysis presented above, concerns the way of asking about coercion. To get adequate information on coercion, one should explicitly make inquiries about *all coercion and aggression associated with child sexual abuse* and not only about coercion as a means to obtain compliance for sexual contact.

Data presented in table 4-7 concern only severity of coercion during sexual abuse applied by the 'main' perpetrator. But, not all coercion associated with sexual abuse is applied during the sexual abuse, and 41% of the women experienced sexual abuse at the hands of multiple perpetrators as a child, (see table 4-10). Abuses by other perpetrators, especially when this other perpetrator is a close family member, may involve similar complex situations as described above. For an adequate understanding of the impact of child (sexual) abuse, it is necessary to get information on all (sexual) abusive experiences. Hence, severity of coercion associated with sexual abuse applied by the first, second and third perpetrator has also been coded in our study. Table 4-8 contains data concerning the most severe coercion ever experienced by a girl as result of sexual abuse applied by one or more perpetrators.

Table 4-8: Severity of coercion associated with child sexual abuse exerted by one or more perpetrators, (percentages)

N=97	coercion ever experienced
	%
No coercion at all.	3
Psychological aggression	33
Physical aggression	37
Life-threats	27

Only a small fraction of the women (3%) reported that they had sexual contacts with adult or older men, while no coercion at all was associated with it. A third of the women has been sexually abused by a perpetrator who was bad tempered when she resisted, blamed her for the abuse, or isolated her by preventing contact with peers (psychological aggression). The majority of the women were at least once subjected to physical aggression (37%) or experienced a verbal threat or actual attempt of murder (27%). These numbers presented concern the most severe means of coercion associated with child sexual abuse, ever experienced.

Severity of coercion ever experienced is of course just one aspect of the abusive situation. Abusive relations may have rewarding as well as violent aspects; often these relations are better characterised as ambivalent.

Kitty (B44) was raped by her brother and his friends. During these abuses she was reduced to a nobody by this brother, who also protected her against his friends when they teased her at school.

Cynthia (B11) was abused by her father who hardly paid any attention to her, except during the times he wanted sexual contact. Then he devoted much attention to her and was tender and caring.

Sometimes, children are subjected to rapidly changing attitudes, (Summit, 1983; Spiegel, 1986). For instance, the father of Floor (B23) used to compliment her before sexual contact was established and used to blame her for this contact just after reaching an orgasm by saying 'fuck you bastard'. Some perpetrators create situations with enormous contradictions.

Lia (B46) states that her father was always cold and punitive. If only a little thing went wrong she was sent to the bathroom and there she was beaten with a rod. When her father wanted to have sexual contact with her he was nice to her. At night after the assaults he came in her bed to make it up. Sometimes he instructed her to misled her mother: she had to pretend being beaten, by screaming aloud while, he raped her in the mean time.

It is difficult to code ambivalent situations. The relation between perpetrator and girl is defined as non-ambivalent when either the relationship is characterized by no coercion or when the relationship is completely coercive. Women reporting that the perpetrator neither paid attention to them outside the situation of abuse nor during sexual abuse were considered as living in an unambivalent situation. A perpetrator shows ambivalent behaviour when: (a) He is nice to the girl outside the sexual abuse situation but coercive during abuse or when he is violent or neglecting outside the abuse situation and warm and nurturing during sexual abuse, (b) is nice or misleading when trying to establish sexual contact, and denigrating to the girl after sexual satisfaction is obtained.

The prevalence of ambivalent attitudes in the main perpetrator is presented in table 4-9.

Table 4-9: Ambivalent attitudes of the perpetrator, (percentages)

N=94	ambivalence
	%
No ambivalence, no-coercion	3
Ambivalence attitudes	59
No ambivalence, overall coercive.	37

Most perpetrators (59%) had ambivalent attitudes to the girls they abused. Negative attitudes and punishments alternated with positive attitudes and rewards. However, 37% of the women reported that child sexual abuse occurred in a relation characterised by a complete lack of positive attitudes on the part of the perpetrator.

Above, the expectation was formulated that more severe means of coercion are being applied when a girl grows older, starts to resist or threatens with disclosure. In literature, special attention is paid to the father (-figures) who feel particularly threatened by the possibility of discovery of their abusive practices. We investigated the relation between severity of coercion and respectively type of perpetrator and duration of the sexual abuse.

A correlation exists between severity of means of coercion and duration of sexual abuse, (r=.34, p<.001). When sexual abuse lasted longer, the probability is larger that severe means of coercion were used by the perpetrator. When women are selected, who were sexually abused by father (-figures), a similar correlation is found between duration of sexual abuse and severity of coercion, (r=.40, p<.001). When women are selected, who are sexually abused by other perpetrators, the correlation between severity of coercion and duration of abuse does not reach a level of significance, (r=.22, p=n.s.). Another question is whether working class fathers are more inclined to use physical aggression and threats of murder than fathers with middle- or higher-class jobs. We found that there is no correlation between socio-economic class of the father and severity of coercion, (r=-.02, p=n.s.). When we select women abused by father (-figures), we find similar results, (r= -.17, p=n.s.).

In a multiple regression analysis two characteristics show an independent and significant contribution to the severity of coercion: severity of coercion applied by the perpetrator preceding sexual abuse, and duration of sexual abuse. Appendix 4-2 gives detailed information on the multiple regression analysis. The multiple correlation R=.46, p<.001, the explained variance is 21%.

4.4.5 Multiple perpetrators, sexual networks and group rapes

Most studies pay attention to the number of perpetrators by whom the child has been sexually abused. However, they report only the number of perpetrators, no detailed information is given on abuses by a second or third perpetrator. Only in studies in which sexual networks or sex rings were the focus of interest, abuses at the hands of more perpetrators are discussed in more detail, (Burgess, Groth and McCausland, 1981; MacFarlene and Korbin, 1983; van Stolk and Frenken, 1986). Descriptions in the literature on child sexual abuse show that children subjected to these abuses are seldom the only children abused by the perpetrators (Herman, 1981, Burgess et al., 1981). The same perpetrators are frequently found to sexually abuse sisters, nieces, younger aunts, and girl-friends too. Moreover, mothers of sexually abused children are found to have a similar history, more often than mothers of non-abused children, (Goodwin, McCarthy & DiVasto 1982). Van Stolk and Frenken (1986) assume that sexual networks, in which sisters and other female family members are sexually abused by multiple men, are typically found in working class families. In such families, girls are 'reared', for the occupation of prostitute.

Our findings concerning the number of perpetrators at the hands of whom women are sexually abused as a child, are presented in table 4-10. In our study, 59% of the women are sexually abused by one perpetrator and 41% are subjected to child sexual abuse at the hands of more than one perpetrator. The 97 women participating in this study were sexually abused at the hands of 175 perpetrators.

Table 4-10: Number of perpetrators by whom girls were sexually abused, (percentages)

N=97	number of perpetrators
	_%_
One	59
Two	23
Three or more	18

Of the women, 18% were sexually abused at the hands of three or more perpetrators and nine women report having been sexually abused by five or more perpetrators.

Helmi (B33) was sexually abused by her oldest brother (twenty-one years old) when she was seven, but she does not remember anything of these abuses. She has information about this abuse only via others. She has been told that her brother was put in jail for one year and a half, because of this sexual abuse. Another brother (eighteen years old) sexually abused her, she can't remember exactly how old she was when that started, she puts it down at nine years. This brother gave her money for it. Her father sexually abused her when she was nine to ten years old. He had sexually abused Helmi's elder sister too. This sister had been placed in a psychiatric institution, after she had revealed this sexual abuse to her mother. This uncovering of the incest made her sister the scapegoat of the family. When the elder sister was placed away from home father started to abuse Helmi. Helmi knows he has also abused another sister.

Eleven women were as a child subjected to group rapes. When the women being abused by more perpetrators are selected, it appears that half of them report that a father (-figure) was involved. In our study, family-friends and unknown perpetrators in majority are 'invited' to the sexual abuse by father or brother. None of the unknown perpetrators are the first or main perpetrator (four were involved in group-rapes). The majority of women sexually abused by more than one perpetrator thought that the perpetrators were aware of each other's sexual abuse: 40% had observed interactions among different perpetrators and 24% have reasons to assume that the perpetrators have known it from each other.

Some women got involved in a new abusive situation by means of blackmail. The blackmail concerned the knowledge by a second perpetrator of the sexual abuse by the first.

Elsbeth's (B21) father was a grocer. She used to help her father in the shop. Her father start to fondle her breasts when she was ten years of age. When she was sixteen years he tried to rape her several times, but she resisted fiercely. Her father's health declined, a servant came to help them in the shop. When this servant observed what her father tried to do, he started to blackmail her. If she would not have sex with him, he would inform her mother. From this time on she was sexually assaulted by two men.

Some men think that as soon as a girl or woman is stigmatized by 'breaking a taboo', she is willing to have or must tolerate 'sexual contacts' with other men too. It seems that girls subjected to child sexual abuse are vulnerable to new sexual traumatization, because of these stigmatization processes.

In table 4-11 findings are presented on child sexual abuse experienced by other girls in the direct environment, (as far as women know).

Table 4-11: Others in direct environment who are also sexually abused, (percentages)

N=90	others are also sexually abused
	%
No others	37
Mother	8
Sister(s), brothers	42
Nieces, aunts	11
Girl-friends	2

In total, 55% of the women found out that others in the direct environment, mostly of similar age, were sexually abused by the same perpetrator(s). Not all women dared to talk with family-members about child sexual abuse, so the real figure may be higher than reported in this study. Eight mothers of our respondents were sexually abused as a child. One women was sexually abused by her grandfather who had sexually abused her mother, and she was born out of these sexual contacts.

Sometimes the girl knows about sexual abuse of others by direct observation:

Jaqueline (B46) slept with her two sisters in one room. Her father often came to their room to fondle her elder sister. Her sister got money and nice dresses from her father and initially Jaqueline was jealous of her. This jealousy ended, when her father started to fondle her too. She was forced to oral sex with him and this she experienced as horrible.

Other women discovered that the perpetrator abused other sisters/brothers, but they did not know it as a child. They were informed about the sexual abuse of the others when they disclosed their own incest-secret years later.

To obtain an impression of the prevalence of sexual networks in our sample, data about multiple perpetrators and sexual abuses of other children were combined. Data about the prevalence of networks shown in table 4-12 demonstrate that only a fourth part of the girls had an 'exclusive contact' with the perpetrator, another quarter were sexually abused by more than one perpetrator and know that others as children had similar experiences with those perpetrators.

Table 4-12: Prevalence of sexual networks, (percentages)

N=90	sexual networks
	%
One perpetrator-one child	25
One perpetrator-more children	33
Multiple perpetrators-one child	18
Multiple perpetrator-more children	24

We have examined the assumption of van Stolk and Frenken (1986), that sexual networks are predominantly found in working class families. An analysis of variance (one-way ANOVA) shows that daughters of fathers with working class jobs were sexually abused at the hands of multiple perpetrators (N=52, M=2.04, s.d=1.39) more frequently than daughters of fathers with a higher level of occupation (N=28, M=1.43, s.d.=.88), (F=3.6, p<.05). When the father was the main perpetrator, a similar association between level of occupation and number of perpetrators has been found to exist, (F=4.01, p<.05). These findings suggest that the likelihood that 'lower class fathers' stimulate others inside or outside the family to abuse their daughter(s) sexually is somewhat higher than that fathers in other socio-economic groups will do so. Inspection of the interviews showed that all girls sexually abused by five or more perpetrators came from 'lower class' families, for at least three girls the (step-) fathers functioned as a kind of pimp. They exploited the sexuality of their daughter(s) by inciting friends to sexual abuse, and they received money or rewards for these practices. Moreover, three mothers received rewards when they permitted (step-) father and others to abuse their daughter.

An analysis of variance shows no association between level of occupation of father and sexual abuse of other children in the family. When the group of women sexually abused by their father is selected, similar findings are found,

(F=1.36, p=n.s.). Fathers with 'higher class jobs' abuse other children in the family equally frequently as fathers with 'working class jobs'.

4.4.6 Hiding child sexual abuse from mother

Findings presented above imply that secrecy around sexual abuse is too general a concept. Secrecy can refer to hiding sexual abuse from mother, from the family in general or from 'society outside'. In case of multiple abuse within the family, it seems as if these sexual abuses are communicated somehow. When sisters are present during sexual abuse or recognise what is happening, there may exist a secret, but not for all the family-members. Within the family, mother is the most important person from whom perpetrators and girls try to hide sexual abuse. Data on (attempts of) hiding sexual abuse from mother are presented in table 4-13.

Table 4-13: Hiding sexual abuse from mother, (percentages)

N=97	hiding sexual abuse from mother
	%
Mother can impossibly know C.S.A. [a]	56
Girl surprised mother don't know C.S.A.	15
Mother knows C.S.A.	23
Mother involved in C.S.A. or is perpetrator	5

[a] C.S.A. means child sexual abuse

More than half of the women (56%) said that sexual abuse was carefully hidden from mother. In these cases it was impossible that mother could have known sexual abuse to take place, because it always happened when mother was not at home, it occurred in another place than at home, or mother was hospitalized. Some of the women (15%) were astonished that mother said she knew nothing, because sexual abuse wasn't carefully hidden, it happened also when mother was at home. Almost one-quarter of the women (23%) have told their mother explicitly about the sexual abuse in the period that it took place and five percent of the women mentioned that mother was involved in sexual abuse or was a perpetrator herself.

What makes perpetrators and children hide sexual abuse from mother? It is likely that both perpetrator and girl try to hide these abuses, the perpetrator because he fears the consequences of disclosure and the girl because she wants to prevent mother from becoming upset. First we explored whether the relation between mother and daughter was an important factor contributing to hiding behaviour. A strong positive association appears to exist between emotional neglect by mother and not hiding abuses from mother, (F=18.89, p<.0001). The majority of the women (78%) who had a normal to good relation with their mother said sexual abuse was carefully hidden. When a girl was emotionally neglected by mother, sexual abuse was not that frequently hidden from her, or mother was even involved. Another question concerned the extent to which girls or perpetrators hide sexual abuse from mother. We found an association between hiding behaviour and number of perpetrators, (F=19.1, p<.0001): of the women sexually abused by one perpetrator, 80% reported that it was carefully hidden and 65% of the women being abused by three or more perpetrators either told their mothers about these abuses, or their mother was involved herself. Another contributing factor to the disclosure appears to be the duration of sexual abuse. The longer the sexual abuse lasted, the less carefully it was hidden, (F=5.88, p<.001). Some mothers (4%), who were informed about sexual abuse by their daughters, stopped the situation of sexual abuse. Inspection of the interviews shows that some mothers were themselves heavily assaulted by the perpetrator (usually their husband) and had no power at all.

In a multiple regression analysis, emotional neglect by mother, number of perpetrators, and duration of sexual abuse, all three appear to have an independent and significant contribution to hiding behaviour, (R=.65, p<.0001; the explained variance is 43%). Detailed information about the multiple regression analysis is presented in appendix 4-3.

4.4.7 Explicitness of resistance

How do children resist sexual abuse? There was no need to resist, because sexual abuse was non-coercive for three of the women. Most women report several forms of resistance, the most explicit way of resistance has been coded. Girls who, from the start used intra-psychic ways of resistance, like dissociation, have resisted the abuse the least explicitly. Girls who have been fighting when the situation escalated, possibly have also been using intra-psychic ways of resistance, but they certainly have been very explicit towards the perpetrator in their protest against the abuse. Table 4-14 presents figures on explicitness of resistance.

Table 4-14: Explicitness of resistance, (percentages)

N=76	explicitness of resistance
	%
Intra-psychic	24
Avoiding	41
Nagging	5
Physical	30

Avoiding the perpetrator was the most common explicit way of resistance (used by 41% of the children). The children remained outside until somebody else than the perpetrator was at home, they were hiding in dark corners of the house, they tried to get another room together with their sister, they avoided visiting their grandfather or covered themselves with the blankets. Almost a third of the children (30%) explicitly resisted the perpetrator by fighting with him or threatening him with a knife. For almost a fourth part of the women, dissociation was the way of coping with the abuses. Explicitness of resistance is associated with severity of coercion, (χ^2=24.84, df=9, p<.01). Children being denigrated or isolated by the perpetrator predominantly tried to avoid him. Children experiencing physical coercion or threats with murder either physically resisted, (N=20), or dissociated, (N=15).

4.5 Characteristics of child sexual abuse and psychological impacts

Above we described many different categories that can be distinguished in order to systemise and describe very different histories of child sexual abuse. By distinguishing among different categories, one gains an important reduction of information. A question is whether it is possible to obtain even more reduction of information. Most authors consider the question of 'severity' of child sexual abuse. Which of the characteristics as described above may constitute a measure of severity of child sexual abuse?

Several methods exist to attack this problem. For instance, by comparing characteristics of child sexual abuse in studies using a sample of a general female population with those characteristics in studies using a sample of women in therapy or women admitted to psychiatric institutions. Such a study has been performed in the United States by Herman, Russell and Trocki (1986). They found women in therapy with a history of child sexual abuse to be more frequently sexually abused by their father, to have experienced more intrusive sexual acts, and more frank violence, to be sexually abused for a longer period than women reporting child sexual abuse in a community sample. In chapter 2, section 2-6-3, characteristics of child sexual abuse reported in three Dutch studies are compared, (see scheme 2-3). We saw that in the Netherlands a similar difference in characteristics of child sexual abuse exists as has been found by Herman et al.

Systematic collection of information on histories of child sexual abuse shows that in almost all samples of women known to psychiatrists or psychologists similar characteristics of child sexual abuse are reported, (Herman, 1980; Frenken and van Stolk, 1987; Silver, Boon & Stones, 1983; Mrazek, Lynch & Bentovim, Pierce & Pierce, 1985; Friedrich, Urquiza & Beilke, 1986; Kendall-Tackett, 1987; Brière and Conte, 1989; Chu and Dill, 1990). The study of Mannarino and Cohen (1986), in which children are predominantly reported to be sexually abused only a few times and not by father (-figures), forms the only exception.

Another way to solve the problem of 'severity of child sexual abuse' concerns the relation between characteristics of child sexual abuse and 'long-term effects'.

Russell (1986) reports that five characteristics of child sexual abuse are related to women's evaluation of the psychological impact: father being the perpetrator; physical aggression associated with sexual abuse; sexual penetration; sexual abuse lasting more than two years; and an age difference of ten or more years. In a multiple regression analysis, these five characteristics were found to contribute independently to long-term effects. As we already mentioned in chapter one, Browne and Finkelhor (1986) reviewed all studies investigating relationships between different characteristics of child sexual abuse and psychological impact [31]. They report that six characteristics are more or less associated with long-term effects: being sexually abused at the hands of multiple perpetrators, severity of coercion, father as perpetrator, duration or frequency of child sexual abuse, intrusiveness of sexual acts, and age-difference between girl and perpetrator. On the basis of the review of Browne and Finkelhor and the findings of Russell we assume that the six characteristics of child sexual abuse mentioned above are related to the 'psychiatric' symptoms included in our study.

In our opinion, Herman, Perry and van der Kolk (1989) constructed the most sophisticated measure of severity of childhood traumatization. They composed a cumulative trauma-score in which all forms of abuse are taken into account and attention is paid to the age at which these abuses took place. In scoring the severity of sexual abuse they include four of the six characteristics specified by Browne and Finkelhor. The construction of this cumulative trauma-score has been elaborated in chapter 2-5-1. In appendix 4-4 the mean cumulative and sub trauma-scores are presented.

4.6 Summary and discussion

This chapter has several purposes: to describe the characteristics of family dynamics and child sexual abuse as reported in our study, to gain understanding in the meaning of different characteristics, and to examine several assumptions developed in other studies.

The women in our study were predominantly sexually abused by father (-figures) and the abuse lasted for a long period of time. The longer the sexual abuse continued, the more the girl started to resist and the more severe means of coercion were used by the perpetrator when sexual contacts did not stop. We found that severe means of coercion are rarely used at the onset of child sexual abuse, but the use results from an escalating situation. In coercive long-lasting sexual abuse, girls try to stop the abuse, they threaten with disclosure and behave rebelliously. In this escalating situation perpetrators resort to massive oppression in order to keep control over what is happening. We find that the use of physical aggression or threats of murder by the father is not associated with socio-

---

[31] A serious defect of their review is that they do not differentiate between the various psychological impacts.

economic class of the family. This finding is rather exceptional. Non-sexual physical child abuse is strongly correlated to the socio-economic class of the family, (Strauss, Gelles and Steinmetz, 1980). Our finding makes it plausible that the use of physical aggression by the father is inherently related to long-lasting coercive sexual abuse.

A quarter of the women participating in this study had an 'exclusive' relation with the perpetrator. Most women either reported that the perpetrator sexually abused other children too, or they had themselves been abused at the hands of multiple perpetrators. The finding that more than half of the women knew that other children were abused by the same perpetrator has an implication. Several Dutch studies show the prevalence of sexual abuse of girls to be around 10 to 15%, (Ensink and Albach, 1983; Vennix, 1983; Draijer, 1988, 1990). When most perpetrators do abuse more than one girl, the general prevalence of perpetrators sexually abusing female children might be lower than 10-15%.

Most perpetrators and girls try to hide sexual abuse from the mother. This is especially so when a girl has a normal or good relation with her mother. It is likely that both perpetrator and girl try to hide these abuses, the perpetrator because he fears the consequences of disclosing and the girl because she wants to prevent mother from being upset. If the mother has emotionally neglected her daughter, the perpetrator nor the girl tries to hide sexual abuse from mother, and mother may even be involved. When sexual abuse lasts longer, attempts to hide become less rigidly; the perpetrator may think that mother will not notice it anyway and the girl may decide to tell it to mother. Multiple sexual abusive experiences are seldom hidden from mother; mother may be involved or considered by the perpetrator as too powerless to intervene.

Child sexual abuse is found to occur in families with many children. In these families, elder brothers are predominantly the perpetrators. Moreover, parentification does increase the risk of child sexual abuse by father (-figures).

With regard to findings as reported above, several remarks should be made:

- The histories of child sexual abuse are reported as seen through women's eyes. We did not take into account reports of others, like the mother or the perpetrator. We do not claim to present the 'truth'. But, we have no reason to doubt the reported histories.

- The group of women participating in our study is not selected in a random manner and this evokes the question of generalizability. By comparing women who participated in our study with those participating in two other, recently executed Dutch studies, we learn that women in our study have similar child sexual abuse characteristics as women soliciting for therapeutic help. Findings of our study may be generalized to women in poli-clinical or psychiatric settings. This means that therapists engaged with women asking for help, in majority are dealing with women who have a rather severe history of child sexual abuse. Many therapists appeared to be not successful in dealing with those problems. Women with such histories frequently have many different therapeutic contacts before they find a satisfying therapeutic relation, (Frenken and van Stolk, 1987). A considerable part of the women participating in our study (44%) received the most satisfying help from 'volunteers' guiding those 'incest-survival' groups.

- Repression of memories may form a major problem for retrospective studies on traumatic events: traumatic events are generally repressed and this is especially the case when memories concern child sexual abuse associated with severe means of coercion, (Brière and Conte, 1989). By our recruitment strategy we have tried to prevent this problem of repression. A study with a retrospective character struggles with the question of reliability of information on childhood incidents. The problem with retrospective data is that rehearsal of memories may change the incidents experienced in childhood. However, we do not know whether 'flashbacks', involuntary intrusions of images of traumatic incidents, follow the same principle of memory rehearsal as described to occur in 'normal' retrieval processes. The majority of our respondents reported flashbacks, (Albach, 1991). The flashbacks may constitute an accurate source of information. Retrospective information via flashbacks is more reliable than retrospective information of non-traumatic memories. We frequently observed reconstruction activities of childhood incidents when we asked formal questions like: 'At which age did sexual abuse start?' 'How often did it take place?' Other reconstruction activities, often mentioned, concern the explorations by women whether 'vivid images of incest' are based on real incidents. For more information on these reconstructions, see chapter 6.

- Some researchers discuss the possibility that reported threats of murder are mainly based on the perception of women and not on real threats, (see Conte, Brière and Sexton, 1989). In our study, women were asked to report why the question on 'threats of murder' was answered positively. The answers of the women incorporated real dangers, such as cushions tightly pressed on the face, hands around throats, illegal abortion practices, fighting with knives, severe physical assaults, or reckless car-driving. Perpetrators might not have the intention to kill, but might have used severe means of oppression only to prevent disclosure and to continue sexual abuse. In any case, according to the answers of the women, the experienced threats of murder were based on realistic perceptions of the situation and not on vague feelings or on free-floating anxieties.

Six characteristics of child sexual abuse are thought to represent the severity of child sexual abuse experiences: sexual abuse by multiple perpetrators, severity of coercion, father as perpetrator, duration of sexual abuse, intrusive sexual acts, and age-differences between girl and perpetrator. The assumption is put forward that these six characteristics of child sexual abuse are related to the 'psychiatric' symptoms considered in this study.

Chapter 5

You don't see, hear, feel anything

child sexual abuse and level of dissociation

Marlene (F36) scored extremely high on the Dissociative Experience Scale (D.E.S.). At the time of the interview, she lived with her three children in a shelter for one-parent families. She has been beaten badly by her former friend. She reports having been sexually abused by her father from her seventh until her twenty-seventh year. Because child sexual abuse was suspected, she was placed in a children protection centre by a child court when 11 years old. When her parents divorced, she returned to live with her mother. But, after a short period the father again joined the family. Her mother was frequently ill, and 'she did not want me'. She also lived in a foster family for some time. Her father had intercourse with her, strapped her, threatened her with a knife and locked her up. 'He always said the same, I'll kill you'. He said that before and after he raped her. 'You are not allowed to tell it to anybody'. She has frequently told her father 'I'll stab you' (certain periods she used to sleep with knives under her pillow).

5.1 Introduction

Early psychological theories assumed a causal connection between childhood (sexual) trauma and repression or dissociation. After the abandonment of the role of childhood trauma by these early psychological theories, other trauma theories have been developed. Literature has been reviewed on this development in thinking regarding the connection between childhood trauma and repression or dissociation (5-2-1). Experiments have been performed to gain insight in the way adult people react during severe traumata (5-2-2). Theories on the connection between traumata in childhood and dissociative disorders in adult life are presented (5-2-3), studies on these connections have been performed (5-2-4), more specific impressions of therapists are formulated (5-2-5), different assumptions deduced from clinical descriptions are summarised (5-2-6). The section on research methods describes the problems to be met when asking about severe disturbances in consciousness (5-3-1), and contains information on the Dissociative Experience Scale (5-3-2). Almost no descriptions exist about the phenomenology of the most extreme disturbance in consciousness, the time-gap. Statements are presented about indirect registration of time-gaps (5-4-1), direct registration of time-gaps (5-4-2), function and implications of time-gaps (5-4-3), antecedents of time-gaps during adult life (5-4-4), and during child sexual abuse (5-4-5). Section 5-5 starts with the presentation of the general level of dissociation (5-5-1) and in this section assumptions are investigated on the relation between level of dissociation and severity of child (sexual) abuse (5-5-2), cumulation of abusive experiences (5-5-3), ambivalent attitudes of the perpetrator (5-5-4), parental neglect (5-5-5), age at which the sexual abuse occurred (5-5-6), and new traumatic incidents in adult life (5-5-8). The relation between cumulative childhood trauma and level of dissociation is compared with other symptoms included in our study (5-6). The chapter concludes with a summary and a discussion of the implications of the research findings (5-7).

5.2 Traumata and dissociation

5.2.1 General developments in thinking on childhood trauma, repression, and dissociation

In coercive long-lasting sexual abuse, girls try to stop the abuse, they threaten with disclosure and behave rebelliously. In the escalation of this situation perpetrators resort to massive oppression in order to keep control over what is happening. Massive means of oppression consist of threats of murder or repeated physical assaults, (see chapter 4). Children who are subjected to massive oppression somehow have to find ways to cope with the situation. Already at the end of the 19th century, authors like Janet and Freud mentioned dissociation and repression as ways of coping with childhood trauma. These concepts, initially introduced by Janet (1911) and Freud (1896), lost their connection with childhood trauma. Freud himself disconnected the repression concept from early childhood trauma; universal conflicts in childhood, such as the oedipus complex, became the main subject of repression, instead of childhood trauma. Janet stressed 'mental weakness' in patients using dissociation to prevent consciousness of 'idées-fixes'. Janet's 'idées-fixes' have the character of 'accidentels pénibles'. These incidents were especially painful for the patient, but they had not the character of overwhelming traumata.

The renewed attention to the role of overwhelming traumata in childhood and their relation to dissociative disorders is of a recent date. At present a debate is going on whether or not dissociative disorders should be conceived as a special form of post-traumatic stress disorder, as representing an 'extreme adaptation to very severe chronic child abuse', (Spiegel, 1986; van der Kolk, 1987; Kluft, 1988; van der Kolk and van der Hart, 1989).

In the next sections existing concepts on the relation between trauma and dissociation are elaborated.

5.2.2 Studies on trauma and dissociation

In general people are inclined to react with denial, depersonalization or dissociation when confronted with overwhelming traumata such as life-threatening dangers, (Noyes, Hoenk, & Kupperman, 1977; Putnam, 1985; Horowitz, 1986; van der Kolk, 1987). Noyes et al. used the concept 'transient depersonalization syndrome' in describing these reactions. This depersonalization syndrome consists of 'alterations in awareness of the self', 'feelings of strangeness or unreality', 'loss of emotion' and 'sense of detachment', 'altered perception of time and space', 'loss of sensations', 'loss of control' and 'disturbance of memory', (these symptoms are conceived to be signs of disturbance of consciousness). Besides these effects, contrasting experiences are reported, such as 'speeded thoughts', 'heightened bodily sensation', 'vivid mental imagery', 'intense emotions', 'a sense of increased control', and 'panoramic memory', (these symptoms are conceived to be signs of hyperalertness), (Noyes et al. 1977, p.401). This study concerned reactions of persons involved in car-accidents. During those accidents most persons reacted with hyperalertness, but a small portion of the persons reacted with mental clouding, (dreamlike alterations in consciousness accompanied by dull thoughts, and blurred vision and hearing). These severe reactions are also denoted with the concept dissociative reactions. Mental clouding, Noyes et al. assume, is a severe form of depersonalization developing in response to extreme experiences of anxiety and threats to life.

In the period after the trauma most persons show biphasic reactions. A phase of denial alternates with a phase of intrusion by memories, (Horowitz, 1978; van der Kolk, 1987). In the phase of denial a person is often in a daze state, staring blankly into space. There may be a narrowed focus of attention and a failure to react appropriately to new stimuli. This may be accompanied by an inner sense of clouded perception, including a diminished awareness of bodily sensations[32]. During involuntary intrusions of memories, mental images of any sense modality may be experienced as if they were real perceptions, (Horowitz, 1986, p.24-25).

A few laboratory experiments have been performed to study reactions on traumata. For self-evident reasons traumatic events employed in experiments can not be severely traumatic, and memories of these traumata used to have a 'panoramic' character. However, certain laboratory experiments are designed in

---

[32] Horowitz describes that traumata are followed by 'denial states'. In this denial states the person may experience depersonalization. Horowitz does not make a link between depersonalization feelings during the trauma and denial states in the phase immediately following this trauma. We assume that the denial states after the trauma consist of depersonalization feelings which may correspond with the depersonalization feelings during the trauma and that these denial states may as well be an indication of intrusions of traumatic memories.

such a way that traumatic events induce memory impairment, (Loftus and Burns, 1982; Christianson and Nilsson, 1984). In these experiments three different theoretical causes for memory impairment were considered. This impairment may be the result of (a) disturbed encoding processes, (b) inadequate storage processes, (c) difficult retrieval of traumatic events. Christianson and Nilsson's (1984) findings indicate that impaired memory of traumatic events has to be primarily understood as a disturbance of encoding processes. Retrieval processes were also deteriorated, when no cues were present eliciting recognition. Disturbed encoding processes concern aspects of traumatic events not entering consciousness. So, the outcomes of Christianson et al. indicate that memory impairment of traumatic events is mainly caused by mental clouding during the traumatic event.

5.2.3 Theoretical notions on childhood trauma and dissociative disorders

A dissociative reaction during a severe trauma is thought to have an important psychological function: it provides protection against immediate, overwhelming emotional experiences. Spiegel writes on this function:

> *Along with the fear and the pain that are associated with rape, combat trauma, or natural disaster, comes an overwhelming and marginally bearable sense of helplessness, a realization that one's own will becomes irrelevant to the course of events, leaving a view of the self which is either damaged, contaminated by the humiliation, pain and fear that the event imposed, or a fragmented sense of self. The pre-existing personality is preserved and attempts to carry on as though nothing at all had happened, (Spiegel 1986a, p.124).*

In the previous section it was described that 'mental clouding', based on disturbed 'encoding' processes', is evoked by severe traumatic events. This 'mental clouding' is thought to be of a transient character, it occurs only during the trauma. In patients with a dissociative disorder however, mental clouding has a permanent character, it is experienced over a longer period of time. Moreover, as we will show in next sections, these patients have often experienced severe traumata as a child. So, adult patients with a dissociative disorder experience 'mental clouding', whereas they used to be, but are not in a traumatic situation any more. The question is, how 'permanent' mental clouding during adult life is related to 'transient' mental clouding during severe trauma as a child.

Two notions are relevant in this respect. The first notion concerns a person's coping strategies. Adults have their own characteristic way of coping with emotional situations, but children still have to develop their own way. When a child is repeatedly confronted with overwhelming trauma, dissociation may become the child's characteristic way of coping with negative emotions. If dissociation is the person's characteristic coping strategy, the person is said to have a dissociative disorder. Spiegel (1986a) speaks in this respect of dissociation as a 'character armour'.

The second notion concerns an innate capacity to react with dissociation. Not every person is inclined to react on trauma with dissociation. Only people with a predisposed capacity respond in such a way, (Frischholz, 1985). The predisposed capacity to dissociate is thought to be closely allied to the capacity to be hypnotized, (Janet; 1911; Frischholz, 1985; Hilgard, 1986; Bliss, 1986; Spiegel, 1986a, 1986b). Children are found to be more susceptible to hypnosis than adults. Based on similarities between hypnotic capacity and inclination to dissociate, children in the age period of 10 to 12 years are thought to be the most inclined to react with dissociation when traumatized. After this age the predisposition to dissociate is less pronounced, (Bliss, 1986; Putnam, 1989).

These notions suggest that dissociative disorders are predominantly found in persons who were severely and repeatedly traumatized in a critical age period.

5.2.4 Studies on relation between child (sexual) abuse and dissociation

Several researchers studied the relation between childhood trauma and dissociative disturbances. Detailed information on these studies can be found in appendix 5-1. Their results can be summarised as follows:

- Persons with a diagnosis of dissociative disorder, most likely multiple personality disorder, have a history of childhood traumata. Several studies show a majority of patients with the diagnosis of multiple personality disorder to have a childhood history with traumatic incidents. These studies reveal that more than three-quarters of the patients with a diagnosis of 'multiple personality' have a history of sexual or physical or both types of abuses, (Saltman and Solomon, 1982; Putnam, Guroff, Silberman, Barbaran & Post, 1986; Ross, Norton , & Wozney, 1989; Ross, Miller , Reagor, Bjornson, Frase & Anderson, in press).

- Persons with a history of frequent child sexual abuse tend to have a high level of dissociation. This is especially so when physical abuse was also present. Chu and Dill (1990) found that child physical abuse as well as child sexual abuse independently predict a high level of dissociation in adulthood. The level of dissociation is particularly high in patients having experienced both types of abuse. Remell (1990) uncovered a high frequency of child sexual abuse to be correlated to a high level of dissociation, in a significant way and independent of other relevant characteristics.

- Persons with a history of child sexual abuse, who get no emotional support from their direct environment tend to have a high level of dissociation. In a multiple regression analysis, Remell (1990) found, that 'emotional support from direct environment' contributed significantly and independently to the level of dissociation.

- A high level of dissociation seemed to be more specific for persons with a history of severe childhood traumata then neurotic complaints or borderline symptomatology. Chu and Dill (1990) consider the relation between a history of child abuse and respectively general neurotic symptoms[33] and level of dissociation. They report a high level of dissociation to be a better predictor for child sexual abuse than general neurotic symptoms. Herman, Perry and van der Kolk's (1989) recruited subjects with borderline and associated disorders such as schizotypical and antisocial disorders. They note the correlation between the cumulative trauma score and level of dissociation to be stronger than the correlation between the cumulative trauma score and the diagnosis borderline psychopathology.

5.2.5 Characteristics of childhood trauma in patients with dissociative disorders

Researchers have examined several relations between childhood trauma and level of dissociation. Therapists, giving their clinical observations, describe rather specific childhood trauma in persons with the diagnosis 'extreme dissociative disorder' (mostly multiple personality disorder). In persons with the diagnosis of multiple personality disorder, the most common form of sexual abuse is father-daughter or stepfather-stepdaughter incest, in addition to which mother and other siblings were frequently actively involved, Putnam (1989). These incest experiences have 'the quality of extreme sadism': many persons with an extreme dissociative disorder have been subjected to group rapes or were forced into prostitution by family members.

> *Confinement abuses seem to be exceptionally common in the retrospective accounts of Multiple Personality Patients. This form of abuses involves the repeated confinement of a child through various means, such as tying the child up, locking the child in closets, cellars, or trunks; stuffing the child in boxes or bags; or even burying alive, (Putnam, 1989, p.49).*

Kluft, Braun and Sachs (1984) state that usually there is concomitant neglect of major needs and intermittent or total abandonment, extreme and inappropriate punishment, as well as physical and sexual abuse in all varieties. Spiegel (1986a) notes that patients with a diagnosis of multiple personality have often been exposed to conflicting or double bind-messages. Sexual abuse consists of an intrinsic double-bind: the child is on the one hand the recipient of wanted attention from a parent and on the other hand victimized by it. The parents often expect their children to be caring at all times for their parents' needs, and at the same time are impossible and selfish themselves. Other characteristics of childhood trauma in persons with a diagnosis of multiple personality disorder are described by Saltman and Solomon (1982) and Braun and Sachs (1985). The

---

[33] The general neuroticism symptoms were measured with the SCL-90.

traumata have the character of being frequent, unpredictable and inconsistent: abuse alternates with love, so the abuse is inconsistent with the parental behaviour immediately preceding that abuse. The atmosphere of extreme ambivalence creates 'emotional polarization' in a child and this polarization is important in the etiology of the multiple personality disorder.

After the child has grown up, dissociation, originally activated as a defense against overwhelming traumata, continues as a symptom when new traumata occur or it remains at a high level when insufficient restorative experiences exist, (Spiegel, 1986a, 1986b; Kluft, Braun & Sachs, 1984).

5.2.6 Assumptions on relations between trauma and level of dissociation.

Clinical observations and theoretical speculations, as summarised in the previous section, lead to assumptions on the character of child sexual abuse experiences in persons with a high level of dissociation and vice versa. Summarising, high levels of dissociation are to be expected in persons with:

- A childhood in which a person experienced overwhelming trauma, like sexual abuse of a sadistic character, group rapes or being forced into prostitution.
- These overwhelming traumata took place repeatedly.
- They occurred in a family context evoking ambivalent emotions.
- They occurred in family context of parental neglect or abandonment.
- New traumata occurring later in life may reactivate high levels of dissociation.
- The traumata occurred in a critical age-period.
- The level of dissociation is more specific for persons with a childhood history of severe and repeated traumatization, than other psychiatric symptoms.

These assumptions will be examined in the next sections.

5.3 Research methods

This section deals with research strategies concerning dissociative symptoms. Detailed information about the research strategy has been given in chapter 2. In sections 2-5-2 and 2-6-1 the Dissociative Experience Scale (D.E.S.) has been discussed.

5.3.1 Questioning on disturbances in consciousness

Questioning an individual about dissociative symptoms, particularly time-gaps, has met with certain objections and is considered to be a risky enterprise. The first objection is intrinsically related to the symptoms under study. William James wonders whether or not consciousness has the capability to always record such disturbances as time-gaps, (see chapter 3). Similar problems are posed by Kluft, Steinberg and Spitzer (1988), and Braun (1988). Persons with a diagnosis of multiple personality disorder need not be aware of their amnesic periods (read 'time-gaps')[34]. On the other hand, case histories and studies using a self-report questionnaire on dissociative symptoms indicate persons to be aware of 'time-gaps' (see next paragraph on the Dissociative Experience Scale). In our opinion, a distinction should be made between direct and indirect registrations of disturbances in consciousness. Self-report questionnaires primarily inquire for indirect registration of disturbances of consciousness, such as, a person can't remember what happened, but relevant others told how was acted, a person suddenly found him or herself to be in another city, a person noticed many things to be moved, or many things to be bought, without remembering having done it. If persons with disturbances in consciousness are living alone, they are less likely to get feedback from relevant others, they get fewer indirect signs on 'disturbances in consciousness'. The first objection may thus be especially important for persons who live alone and have severe disturbances in consciousness.

The second objection concerns the question of suggestibility. Reports on disturbances in consciousness may be the effect of suggestions made by therapists, or suggestions originating from popular case histories like 'Sybil' and 'Eve', (see Aldridge-Morris, 1989). When planning this study the issue of suggestibility was taken into account. The way we have tried to deal with this problem is described in section 2-3-1.

5.3.2 The Dissociative Experience Scale (D.E.S.) in our study

Certain research instruments are based on the concept that dissociative phenomena lie on a continuum, they measure frequency and intensity of several dissociative phenomena. An example of such a research instrument is the Dissociative Experience Scale [35].

Out of 97 women, who participated in this study, 87 completed the D.E.S. The scores on the D.E.S. in this group showed a normal distribution. Only one respondent (F36) scored extremely high on the D.E.S. (mean=72). Her interview

---

[34] The observation that some persons have an 'amnesia for the amnesia' was one of the reasons to drop the criterion 'amnesia' for the diagnosis of multiple personality.

[35] We learned about the existence of the D.E.S., just before we started the field-work in this research and when a questionnaire on dissociative phenomena had already been constructed. Because I obtained the D.E.S. late and both questionnaires overlapped, I decided to merge them. The D.E.S. seemed to me a rather heterogeneous questionnaire. The structured questionnaire constructed by us, contained more questions about several dissociative features, see appendix 2-2. However, for reasons of standardization, only the results of the D.E.S. items are reported here. In our questionnaire a distinction was made between recent experiences of dissociative features (that is one year before the interview) and past experiences. Only the recent experiences are reported here.

is excluded and interviews with missing D.E.S. were also omitted from the statistical analysis on the D.E.S[36].

In our opinion the D.E.S. inquires about rather heterogeneous problem areas. In order to check the intercorrelations a principal component analysis has been performed on the D.E.S. items. This analysis showed that these items were highly intercorrelated, (the lowest correlation between one item and the communality being 0.42), and that 11 factors were distinguished, that explained all the variance in the D.E.S. scores: the variance explained by each factor ranged from 7% to 12%. The factor loadings of the items of the D.E.S. and the interpretation of the factors are presented in appendix 5-2.

The principal component analysis showed the D.E.S. to be a questionnaire of a heterogeneous character. It measures a number of different aspects of 'dissociation', but the items measuring these different aspects do have a high mutual cohesion. Thus the combined score is meaningful.

5.4 Phenomenology of severe disturbances in consciousness, descriptive results

5.4.1 Indirect registration of time-gaps

In the semi-structured interview, 32 women mentioned time-gaps. The consciousness of time-gaps may evolve from indirect registrations. Most women became aware of having time-gaps by the information important others had given about complex behaviour these women did not remember performing.

Another source of information consisted of traces of things that happened. Various kinds of traces were mentioned by women in our study. For instance, four women found notes or diaries in which thoughts, actions, visits were mentioned, while they could not remember anything of what had been written. For instance, Anna (B1) told: 'After watching a television program on self-injury, I lost four days. When my mind got clear again, I found on my desk telephone numbers of incest-survivor groups. Several notes were made about conversations I seem to have had. I phoned these numbers again and asked them what I told them during the previous days. They informed me that I told them about my incest experiences. In this way I became aware of my history of child sexual abuse'. Other signs women mentioned concern self-injury or suicide attempts (see chapters 7 and 8).

---

[36] Some of the women who were fatigued after the semi-structured interview, were insufficiently motivated to fill in the questionnaire. Since it could not be taken for granted that the missing D.E.S.-scores are randomly distributed, a check was made to determine if the missing D.E.S.-scores correlated differently with the characteristics of child sexual abuse, compared with the non-missing ones. No differences were found. Therefore the missing D.E.S.-scores are assumed to be randomly distributed.

Some women noticed that things in the environment had changed. They woke up in a city and didn't remember how and why they came in that particular place. For instance, Gea (B26) reported: 'Once I found myself back in a town, while I didn't know why and how I came there'. Some women felt uncertain whether they had done things they could not remember. For instance, Anna (B1), who is living alone, said about her present state of mind: 'I do not trust myself. In the past I lost time, I do not think I'm experiencing this now, but I'm afraid of it. I may not know, because I'm living alone. Some persons may know I do things, but not the persons I usually meet. Maybe I go on the streets at night and throw stones through windows. Maybe that is why I'm so afraid at night'.

Some women got signs about disturbances in consciousness but did not note to experience time-gaps. Six women said that they as adults had periods of sleep-walking or periods of consistent conversations while asleep. Roaming around without consciousness is called sleep-walking, if the person has been asleep for at least 3/4 hour before starting to roam around, (Diagnostic Classification of Sleep and Arousal Disorders 1979). Sleep-talking is very common, but sleep-talking seldom has a coherent character. Consistent talking while asleep is very rare (Arkin, 1981). To others it is usually obvious that one is asleep, while sleep-walking or sleep-talking. Some women reported such behaviour while it was very unlikely they were or had been asleep. For instance, Floor (B23) said: 'When I am asleep and my husband comes home, I start asking him questions. If he answers my questions, I keep asking more, but otherwise I fall asleep. The next morning I ask the same questions. My husband is surprised, that I can not remember having asked those questions before'. The husband had not noticed she was asleep. If he had noticed she was asleep, he would not have been surprised she was asking the same questions.

Other women said they had an extremely bad memory[37]. A bad memory may indicate the experience of time-gaps, (see section 3-3). For instance, Inge (B36) reports that she had a meeting at her house with some of her aunts and her stepmother. Aunts as well as stepmother had taken care of her during childhood. It appeared that during this meeting they were talking about her father, who sexually abused her. The next day she got several telephone calls. Her stepmother accused her of permitting the aunts to blacken her father's name, but she could not remember anything of what had been said. Inge said she had learned to forget quickly. This was bothering her, because sometimes she did not know if she had or hadn't put her child to bed. She missed 'time' during the day, but acted 'normally' during time-gaps.

---

[37] Extensive forgetting may result from excessive use of alcohol, drugs, illness, or ageing. Forgetting resulting from such conditions has not been not coded as dissociative symptoms, (see section 2-4-3).

5.4.2 Direct registration of time-gaps

William James's question, whether or not consciousness has the capacity to record such disturbances as time-gaps, implies that consciousness may not have this capacity, (see 3-6). A remarkable finding in our study is that about half of the women, mentioning time-gaps, learned to register these (non-) experiences. They noticed feelings preceding time-gaps and combined this with information given by important others or signs about behaviour that they can't remember performing. Most women used similar metaphors in denoting time-gaps, like 'you are gone, you are in a black hole, in a vacuum, you are nobody or you are not there any more'. In scheme 5-1, a selection is presented of statements on time-gaps and metaphors used.

Scheme 5-1: Conscious registration of time-gaps [a]

Elsbeth (B21): 'In one way or the other I'm gone, I'm simply gone. You do not know any more. It is a strange black feeling -very strange- it is totally black inside you. First I start to be light in my head, then you are looking to yourself and then you have stepped outside yourself. You know that you will come back, but you do not know when'.
Hanna (B31): 'I'm turning inside. I'm getting into a vacuum. And then I do not know anything any more. Then I'm in a nowhere area, in a vacuum'. Q: 'Is your time feeling lost?' A: 'It is completely gone. I talk in a different way'. Q: 'How do you know?' A: 'Others have tape-recorded me'. Q: 'You do not remember what was said?' A: 'No I'm not there, because I want to sleep or do not feel'.
Hilly (B32): 'I do have the feeling that I'm sinking into a pit. I go on, but I do not know what has happened when I'm back again. It is a bad feeling because you are standing outside, you are not participating in life. Sometimes it seems as if I'm moved from one place to the other -it is very creepy- it is as if it is not me that has moved'.
Inge (B36): 'If I talk about my father it is as if I shut off. I'm not there any more'. A: 'They say to you that you are staring?' A: 'No'. Q: 'Do you know where you are with your thoughts?' A: 'No. It seems as if I'm not there. I have the feeling I do everything just normally. I do not know what is happening then'.
Joan (B38): 'I frequently feel myself to be nobody, I'm completely empty. Sometimes I'm gone, then I'm nobody any more. You do not feel anything. You do not see anything. You do not hear anything'.

[a] Statements are selected on explicitness and variation.

These metaphors used to describe time-gaps, are similar to the metaphors used to describe intense depersonalization feelings. Time-gaps are experienced or conveyed in language as extreme depersonalization feelings. Extreme depersonalization feelings and time-gaps differ in the presence of complex behaviour during time-gaps, that is not present during extreme depersonalization.

When persons regain consciousness they describe the time-gap with metaphors as 'at a certain moment you wake up with a start' or 'you find yourself back'. These metaphors are based on experiences of time-gaps in the stream of consciousness everybody experiences every day, namely sleep.

Although some women notice signals preceding time-gaps, they have no control over the occurrence of time-gaps. Kitty (B44) expressed it in the following way: 'I feel I am going, but I can't stop it. The switches are much stronger than I am'. However, a few women learned to control experiences of time-gaps, mainly by discussing these time-gaps in therapy. For instance Erna (B20) said; 'Before I was wandering, I did not know I was existing. Now I do not lose time any more, I can keep in mind that there are persons caring about me. When I feel I'm disappearing, I start writing and drawing. At present these time-gaps occur less frequently than before'.

5.4.3 Function and implications of time-gaps

Dissociation is assumed to be a reaction to overwhelming trauma with the function to protect the victim against unbearable emotions, Spiegel (1986a and 1986b), Summit (1983). Besides this positive protective aspect of time-gaps, these experiences have several negative aspects: one is not aware of one's own behaviour, one lacks voluntary control over one's own behaviour, and one loses self-reference, (see chapter 3).

If dissociation is a protection mechanism against overwhelming feelings, it need not be a negative (non-) experience. Indeed, some women describe relief from free-floating anxiety or internal conflicts when 'being nowhere'. However, most women had problems with the experience of time-gaps. Not the time-gaps per se, but the implications of time-gaps are experienced as negative. During time-gaps eleven women performed self-destructive behaviour, over which they had no voluntary control. For instance, Marieke (F16) told that she set herself afire. She didn't want to commit suicide, she had no memories of doing it. She, her environment and her therapist were very worried, because she really could not be trusted. This feeling of uncertainty, caused by experiencing time-gaps, is also present when less dramatic things occur. For instance, Kitty (B44) said: "When I get angry, he (her husband) does not exist for me, then 'one' is gone. I can not remember what I said to him and then I get angry with myself, I can't stand it. One can not apologise for what 'one' has done. Sometimes I think I should not have said such a thing, but 'one' does not even remember. Nowadays I try to get stronger and stronger proofs that I really said those things. I'm afraid that he will abuse the situation".

The experience of time-gaps implies that the person does not have a 'self-reference' about behaviour during time-gaps. Behaviour during time-gaps is experienced as ego-dystonic. Dieuwertje (B14) said, 'I always have to be there, if I am not, terrible things may happen. When I'm driving my car, I see the image that I drive my car into a tree at the end of the street. Then I disappear, when I wake up, I'm just a few meters away from that tree. I have to pull the wheel to prevent an accident'. The same theme recurrently expressed itself during her dreams, too. 'She' had to be awake in time, to be in control to prevent terrible things.

5.4.4 Triggers for time-gaps in adult life

We inquired in a general way about the antecedents of time-gaps. Almost half of the women (17 out of 32) reported connections between child sexual abuse and time-gaps experienced during adult life. Some women mentioned flashbacks preceding time-gaps. Ans (B4) said: 'I see all those things I don't want to see (things her stepfather did) and then I'm in this black-hole'. Kitty (B44) told: 'First I see all those hands (of friends of her brother who committed a gang rape) and then I'm disappearing'. Thirteen women reported flashbacks immediately preceding 'all' or 'some' time-gaps and four women mentioned time-gaps in the period of intrusion of memories about child sexual abuse. Rie (F23) said: 'Once I had a rather extensive time-loss. It happened just before I got my memories back about the incest with my father'.

Other women experienced time-gaps that were triggered by situations associated with child sexual abuse. For instance, Tilly (F33) told: 'I saw that movie (about sexual abuse) and then I wasn't existing any more, I have no images of that period'. Dieuwertje (B14) reported: 'When I walk near the train station in the evening and I see a man walking, I get scared and I feel disappearing. When I regain consciousness at home, I do not know what has happened'. Some women noticed that they have been wandering after intense therapy sessions about their history of (sexual) abuse. They find themselves back hours later and do not know where they have been.

5.4.5 Time-gaps during child sexual abuse

Of the women participating in our study, 56% reported to have experienced symptoms associated with the depersonalization syndrome during child sexual abuse. Almost a third of the women reported time-gaps during sexual or physical child abuse. For instance, Floor (B23), being sexually abused by her father from early age on, does not know how and when sexual abuse ended. She has memories of her father's shop, in which she was helping at age of seventeen and how her father would approach her after closing-time. She remembered she was running away and then there was this black gap. She does not know whether sexual abuse had stopped at that age or was still going on. She describes it as a very creepy situation.

At least nine women reported to 'practice' selective attention during child (sexual) abuse, these practices resulted in dissociative symptoms. These women said that they concentrated extremely on the environment, solved problems, used fantasies, were counting etc. Some do have sharp memories of their own active practices to block sexual abuse out of consciousness.

5.5 Characteristics of child sexual abuse and level of dissociation, statistical analyses

When a child is repeatedly confronted with overwhelming trauma, dissociation may become the child's characteristic way of coping with emotional situations. If dissociation is a person's characteristic way of coping with emotional situations, the person is said to have a dissociative disorder. An excerpt of statements of leading authors on dissociative disturbances has led to well described assumptions. Before these assumptions will be investigated, information is given on the general level of dissociation of this group of women, as compared with standards, and with other relevant data.

5.5.1 General level of dissociation

Is the general level of dissociation in our group higher than in comparable control-groups? The general level of dissociation can be expressed by the mean, the median and the standard deviation, (for information about the D.E.S. questionnaire, see 2-5-2). Women in our study had a mean of 25 on the D.E.S., the standard deviation is 14 and the median is 24. The median D.E.S.-score found in our study has been compared with median D.E.S.-scores obtained in other studies. In appendix 5-3 these figures are presented. It is difficult to find a suitable control-group for the women participating in this study. For instance, it is found that level of dissociation is higher in adolescence than in adulthood. The mean scores on the D.E.S. are decreasing when age is increasing: adolescents and students score higher on the D.E.S. than adults, (Ross, Ryan, Anderson, Ross & Hardy, 1989). The D.E.S. is also susceptible to context-variations, (van Otterloo, 1987, Ensink and van Otterloo, 1990). The best available group of reference for the women in our study are psychology students older than 22 years, who scored a D.E.S. questionnaire with dummy questions[38] included, (see 2-6-1 for information about the study of van Otterloo). This group had a mean D.E.S.-score of 16. We see that the scores on the D.E.S. obtained in our group are higher than the scores on the D.E.S. of the best available study using a sample of the normal population.

In the United States of America therapists rather frequently use the diagnosis 'multiple personality disorder'. This diagnosis coincides with a cut-off score of 30 on the D.E.S., (Putnam, 1990, personal communication). This cut-off score

---

[38] Dummies consisted of questions about common dissociative phenomena, but they did not count in statistics.

appears to have reasonable specificity and sensitivity for diagnosis 'multiple personality disorder' as is given in the United States. Scheme 5-2 represents the scores of our respondents on the D.E.S.

Scheme 5-2: Scores on the Dissociative Experience Scale

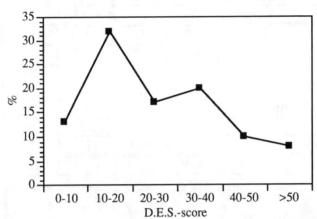

D.E.S.-score

According to the data presented in scheme 5-2, more than a third of the women (38%) had a score on the D.E.S. exceeding 30. Sixteen persons (18%) had a score exceeding 40 and seven persons (8%) had a score above 50. Therapists willing to give the diagnosis 'multiple personality disorder' would assess this disorder in more than a third of the women participating in our study. Four women told during the semi-structured interview, that Dutch therapists had diagnosed them as having a multiple personality disorder.

5.5.2 Overwhelming childhood trauma and level of dissociation

In section 5-2-6 we formulated several assumptions about the characteristics of trauma experienced as a child and level of dissociation. The first assumption concerned the severity of childhood trauma: the more severe child sexual abuse has been, the higher the level of dissociation will be in adult life. In section 4-5 we saw that in general six characteristics of child sexual abuse are found to be related to the (general) psychological impact. These six characteristics are: sexual abuse at the hands of multiple perpetrators, severity of coercion, intrusiveness of sexual acts, abuse by father (-figures), duration of sexual abuse, and age difference between girl and perpetrator.

First of all we examined the question whether these six characteristics are associated with the level of dissociation, (as measured by the sum-score on the D.E.S.). Findings are presented in table 5-1.

Table 5-1: Severity of child sexual abuse and level of dissociation (D.E.S.), (Pearson correlations and F-values and multiple correlations; ß-coefficients, Standard coefficients and t-values)

N=86	level of dissociation				
	r	F	ß-Coeff.	Std Coeff	t-value
Multiple perpetrators [a]	.36***	12.09	.34	.30*	2.82
Severity of coercion	.29**	7.63	.3	.18	1.54
Father (-figure) as perpetrator	.15	2.01	.52	.18	1.69
Intrusiveness of sexual acts	.13	1.41	.02	.01	.05
Duration	.12	1.19	-.05	-.04	.39
Age difference girl-perpetrator	.05	.24	-.17	-.04	.81
Multiple R	.43**	2.96		.18	

[a] More information about the way of inquiring and coding characteristics of child sexual abuse was given in chapter 4.

* p<.05, **p<.01, ***p<.001

As is shown in table 5-1 sexual abuse at the hands of multiple perpetrators and severity of coercion applied by the perpetrator are correlated with level of dissociation, (resp. r=.36, p<.001 and r=.29, p<.01). We see that in a multiple regression analysis, sexual abuse at the hands of multiple perpetrators contributes independently and significantly to level of dissociation, (the standard coefficient, Std Coeff=.30). 'Severity of coercion' does not contribute in an independent way to level of dissociation, (std Coeff.=.18). When a woman has been sexually abused as a child at the hands of multiple perpetrators she will tend to experience a high level of dissociation as an adult.

We found no indication that 'intrusiveness of sexual acts' does contribute to level of dissociation. Neither did we find an association between being abused by the father (-figures) and level of dissociation.

The characteristic 'severity of coercion' is based on the most extreme form of coercion applied by the perpetrator. A more specific differentiation with respect to the period in which the perpetrator has exerted coercion: in the period of, during, or after termination of sexual abuse. In table 5-2 findings are presented about level of dissociation and conditions in which coercion has been applied.

Table 5-2: Severity of coercion during, in the period of or after child sexual abuse and level of dissociation (D.E.S.), (Pearson correlations and F-values)

N=86	level of dissociation	
	r	F
Coercion during child sexual abuse	.36***	12.85***
Coercion in period child sex abuse	.08	.50
Coercion after child sexual abuse	.18	2.89

* p<.05, **p<.01, ***p<.001

As we can see in table 5-2, coercion used during the sexual abuse is correlated with level of dissociation, (r=.36, p<.001). When a woman during sexual abuse had been subjected to physical violence or physical restraint or threats of murder, she tends to have a high level of dissociation as an adult. This finding suggests that overwhelming or sadistic sexual abuse contributes to level of dissociation.

Group- or gang-rape is mentioned as another overwhelming trauma frequently observed in women with severe dissociative disorders. Women who as a child were subjected to group rape, tend to have a higher level of dissociation than those without such experiences, (F=4.49, p<.05). Inspection of the data showed that especially women, who as a child were subjected to gang-rapes or arrangements in which the main perpetrator involved men unknown to the girl tend to have a high level of dissociation as an adult, (F=7.26, p<.01).

These results suggest that not all the 'general' characteristics indicative for severity of child sexual abuse are associated with level of dissociation, only very overwhelming trauma in childhood seems to result in severe and frequently recurring disturbances in consciousness.

5.5.3 Accumulation of trauma and level of dissociation

The second assumption we formulated concerns the repetition of childhood trauma and level of dissociation. In table 5-1 we presented two characteristics concerning repetition of childhood trauma: sexual abuse at the hands of multiple perpetrators, and duration of sexual abuse. We already discussed the correlation between multiple perpetrators and level of dissociation. However, duration of sexual abuse did not correlate with level of dissociation, (r=.12, see table 5-1).

A further exploration of the data shows that only within the group of women who have experienced physical violence or threats of murder (N=55), duration of child sexual abuse is significantly correlated with level of dissociation, (r=.26, p<.05). This finding indicates that only when women as a child experienced severe coercion at the hands of the perpetrator, the duration of abuse is correlated with level of dissociation.

In section 2-5-1 we described the construction of a cumulative trauma-score, representing the repetition of childhood trauma. As was to be expected the cumulative trauma-score is correlated with level of dissociation, (r=.39, p<.0001).

These results suggest that the repetition of severe trauma, experienced as a child, increases the risk of a high level of dissociation.

5.5.4 Ambivalent child sexual abuse and level of dissociation

The third assumption we formulated concerns the ambivalent family context and level of dissociation, (see 5-2-6). In persons with a high level of dissociation, traumatic situations appeared to be characterized by inconsistencies evoking ambivalent emotions. In chapter 4 we described ambivalent attitudes of the perpetrator with regard to application of coercion. Another inconsistent attitude described in chapter 4 concerns emotional parentification. Emotional parentification by a parent means that the parent involves the child in intense emotional problems and the child feels responsible for lifting the parent out of his or her misery.

Table 5-3: Ambivalent attitudes and level of dissociation (D.E.S.), (one-way ANOVA) [a]

N=82	level of dissociation
	F
Ambivalent attitudes [b]	2.41
Emotional parentification father [c]	.21
Emotional parentification mother	.53
Parentification household duties	.28

[a] More information about the way of inquiring and coding characteristics of child sexual abuse was given in chapter 4. [b] Only a few women had an unambivalent sexual abuse history without coercive elements (N=4). Those women were excluded from this analysis. [c] The association between emotional parentification by father (-figures) and level of dissociation is investigated only within the group of women who were sexually abused by their fathers (-figures), (N=65).

* p<.05, **p<.01, ***p<.001

As the findings in table 5-3 show, an analysis of variance shows no significant differences between level of dissociation in different groups of women who either were or were not confronted with ambivalent attitudes of the perpetrator. Neither did we find any association between task oriented, or emotional parentification by mother or father and level of dissociation. The lack of association is contradictory to what has been described in literature.

5.5.5 Parental neglect and level of dissociation

The fourth assumption we formulated concerns the emotional neglect and abandonment by the parents and level of dissociation. In 4-3-4 we reported that more than a third of the women in our study can not remember ever having had a warm and emotional relation with their mother. Another indication for emotional neglect by the mother concerns her involvement in child sexual abuse, (4-4-6). Moreover, a quarter of the women reported that their relationship with the perpetrator (more particularly the father) preceding sexual abuse was characterised by emotional neglect and physical assaults, (4-3-5).

We found no association between emotional neglect by mother and level of dissociation, (F=2.53, p=n.s.). An analysis of variance was calculated to examine the inolvement of the mother in child sexual abuse and level of dissociation. These findings are presented in table 5-4.

Table 5-4: Hiding sexual abuse from mother and level of dissociation
(D.E.S., one-way ANOVA) [a]

N=86		level of dissociation	
	n	M	s.d.
Mother can't know C.S.A.[b]	50	24	12
Surprised mother doesn't know	14	25	15
Mother knows C.S.A.	17	26	20
Mother involved or perpetrator	5	46*	9
F= 3.62, p<.01			

[a] More information about the way of inquiring and coding characteristics of child sexual abuse was given in chapter 4. [b] C.S.A. means child sexual abuse

* significant at a 5% level Fisher PLSD.

We find that only women with a mother involved in child sexual abuse differed significantly in level of dissociation (mean D.E.S.-scores) from other women.

Findings concerning the relation between girl and perpetrator preceding child sexual abuse and level of dissociation are presented in table 5-5. Women who reported to have been physically assaulted by the perpetrator before the onset of sexual abuse show a significantly higher level of dissociation than the others.

**Table 5-5: Relation between girl and perpetrator preceding sexual abuse
and level of dissociation (D.E.S.), (one-way ANOVA) [a]**

N=64 [b]		level of dissociation	
	n	M	s.d.
Normal relation precedes C.S.A.[c]	30	22	13
General neglect precedes C.S.A.	26	26	13
Physical abuse precedes C.S.A.	8	37*	15
F= 4.01, p<.05			

[a] More information about the way of inquiring and coding characteristics of child sexual abuse was given in chapter 4. [b] Women who couldn't remember their relation with the perpetrator preceding sexual abuse were excluded from analysis. [c] C.S.A. means child sexual abuse

* significant at a 5% level Fisher PLSD.

These findings suggest that it is not emotional neglect in general, but more specific aspects of neglect and abuse, like early physical assaults preceding sexual abuse and involvement of the mother in sexual abuse, which contribute to level of dissociation.

5.5.6 New trauma in adult life and level of dissociation

The fifth assumption we formulated concerns new traumata occurring later in life and level of dissociation. We inquired whether women were subjected to spouse-beating, (scored as never, irregular and regular). We found no significant association between spouse-beatings and level of dissociation, (F=.63, p=n.s.). Women with a history of child sexual abuse who additionally were subjected to regular physical assaults by their spouse, did not tend to have a higher level of dissociation than women with a history of child sexual abuse who were never subjected to physical assaults by their spouse.

5.5.7 Age at onset of child sexual abuse and level of dissociation

The last assumption formulated concerns the age period in which child sexual abuse took place. It is assumed that children between 10 and 12 are most susceptible to react to trauma with dissociation. In order to investigate this assumption three age groups were distinguished: in the first group sexual abuse terminated before the age of 10, in the second group sexual abuse started after the age of 12 and in the third group sexual abuse had taken place between the age of 10 and 12 and possibly beyond. In table 5-6 the mean D.E.S.-scores for these different age-groups are given.

Table 5-6: Critical age period and level of dissociation (D.E.S.), (one way ANOVA)

N= 86		level of dissociation	
	n	M	s.d.
C.S.A.[a] before age 10	18	19	1.3
C.S.A. during age 10-12	43	29*	1.62
C.S.A. after age 12	25	26	1.25
F= 2.89, p<.05			

[a] C.S.A. means child sexual abuse.

* significant at a 5% level Fisher PLSD.

As demonstrated in table 5-6 the majority of women was sexually abused between 10 and 12 years of age. This group of women showed a significantly higher D.E.S.-score than the women sexually abused before the age of 10-12, (but the score was not significantly higher than the group of women sexually abused after the age of 10 to 12). This finding may be attributed to (for instance) the duration of sexual abuse. The women who were abused in the period 10-12 years and beyond, generally were sexually abused for four or more years, whereas women who report that sexual abuse stopped before the age of 10 generally were abused for a shorter period. But, as has already been reported, duration of sexual abuse is not associated with level of dissociation. Another important factor may be the severity of coercion applied by the perpetrator. In a two-way analysis of variance, including three age groups together with severity of coercion and level of dissociation did not show significant interaction effects. These findings suggest that children between 10 and 12 are most susceptible to react with dissociation when traumatized.

5.5.8 Multiple regression analysis characteristics of child sexual abuse and level of dissociation.

One may wonder how much variance in level of dissociation is explained by the characteristics of child sexual abuse presented above and which of these characteristics have an independent contribution to level of dissociation. To answer this question a multiple regression analysis was performed. The results of this multiple regression analysis are presented in appendix 5-4. In this analysis we found that 4 characteristics contribute significantly and independently to level of dissociation, the cumulation of childhood trauma, age at onset of child sexual abuse, relation between perpetrator and girl preceding child sexual abuse and being subjected to sexual abuse at the hands of a unknown perpetrator. The multiple correlation is R=.52, N=86, p <.0001, the explained variance is 27%.

5.6 Cumulative trauma-score and psychological symptoms, a comparison

Certain researchers, like Herman, Perry and van der Kolk (1989), and Chu and Dill (1990), find dissociative symptoms to be more than other symptoms associated with the accumulation of traumatic experiences. In our study, several other symptoms are included. Special attention has been paid to one aspect of dissociation, namely the time-gaps.

Table 5-7 gives findings about the correlations between the cumulative trauma-score and other psychiatric symptoms included in this study, (see chapter 1). In section 2-5-1 and appendix 4-3 we discussed the cumulative trauma-score. For a description of the way of inquiring these psychiatric symptoms we refer to section 2-3 and appendix 2-2. More detailed information about visual hallucinations, auditory hallucinations, and repression of memories can be found in chapter 6. Chapters 7 and 8 contain descriptions of respectively self-injurious behaviour and suicidality.

Table 5-7: Cumulative trauma-score and psychological symptoms,
(Pearson correlations)

N=97	cumulative trauma-score
	r
Time-gaps [a]	.48****
D.E.S.	.39***
Visual hallucinations	.37***
Reliving the trauma [b]	.36***
P.T.S.D. [b]	.29**
Pain feelings [b]	.29**
Depersonalization [b]	.26**
Repression of memories about C.S.A. [c]	.24*
Self-injury	.23*
Derealization	.21*
Auditory hallucinations	.13
Suicidality	.13

[a] The items 3, 4, 5, 6, 8 of the D.E.S. inquire about experiences of time-gaps. The scores on these items are added in order to construct a time-gap score. [b] See appendix 2-2 for a description of the items concerning P.T.S.D., reliving the trauma, pain feelings, depersonalization 'disturbances in self-reference', and derealization. [c] C.S.A. means child sexual abuse.

* p<.05, **p<.01, ***p<.001,****p<.0001

Findings presented in table 5-7 show that the highest correlation exists between cumulative trauma-score and time-gaps. The more frequently and severely a woman as a child has been traumatized the more frequently she tends to experience time-gaps. We see that cumulation of traumatic experiences is correlated more strongly with level of dissociation than with other psychiatric symptoms, such as post-traumatic stress symptoms, self-injury or suicidality.

5.7 Summary and discussion

Dissociative disturbances consist of 'disturbances in consciousness'. A disturbance in consciousness includes a less adequate monitoring of the environment, a decreased voluntary control to initiate or terminate behaviour, changes in self-reference, amnesic phenomena, a decline in capacity to share one's mental state with others, and a diminished ability for long term planning.

Recently much attention has been paid to the role of severe childhood trauma in the etiology of dissociative disorders. In general, people are inclined to react with depersonalization or dissociation when confronted with overwhelming traumata, such as life-threatening dangers. Dissociative reactions provide protection from immediate, overwhelming emotional experiences. The time-gap (synonyms are: time-loss, blackout, subconsciousness, co-consciousness) is considered to be the most extreme dissociative reaction. Time-gaps are frequently observed in patients who were diagnosed as having a 'multiple personality disorder'. Psychiatrists, like Putnam (1989), stressed the severity of childhood trauma in patients with this disorder. These observations have led to the assumption that a high level of dissociation is to be expected in persons, who as a child, experienced overwhelming trauma that repeatedly took place in family context characterized by neglect and ambivalent attitudes. A considerable proportion of the women participating in our study have severely been traumatized as a child.

We asked about disturbances in consciousness in two different ways, in a semi-structured and in a structured interview. In the structured interview the Dissociative Experience Scale was used to measure level of dissociation. Most questions incorporated in this scale concern disturbances in consciousness.

We found that 38% of the women in our study would have received the diagnosis of multiple personality, if they had been living in the United Stated and had been treated by a therapist willing to give this diagnosis. In the semi-structured interview, a third of the women reported to experience time-gaps. Certain important authors, like William James, wonder whether or not consciousness has the capacity of recording 'time-gaps'. Statements of some women about time-gaps indicate that the registration of time-gaps by consciousness results from a complex learning process. First, a person may notice that things have changed, and they themselves are the only ones being able to have done those things (indirect registration). Second, important others in the direct environment may tell the person that she did seem to be fully aware of some acts she can not remember having done. Finally, a person learns to recognise inner state of feelings, such as 'being in a vacuum, being nowhere', preceding the time-gaps (direct registration). The presence of important others who can give feedback on the behaviour of the person, is crucial in this respect. A person learns to consciously record time-gaps by the (preceding) depersonalization feelings.

With regard to childhood trauma and level of dissociation, we find that a high level of dissociation tends to be reported by: (a) women who have a childhood history in which they feared to be killed during sexual abuse, (b) women who, as a child, were subjected to group-rapes in which unknown perpetrators were involved, (c) women who, as a child, were physically assaulted by the perpetrator before sexual abuse started, (d) women who, as a child, were sexually abused at the hands of multiple perpetrators, (e) women who, as a child, experienced physical aggression associated with sexual abuse for a considerable time, (f) women whose mother was involved in sexual abuse. A multiple regression analysis showed that 4 characteristics significantly and independently contribute to level of dissociation: cumulation of childhood trauma, age at onset of sexual abuse, physical aggression preceding sexual abuse, and being forced to have sexual contacts with unknown perpetrators. Our results confirm most assumptions deduced from observations of psychiatrists about the type of trauma experienced by persons with a dissociative disorder. The anxiety experienced by a child when being beaten, tied or threatened with murder at an early age during sexual abuse, seems to be so overwhelming that a permanent disturbance in conscious monitoring of the environment and voluntary control of behaviour results.

Depersonalization and dissociation during trauma were supposed to have a transient character, (Noyes et al. 1977). The outcomes of certain studies suggest that in adult persons overwhelming trauma, effects may be of a more or less permanent character. For instance, Pitman, van der Kolk, Orr, & Greenberg (1990) found that Vietnam veterans, 20 years after the war report (reversible) reduction in sensitivity of pain feelings, while viewing a war movie in a laboratory. These researchers studied whether reduction in pain feelings has a neurophysiological or a chemical basis. The reduced sensitivity for feelings of pain appears to be mediated by the body's own opioids. These findings suggest that experiencing severe traumata may alter the chemistry of the nervous system. In this research the average age at which child sexual abuse terminated was between thirteen and fifteen years. The mean age of our respondents was between thirty and thirty-five years. This shows that there was a time period of ten to twenty years between the actual trauma and reports of dissociative disturbances. In trauma theory, intrusions of flashbacks are thought to be accompanied by emotional experiences evoked by the trauma (Horowitz, 1986; van der Kolk, 1987). Almost half of the women with time-gaps mentioned connections between child (sexual) abuse and the experience of time-gaps in adult life. Intrusive memories about child abuse often preceded the experience of a time-gap. These results suggest that extreme dissociative reactions during childhood traumata may be reexperienced when memories of overwhelming child abuse are provoked. These dissociative reactions may also be mediated by neurophysiological processes.

There is an on-going debate whether or not dissociative disorders should be conceived as a special form of post-traumatic stress disorders (P.T.S.D.), Spiegel (1986), van der Kolk (1987), and Kluft (1988). Findings reported above suggest that disturbances in consciousness may be conceived as a special manifestation of post-traumatic stress disorder. Dissociative disorders are experienced by persons who have repeatedly been subjected to overwhelming, sadistic or life-threatening trauma at an early age. It was found that severe disturbances in consciousness are more strongly correlated with the cumulation of childhood trauma than any other psychiatric symptom included in this study.

In women who have been subjected to repeated coercive or sadistic sexual abuse, we can expect to find a high level of dissociation. Psychotherapy with the aim to regain conscious and voluntary control over memories of and thoughts about traumatic childhood experiences, may be effective in decreasing the occurrence of disturbances in conscious awareness. A significant correlation is found between level of dissociation and admission to psychiatric institutions. (r=.39, p<.01). Gelinas (1983) suggested that dissociative phenomena may be used as 'signalling complaints' in persons with a 'disguised presentation' of a child sexual abuse. There seems to be certain support for her suggestions, at least when a restriction with regard to more severe of child sexual abuse is taken into account.

Chapter 6

They're all talking at the same time

child sexual abuse and hallucinations

Lieneke (B50) grew up in a family as the only daughter among several brothers. Her brothers had the opinion that she was being spoilt by her father. For instance, at her 18th birthday, she got from her father a beautiful golden ring. But, on the evening of this birthday her father took her downtown and on the way back home, he raped her in the woods. Sexual abuse started at an early age, she thinks before the age of six and continued into adulthood. Her father subjected her to his perverse fantasies. He blindfolded her, tied her to her bed and used several tools during sexual penetration. She used to count steadily while subjected to his sexual activities. She started to hallucinate the voice and image of her father after his death. She had periods of terrible nightmares, which sometimes also emerged during waking consciousness. She reports: 'I see the image of my father, he calls me and commands me to come to him. He says: 'for you there is no heaven, there is only hell. Sometimes I see a small chap, sometimes a gnome, but the person I see is always my father. In the evening I see him appearing on the television screen. When he appears I say to my husband "look!", but my husband doesn't see my father. If my husband is away from home, I don't dare to move. I'm afraid my father will call and do these queer things again. I stay knitting and counting, I always count everything. My therapist says to me that I should chase my father away, I try but I do not succeed'. Lieneke prefers not to disclose too much about the contents of the commands she gets from her father. These commands concern suicidal acts and forms of self-injury.

6.1 Introduction

In this chapter we will first discuss the confusion surrounding psychiatric diagnoses of schizophrenia and multiple personality (6-2-1), and the criteria specified to distinguish between dissociative hallucinations and 'psychotic' hallucinations (6-2-2). The conclusion is drawn that hallucinations should be studied as symptoms regardless of psychiatric diagnoses (6-2-3). Freud assumed that hallucinations refer to relivings of childhood trauma. One study indicates that psychotic decompensation contains memory traces of child sexual abuse experiences (6-3-1). Several impacts of trauma contributing to the risk of hallucinatory experiences are considered. Such impacts concern extreme deployment of attentional strategies (6-3-2), involuntary vivid intrusions of memories (6-3-3), repression of memories (6-3-4), disturbances in sleep-wake cycles (6-3-5), a chronically increased level of arousal (6-3-6), and distorted learning of reality-discrimination (6-3-7), the different assumptions are summarised (6-3-8). Information is given on validity of questions about hallucinations (6-4). Insight in the phenomenology of hallucinatory experiences is given (6-5-1 to 6-5-10). The prevalence rate of hallucinatory experiences reported in our study is compared with prevalence rates reported in other studies (6-6-1). Relations are considered between cumulation of childhood trauma and respectively hallucinatory flashbacks (6-6-2), visual hallucinations (6-6-3) and auditory hallucinations (6-6-4). Finally the specified assumptions are investigated (6-6-5). In a summary and discussion our research findings are evaluated (6-7).

6.2 Hallucination as a psychiatric symptom

6.2.1 Confusions around diagnoses multiple personality disorder and schizophrenia

As described in section 3-2, the acceptance of the diagnostic category schizophrenia was accompanied by a sharp decline in publications on multiple personality disorder. Bleuler (1911), who introduced the group of schizophrenic disorders, not only incorporated this disorder in his new diagnostic category, but also included certain symptoms of dissociation. At present there is an upsurge in interest among psychologists and psychiatrists in the concept of dissociation, especially in the United States. The renewed interest has evoked a need to distinguish both disorders[39]. This need is rather strong, because studies report a

---

[39] In several publications we find a comparison between patients with a diagnosis of schizophrenia and patients with a diagnosis of multiple personality disorder. Spiegel states that the main difference between those two diagnostic categories concerns the capacity to be hypnotized. Patients who receive a diagnosis of multiple personality disorder have an extreme capacity to be hypnotized, whereas patients being diagnosed as schizophrenic do not have such a capacity (Spiegel, Detrick, & Frischholz, 1982; Spiegel, Hunt, & Dondershine, 1988). Ross, Heber, Norton & Anderson (1989) found that these two diagnostic groups differ with respect to symptoms such as a childhood history of sleep-walking and imaginary playmates.

considerable overlap in symptoms. For instance, both psychiatric categories include hallucinatory experiences. Kluft (1987), found that patients with a multiple personality disorder do have auditory hallucinations meeting the first rank Schneiderian criteria[40]. Such hallucinations were thought to be 'core' symptoms of the mental illness schizophrenia. Other studies have repeated Kluft's findings, (Ross, Heber, Norton & Anderson, 1989). Patients with a multiple personality disorder have even been found to score higher on M.M.P.I.'s 'Schizophrenic' and 'False' scales than persons with a diagnosis of schizophrenia, (Fink and Golinkoff, 1990). Bliss (1980) and Coons and Milstein (1986) report that patients with a multiple personality disorder have not only auditory, but also visual hallucinations. Findings of several studies on hallucinatory experiences of patients with a multiple personality disorder are summarised in appendix 5-1.

Considering this development, it is hardly surprising that a large fraction of patients now receiving a diagnosis of multiple personality disorder, have previously been diagnosed as schizophrenic, (41% according to Ross et al. ,1989). Although the overlap in symptoms is considerable, a dissociative disorder is conceived to be a neurotic disturbance, whereas schizophrenia is understood as a psychotic disorder (D.S.M.-III-R). This means that patients with a multiple personality disorder are supposed to have an intact 'reality-discrimination', (see Aldridge-Morris, 1989). These patients are considered to have 'pseudo-hallucinations'.

6.2.2 Criteria distinguishing dissociative hallucinations

In psychiatry many attempts are made to connect symptoms with psychiatric diagnoses. In the course of history several criteria have been specified in order to distinguish 'dissociative' or 'hysterical' hallucinations from hallucinations associated with other psychiatric diagnoses. These criteria are summarised below:

- Hysterical hallucinations are thought to be experienced in a clouded consciousness, whereas hallucinations in other patients take place in a clear consciousness, (Andrade, 1988).
- Hysterical hallucinations are thought to have a sudden and dramatic onset, to be precipitated by a profound and upsetting event or situation, and to last less than three weeks (the acute period), (Hollender and Hirsch, 1964).
- A hallucination is thought to be of a 'dissociative' character, when the person can have a conversation with the 'auditory' or 'visual hallucination', the

---

[40] Schneider (1959) formulated criteria to differentiate simple auditory hallucination from complex auditory hallucination. He distinguished 11 criteria, which he called first rank symptoms of schizophrenia. The auditory hallucinations concern 'voices commenting', 'voices arguing', and 'hearing thoughts aloud'. Later these criteria were defined more strictly by Mellor (1970). Studies with these Schneiderian criteria report high interjudge-agreements, hence these criteria are well scorable (See De Vries 1992).

hallucinations concern persons with whom the 'hallucinator' has affective bonds, and if heavy sub-cultural systems of religious sects, or other belief systems have influenced the occurrence of hallucinations (Wing, Cooper and Sartorius, 1974).

• An auditory hallucination is thought to be of a 'dissociative character' when voices are predominantly heard inside the head, whereas patients diagnosed as schizophrenic hear voices coming from outside the head, (Putnam, 1989).

It is evident that making a distinction between dissociative/hysterical hallucinations and other hallucinations is a hazardous enterprise, if one only considers this list of criteria. Nowadays, the distinction between voices coming from within and voices coming from outside the head is considered to be the most important discriminating criterion between dissociative ('pseudo'-) and 'real' auditory hallucinations. This criterion is thought to be a difficult one for several reasons, (see Slade and Bentall, 1988). Patients with a diagnosis schizophrenia may initially experience auditory hallucinations as having an external source, (being a public event, coming from outside the head), but after several of such experiences they may learn that these hallucinations have an internal source, (being a private event, coming from inside the head). The patient's attribution of the voices as being private or public events is found to reflect the progress in therapy, (Strauss and Bethesda, 1974; Romme and Escher 1989). One of the first goals in therapy may be to teach patients, that hallucinations are private and not public events. If so, patient's attribution reflects the number of years of therapy.

Moreover, certain studies found that 'schizophrenic' patients do not predominantly experience voices as coming from outside the head. For instance, a carefully performed study on seven different qualities of auditory hallucinations in male patients diagnosed as schizophrenic showed that these patients in majority (2/3) judged their hallucinations to be private and not public events, (Aggernaes, as cited in Slade and Bentall 1988, p.19-24) [41].

Difficulties discussed above are not limited to the distinction between dissociative disorders and other psychiatric disorders. Much research is devoted to the question whether the sense modality (auditory, visual, tactile etc.) in which a hallucination emerges, the form or contents of a hallucination, may function as

---

[41] The relation between ego-dystonic auditory hallucinations and the diagnosis schizophrenia is a complex one. Slade and Bentall (1987) write about this relationship. 'In fact, the existence or not of a unitary schizophrenia disease entity has been a matter of some debate for many years. With respect to the study of hallucinations, the problem can be stated in this way: given that there is a relationship between type of hallucination experienced by a patient and his or her psychiatric diagnosis, different hallucinations may reflect or even be caused by different psychiatric disease entities; on the other hand, the reasoning behind this argument may prove to be circular and patients receive different diagnoses because they suffer from different types of symptoms' (p.51/52). Although one of the criteria of schizophrenic hallucinations is that they are perceived as coming from an external source, psychiatric practices are found to differ considerably in this respect.

an important diagnostic criterion for different psychiatric diagnoses, (Slade and Bentall, 1988). The outcomes of those studies have shown that questions about reliability, construct validity and predictor validity of psychiatric syndromes are rarely met in a satisfactory way. All the research data point towards a dimensional rather than a categorical model of mental disorder, (Bentall, 1991). Instead of investigating hypothetical syndromes, psychopathologists should make particular symptoms the objects of their inquiries.

6.2.3 Hallucinations as a symptom

Several authors advise to study hallucinations in their own right, (Asaad and Shapiro, 1986; Slade and Bentall, 1988; Romme and Escher, 1989; Bentall, 1991). This point of view will also be our starting-point in investigating hallucinations.

Hallucinations are defined as [42]:

Any percept-like experience which (a) occurs in the absence of an appropriate stimulus, (b) has the full force or impact of the corresponding actual (real) perception, and (c) is not amenable to direct and voluntary control by the experiencer, (Slade and Bentall, 1988, p.23).

The first criterion -absence of appropriate stimulus- is a key criterion, an experience may be considered a hallucination only where such stimulation fails to provide the appropriate sensory stimulus for the experienced response. The criterion is used to distinguish between hallucinations and illusions.

The second criterion -a percept-like experience having the full force and impact of an actual perception- is not a simple one. The most important aspect of this criterion is that the hallucination is experienced with the full impact of an actual perception.

The third criterion -a percept-like experience which is not amenable to direct and voluntary control- serves to distinguish hallucinations from other kinds of vivid mental imagery, (Slade and Bentall, p. 23/24).

Hallucinations have been distinguished from various other forms of vivid mental experiences, such as day-dreaming. It should be noted that many observers, whereas accepting the validity of these distinctions, tend to view them as points on a continuum, with mental imagery at one end and 'true' hallucinations at the other[43].

---

[42] Hallucinations are defined in several ways and different criteria are specified. For a systematic review of the different definitions we refer to De Vries (1992). The definition of Slade and Bentall and the criteria they define are surely open to debate.

[43] Hallucinatory experiences may emerge under various circumstances. Many physiological states are conducive to hallucinations, such as extreme brain temperature, conditions of thirst, certain breathing patterns, different types of medical conditions, and alcohol or drug consumption.

6.3 Traumata and hallucinations

6.3.1 Childhood trauma and diagnosis of schizophrenia

Nowadays many persons in the United States, who were severely traumatized as children, and report dissociative and hallucinatory symptoms, receive the diagnosis of multiple personality disorder. The historical development described in previous chapters, leads to the suggestion that a certain percentage of the patients who (previously) received the diagnosis of schizophrenia must have been severely traumatized as a child. This suggestion is in line with the early theories of Freud (1896) and Breuer and Freud (1893-1895). After carefully studying their patients, they postulated, that hallucinations might relate to relivings of trauma, in actual or symbolic form. These childhood traumata are repressed, but are constantly forcing themselves upon the patient, and by this process prove the strength of the trauma. Later Freud (1905) abandoned this notion. He then assumed that hallucinations just like dreams, express wishes unacceptable to the conscious mind[44]. The study of Bleuler (1978) can be considered in the light of Freud's early theory.

Bleuler studied the childhood histories of 208 patients with a diagnosis schizophrenia[45]. He categorizes the childhood of these patients as being normal (living in a family with both parents), doubtful or horrible. Long-term maltreatment, severe physical neglect, regular beatings and being exposed to prostitution or beatings by drunkards, are categorized as horrible childhood circumstances. He found that a third of all persons (men and women) with a diagnosis schizophrenia had grown up in such horrible circumstances. The percentage 'schizophrenic' women with a horrible childhood history was higher, than the percentage of 'schizophrenic' men with such a history. Of the 'schizophrenic' women, 46% had been living under horrible childhood circumstances (child sexual abuse was not mentioned in this study). Only a fourth part of the 'schizophrenic' patients grew up in 'normal' families.

In later textbooks on psychological stress and psychopathology the results of Bleuler (1978) met with scepticism. For instance, Spring and Coons (1982) comment that horrible childhood circumstances are not only reported by patients with a diagnosis of schizophrenia. But, schizophrenic patients often subjectively experience a relationship between childhood trauma and symptoms of schizophrenia. This subjectively felt relationship is the 'single greatest impetus to

---

[44] Hallucinatory symptoms of some patients, interpreted by Freud as 'wish-fulfillment' are redefined by object relation therapists.The most famous case in this respect is the patient Schreber, whose symptoms were interpreted by Freud as manifestations of forbidden homosexual longings for his father. After the discovery of the extreme pedagogic principles of this father his hallucinations were redefined as memory traces of traumatic early life-experiences (Schatzman 1973).

[45] Bleuer (1978) doesn't give figures about hallucinations, but describes 'psychosis'.

research in this domain'. Spring and Coons think that this subjectively felt relation is only important to study because:

> When Freud's neurotic patients reported particular types of childhood sexual experiences, their reports did not correspond to reality. They were nonetheless useful in understanding and treating these patients, because they revealed a particular kind of symbolic thinking that is at least symptomatic, if not productive, of neuroses, (Spring and Coons, 1982, p.49).

After the discovery of the widespread prevalence of child sexual abuse, Freud's early notions have met with some acceptance, (Russell, 1986, Brière and Conte, 1990, van der Kolk, 1987, and many others). The way in which Spring and Coons refer to Freud shows how influential Freud's rejection of early sexual childhood trauma has been as a basis for mental disturbances. So, the recovery of the wide prevalence of (severe) child sexual abuse makes us in turn sceptical about the scepticism of Spring and Coons.

Until now only one study has considered the connections between child sexual abuse and 'psychotic decompensations' of patients in adult life. Beck and van der Kolk (1987) studied a cohort of 26 chronically hospitalized female patients, of whom 12 had incest histories. These 12 women with 'psychotic decompensations', had several times been admitted to psychiatric institutions in which they had received a variety of psychiatric diagnosis, the most prevalent being the diagnosis of 'schizophrenia' [46].

The impact of trauma and its relation to hallucinatory experiences can be considered in several different ways. Results of cognitive psychological studies shed new light on this relation, as will be shown in next sections.

6.3.2 Trauma and excessive deployment of attention

As we have seen in section 5-2-2, persons experience changes in consciousness during traumatic experiences, (Noyes, Hoenk & Kupperman 1977). Under these conditions persons report either 'speeded thought', 'vivid mental imagery' and 'heightened bodily awareness' or 'dull thoughts', 'dream-like alterations in consciousness', and 'loss of sensations'. In case of extreme trauma, persons experience mental clouding. The most extreme form of mental clouding is called a time-gap, (see 5-2-3). Changes in consciousness are associated with disturbances in self-reference; persons confronted with trauma report to feel as if the trauma did not happen to them. Noyes et al. find in their study a remarkable similarity between the 'depersonalization syndrome' experienced during trauma and the 'depersonalization syndrome' experienced by

---

[46] One main difference between women with and women without a history of sexual abuse concerned the delusions with sexual content. Beck and van der Kolk suggest that in their psychotic states, women with an incest history relive earlier traumata. They illustrate this suggestion by giving several case histories. For instance one 'psychotic' woman believed that her body was covered with ejaculate.

psychiatric patients. An increased awareness or a decreased awareness of the environment is often reported by patients receiving a diagnosis of schizophrenia, (Shean, 1982). Patients who received the diagnosis of schizophrenia and have an increased awareness of the environment are called 'reactive schizophrenics' and those who have a decreased awareness of the environment are called 'process schizophrenics', (Heilbrun, 1983).

Heilbrun et al. (1980, 1983, 1986) who studied hallucinations from a cognitive psychological point of view, have developed theories permitting a connection between trauma, depersonalization syndrome and hallucinations. Horowitz (1975) expressed similar ideas. Below, the work of Heilbrun et al. will be considered.

One of the most characteristic features of hallucinations is the disturbance in self-reference. General consensus exists that auditory and visual hallucinations are misrepresentations of a person's own thoughts in lexical (word) and visual (image) form, so that they are treated as perceptions, (Heilbrun, 1980). Heilbrun assumed that individuals susceptible to hallucinations are generally less familiar with the characteristics of their own internal processes, than those who are not. Lack of familiarity explains the misinterpretation of the hallucinators:

> The logic is simple. The more limited one is in recognising one's own thinking, the more likely it is that one will misidentify the source of a thought as being the voice of another (the usual auditory hallucination) when for any reason discrimination is required between its having an internal or an external origin, (Heilbrun, 1980, p.728).

He tested his hypothesis by asking hallucinating psychiatric patients and non-hallucinating patients to identify their own thoughts expressed a week earlier as being or not being their own thoughts. Twelve hallucinators and eight non-hallucinators were requested to recognise words, meaning and grammatical style of their own thoughts as expressed a week earlier and, as hypothesized, hallucinators were less capable of correctly recognising their own expressions. In this study, Heilbrun tried to find a basis for explaining impaired thought recognition in hallucinating patients. Locus of attention deployment by hallucinating patients was distinguished as one possible basis. In further experiments Heilbrun, Blum & Haas (1983) and Heilbrun, Diller, Fleming, Slade (1986) studied the misidentifications of thoughts found in hallucinating patients in relation to attention deployment. Two types of 'schizophrenics' were distinguished: patients with a heightened awareness of the environment who show extreme concentration on the environment, and patients with a decreased awareness of the environment who show extreme concentration on internal processes. Heilbrun et al. assumed that excessive deployment of attention towards the external environment may limit the monitoring of the individual's own thought. On the other hand, excessive deployment of attention inwardly may reduce the individual's ability to correctly label events that have their origin in the external surroundings.

An experiment demonstrated that 'reactive schizophrenics' and 'process schizophrenics' do indeed deploy attentional strategies as hypothesized. The results of these studies also indicated that extreme attentional strategies are significantly more frequently present in hallucinating psychiatric patients than in non-hallucinating patients. Especially patients who turn their attention inwardly had difficulty in locating auditory stimuli in space, (Heilbrun, Blum & Haas, 1983). Heilbrun et al. concluded that excessive deployment of attention in hallucinating patients allows gross misperception of their own thoughts and of the spatial location of the voices heard. They supposed that extreme attentional strategies are used as defense against the distressing meaning of social cues. Extreme attention deployment may help to prevent the 'flooding of aversive stimuli' (for instance, the intrusion of memories about traumatic incidents).

The descriptions of Heilbrun bear much resemblance to the theories and findings referring to disturbances in consciousness as described in chapters 3 and 5. It seems plausible that during traumata a person uses extreme attentional strategies to exclude overwhelming emotions from consciousness. Most persons subjected to severe trauma will temporarily use these extreme attentional strategies to exclude overwhelming emotions from consciousness. If a person constantly uses such extreme attentional strategies, she will hardly monitor what is going on in her mind. She will be less familiar with her own thoughts. This impaired recognition of one's own thoughts may well increase the risk of (auditory) hallucinations.

6.3.3 Flashbacks, perceptual intrusions

Horowitz (1976, revised and extended in 1986) devoted a major piece of work to stress-response syndromes. In the same time period he was also writing about (visual) hallucinations. In his work on the information processing approach towards hallucinations he elaborates the early notions of Freud, (Horowitz, 1975, p.188-191). In both works he describes the intrusion of flashbacks. Flashbacks are involuntary recurrences of thoughts, and especially images about traumatic events. Horowitz calls these intrusions 'unbidden images', that may have a very vivid quality. Those 'unbidden images' may be experienced by the person either as real or as unreal perceptions, but independently from this qualification the person will respond to these images as if they concern real perceptions[47]. In his elaboration of the early notions of Freud, Horowitz develops the idea that in the etiology of hallucinations, involuntary intrusions of 'unbidden images', as well as repressed emotions and thoughts evoked by these intrusions, play an important role, (Horowitz, 1975, p.188-191). The defense mechanism 'isolation', employed

---

[47] Horowitz states that these intrusions may be the source of paranormal phenomena, such as seeing ghosts or hearing ghosts of persons who have died.

to protect a person's concept of self, makes the person unable to recognise repressed ideas and images.

Before Horowitz, Mintz and Alpert (1972) thought the combination of vivid images and impaired recognition to be important for hallucinatory experiences. They did not refer to intrusion of flashbacks, but supposed the vividness of mental imagery to be important. They administered a test of vividness of auditory images to a group of 'hallucinating schizophrenics', a group of 'non-hallucinating schizophrenics', and a 'non-psychotic' control-group. They find the 'hallucinators' to have a high and the 'non-hallucinators' to have a low vividness of auditory imagery. The results indicated that vividness of mental imagery is a necessary but not a sufficient condition for the experience of hallucinations[48].

6.3.4 Repression and disturbances in reality-discrimination

Memories of trauma are normally repressed for a certain period, (Breuer and Freud, 1895; Horowitz, 1986; Kleber, 1986; van der Kolk, 1987; Pennebaker, 1987). Sometimes the repression of these memories is very strong and intrusions do not occur immediately but start many years after the traumatic incidents, (Hartmann, 1984; van der Kolk, 1987).

A person repressing her or his memories often recognises that intrusions of 'unbidden images' concern traumatic experiences. Even if the trauma evokes feelings of unreality, the person cognitively knows that the trauma has taken place. Sometimes persons experience a brief reactive psychosis after a recent traumatic event. This psychosis may last for a few hours or for as long as two weeks, (Horowitz 1986). Other authors report brief psychoses after traumatic experiences too, (for a review of the literature, see Bailly, 1990). After a while a person realizes what is going on. Van der Kolk and Kadish (1987, p.187) report observations that invite a re-evaluation of this description. For instance, they observed that in U.S. Veterans Administration Hospitals many Vietnam-war veterans are admitted who, preceding this admission, have received a diagnosis of schizophrenia in other psychiatric hospitals. Neither the veteran nor the environment had recognised that the 'repeatedly returning hallucinations' referred to relivings of war episodes. This observation suggests a considerable defect in recognising relivings of the past. This deficiency was not of a short and episodic character.

Repression of thoughts and images of traumatic incidents can be related to the finding that hallucinations occur in thát sense modality that is the least preferred by the patient, (Horowitz, 1975). Certain researchers find that auditory hallucinations occur in patients who have an impaired capacity to auditory imagery and visual hallucinations occur in patients who show to have a deficient

---

[48] There exists a considerable controversy about the role of vividness of mental imagery as a prerequisite for hallucinations (see for instance Bentall and Slade, 1985). Bentall and Slade argue that poor 'reality-discrimination' is the most important prerequisite.

visual imagery, (Seitz and Molholm, cited by Horowitz, 1975, p.173; Heilbrun, Blum & Haas, 1983).

From the theory and research summarized above the following notion can be deducted: Trauma are usually repressed and if this repression is strong, a person may not recognise flashbacks as based on real experiences.

6.3.5 Disturbances in sleep, dream and wake cycles and hallucinations

Other indications for a relation between trauma and hallucinations come from studies about nightmares. Hartmann (1984) reports that war veterans with a post-traumatic stress disorder have recurrent nightmares. These nightmares usually manifest themselves during dream (REM) sleep. But, these nightmares manifest themselves in other sleep periods too, and even during waking states. Nightmares in waking states are called 'daymares' by Hartmann.

These abnormal manifestations of nightmares in war veterans have also been described in persons with a diagnosis of schizophrenia. Electro-encephalograms of persons with a diagnosis of schizophrenia show that particular brain waves (called pontine-geniculate-occipital waves) usually present during dreams (in REM-sleep), may emerge in these patients during other sleep periods and even during waking states, (Buchsbaum, Ingvar, Kessler et al., 1982).

6.3.6 Trauma, increased arousal and hallucinations

Hyper-arousal is described as one of the main effects of traumatic experiences. Van der Kolk (1987), in particular, states that the most important post-traumatic stress symptom is loss of the ability to modulate arousal. In many traumatized people this modulation has been disturbed by trauma: they continue to respond even to minor stimuli with an intensity appropriate only to emergency situations. Slade and Bentall (1988) reviewed several studies demonstrating that increased arousal is associated with hallucination. An increased activation of the sympathic autonomic nervous system (skin conductance and finger pulse volume) is observed prior to experiences of hallucinations.

These findings seem to be congruent with the observation that any event may trigger 'psychotic' episodes in patients with a diagnosis of schizophrenia. The event may be very trivial and does not need to have a 'stimulus-based traumatic' character. Events that produce no or only mild stress reactions in most people, may evoke a period of hallucinations in patients with a diagnosis of schizophrenia, (Spring and Coons, 1982).

6.3.7 Distortions in learning reality-discrimination

Children of six years old or younger have not yet developed skills to discern real and imaginary events. Children often report dreams as real events.

Slade and Bentall (1988) devote some discussion to the way reality-discrimination is learnt and how it relates to hallucinations. This question is a difficult one. Private events like images or thoughts or feelings of pain are in essence only available to the person who experiences these events, but it is obvious that people can describe private events with some consistency. Words used to describe private events must be tied to public events. Often adults make inferences about a child's internal state from contextual environment and use words to describe this state. Or a child may observe how an adult connects his or her private feelings to public stimuli. However, sometimes people make wrong inferences about their own mental events. It has been demonstrated, for instance, that some people misattribute their feelings of emotional arousal to an illness, (Pennebaker, 1983).

A child can become profoundly confused in reality-discrimination when its parents use double bind messages, (Bateson, Jackson, Haley and Weakland, 1956; Laing and Esterson, 1964). A child may also have difficulties in learning reality-discrimination, if parents themselves attribute wrong inferences to private mental events.

6.3.8 Assumptions on relations between trauma and hallucination

From the literature and research reviewed above, several assumptions have emerged about how trauma may influence cognitive emotional functioning and how this cognitive emotional functioning may increase the risk of hallucinatory experiences. These assumptions will be summarised:

- When during repeated trauma a person develops an extreme style of attention deployment, in order to exclude overwhelming emotions from consciousness, she will not monitor what is going on in her own mind. She will be less familiar with her own thoughts and the impaired recognition of thoughts as one's own increases the risk of (auditory) hallucinations.

- When memories of the past involuntarily intrude consciousness and have a vivid perceptual quality, this increases the risk of (visual) hallucinatory experiences.

- When repression of trauma is strong, a person may not recognise flashbacks or memories as based on real experiences. The repression results in impaired recognition of memories and increases the risk of hallucinatory experiences.

- When a person has learned to repress emotions connected with trauma, this repression may contribute to 'not recognising emotions as belonging to the self' and may facilitate the attribution of these emotions to ego-dystonic (not self) sources.

- *When traumatic experiences result in a higher level of autonomic arousal, a person may respond to minor 'stressors' with a high level of arousal. This high level of autonomic arousal facilitates the occurrence of hallucinations.

- When persons suffer from chronic nightmares after traumatic incidents, these nightmares may not only occur during during the REM-sleep, but may emerge during day-time too. These 'daymares' may have a hallucinatory character.

- A young child has to learn to distinguish reality from imagination. When parents themselves are not able to discern between reality and imagination very well, a child will not easily learn this difference.
- *A child being abused by one or both parents from young age on, may gain some profit by not learning the difference between reality and imagination, because learning this distinction may be too devastating for the child. The child will restructure reality to provide herself with a safe environment at least at an imaginary level.

Not all assumptions formulated above have been tested in our study. The assumptions, which have not been examined, are marked with a *.

6.4 Research methods

Detailed information about the research strategy is given in chapter 2, questions concerning hallucinations and coding problems are presented in respectively sections 2-3-3 and 2-4-3. This section deals with the reliability of hallucinatory experiences.

6.4.1 Reliability of reports on hallucinatory experiences

In the semi-structured interview we did not enquire directly about hallucinatory experiences. Most visual hallucinations were mentioned when we asked about: quality of flash-backs, emotions surrounding self-injury or suicide attempts, 'daymares', or the quality of dissociative experiences. We only asked about auditory hallucinations when a woman reported to experience 'time-gaps'. The Dissociative Experience Scale contains one item about voices coming from inside the head. This question was put to all respondents and concerns recently heard voices.

A check was made whether coding of hallucinatory phenomena was consistent with other data obtained, whenever possible. Women reporting hallucinatory flashbacks in the semi-structured interview scored significantly higher on a D.E.S.-item about intensely reliving the trauma, than women who did not report hallucinatory flashbacks, $(F= 5.46, p<.01)$.

Auditory hallucinations reported at the D.E.S.-item are divided into two groups: voices absent (score 10 or less on the D.E.S.), and voices present (score 11 or more). Auditory hallucinations reported in the interview are compared with data obtained with the D.E.S. Comparison shows that in response to the D.E.S. women reported auditory hallucinations more frequently than during the interview. This finding may be explained by our strategy of inquiring: as said before we only asked about auditory hallucinations during the interview when a woman mentioned time-gaps. Due to this outcome we have preferred to use auditory hallucinations reported on the D.E.S. Verbal statements about auditory hallucinations are only presented when they have a heuristic value.

The question in the D.E.S. concerns 'hearing voices inside the head'. Women who hear voices solely as coming from outside may have answered this question in a negative way. Exploration of the protocols learned, that nine women report to hear (also) voices coming from 'outside the head'. Of these nine women three did not indicate to have auditory hallucinations on the D.E.S.[49]. The restricted way of inquiring about auditory hallucinations by the D.E.S, excluded some respondents with such hallucinations, but proportionally to all women who answered this item, the percentage is rather low (3%).

A check of the reports on visual hallucinations in the interview with data from the D.E.S. was not possible.

6.5 Phenomenology of hallucinatory experiences, descriptive results

We have arranged hallucinatory phenomena according to two criteria: (a) sense modality in which the hallucinatory perception occurred (visual or auditory) and (b) connection with flashbacks of child abuse. These criteria led to a subdivision of hallucinatory phenomena in: flashbacks with a hallucinatory character (visual and auditory), visual hallucinations and auditory hallucinations. Intrusive vivid flashbacks do meet the criteria of Slade and Bentall (see 6-2-4) for hallucinations, but we only considered flash-backs to be 'flashbacks with a hallucinatory character' when they changed the 'real' perception of the environment. Hallucinatory flashbacks always concerned incidents of child abuse and were recognised as such after a short period. Visual and auditory hallucinations were in no or in a less obvious way connected with childhood incidents. Visual and auditory hallucinations can be divided into several sub-categories. We will first consider the phenomenology of these hallucinations.

6.5.1 Hallucinatory experiences during childhood traumata

It is a matter of definition whether or not time-gaps are conceived as (negative) hallucinations. During time-gaps persons do not notice events present, whereas during hallucinations persons notice events not present, (Hilgard, 1986). Several studies found that hallucinations occur during extreme traumatic experiences. For instance, Amnesty International reports that 80% of the captives hallucinate during tortures, (Verhoeff, 1990). When time-gaps are considered as negative hallucinations, 39% of the women reported hallucinatory experiences during child (sexual) abuse; seven women experienced 'out of body feelings' with a hallucinatory character and 31 women experienced a time-gap, sometimes

---

[49] Of the nine women who reported to hear voices coming from outside the head, two did not complete the D.E.S. and other four women indicated hearing voices on the D.E.S.

immediately, sometimes after experiencing 'out of body-feelings', imaginary walks etc. Of course we have to be careful with the interpretation of these retrospective data.

6.5.2 Flashbacks with a hallucinatory character

Some respondents reported to experience perceptual distortions during flashbacks. For instance:

> Ilse (B37): was sexually abused by her father and badly beaten by him. She reports as one of her present complaints: 'The most horrible thing is that I can't see my husband. When I'm in the bathroom, and he comes in, I have to leave. I do not see my husband coming in, it is my father. I see my father coming into the bathroom. I get really sick of it'.

Ilse's description shows that the actual event (seeing her husband), by triggering a flash-back, is perceived in a transformed way. Her husband changes into the father. The father is perceived in an immediate and compelling way and her statement shows that reality-discrimination takes place only afterwards. 'I see my father coming into the bathroom, but it I know it is my husband'. Some women frequently endured such perceptual distortions.

Others report the flashbacks to be so intrusive that they lose their own adult frame of reference, they really feel like a child again and are 20 years back in time. For instance:

> Janny (B40) was sexually abused by her father from the age of six to twenty-seven. She recalls very well what has happened, her memories don't intrude unexpectedly, but she feels rather numb. In therapy she tried to remember more emotional details of the childhood incidents. "Then something happened that really scared me. I felt I became a child again with the same 'locked-inside a tube' feeling, the feeling that I could not escape from the situation. I really did not know how to escape. I did not realize I had escaped from that situation some time ago".

Some women have periods in which they are reliving childhood memories so intensely, that they need others to help them with reality-discrimination.

Flashbacks are conceived as being hallucinatory when they are accompanied by perceptual disturbances or by a loss of an adult frame of reference or by time-gaps (in 5-4-5 we mentioned that some women experienced time-gaps after flashbacks). All women reporting hallucinatory flash-back said these experiences lasted for short periods.

6.5.3 Visual hallucinations partially related to child sexual abuse

Breuer and Freud (1893-1895/1974), Asaad and Shapiro (1986) and many others supposed hallucinations, just like dreams, to consist of building blocks with memory-traces. Those memory traces present themselves in a disguised symbolic form. Beck and van der Kolk (1987) suggest that 'psychotic decompensations' of women who were sexually abused as children incorporate elements referring to this abuse. In our study eight women mentioned hallucinatory experiences partially, but in various ways related to sexual abuse.

Koos (B42) was sexually abused by her father as a child and went through a rape experience when an adult. 'I have been admitted to hospital after a rape experience. In that period I refused to eat. I saw sperm in my food and in my drinks, I saw sperm all-over'.

The description of Koos suggests that a chain of events relating to child sexual abuse, may trigger transformed perceptions.

6.5.4 Daymares as visual hallucinations

Hartmann (1984) suggests that persons suffering from chronic nightmares sometimes experience daymares too. For a person experiencing nightmares as well as daymares, the connection between those two experiences is obvious: the nightmares and daymares have similar contents. In our study we found five women reporting daymares with similar contents as their nightmares.

Hilly (B32): 'I frequently have this terrible dream that my father comes to kill me. When I awake from a nightmare and my friend sleeps next to me, I can't get rid of the feeling that my friend wants to kill me. In the day-time I often feel that somebody has caught me by my throat and that monsters are jumping on me. It is much more terrible than what my father did to me. Mostly I wake up, because I think that I scream very loud, but that nobody hears me. In reality I do not scream very loud. I often think that my neighbours will climb the stairs and then ...oh...no. I surely have dreamt that I was screaming'.

6.5.5 Somnambulistic experiences as visual hallucinations

Janet (1911) described 'somnambulist periods' in which a person is apparently experiencing terror. He assumes that this terror is based on experiencing 'idées-fixes'. In this study eight women reported somnambulistic experiences during the day in which they experienced terrifying hallucinations so vividly that they found themselves screaming and fighting. For instance:

Els (B18) told after a question about anxiety: 'At a certain moment I see a man coming in, he puts his hands around my throat and tries to kill me. I feel life is slipping away from me. At that moment I think this is what I don't want. I start to beat, to kick and fight. After an incredible fight I throw this man on the floor. He flies out of the door. After this experience I checked if I had locked the door well and went to sleep. After that event all the anxieties I had before were gone (she was agoraphobic). It felt as if I had been fighting with my father. I felt as if this fight really happened, you are awake, you are in your own room, I have been fighting on the floor with him'. However, Els doubted, if it really happened. She had experienced it very vividly, but in a dream-like way. She concludes: 'I think the experience is similar to experiences of people who have been in concentration camps'.

As far as these women remember, such hallucinations did not refer to real (childhood) incidents, (if so we would call it a hallucinatory flash-back), neither did they have similar nightmares (if so we would call it a daymare).

6.5.6 Auto-scopic hallucinations

Bliss (1980) and Putnam (1989) state that hallucinations of persons with a diagnosis multiple personality disorder refer to imaginary playmates that the patient created as a child. These imaginary playmates have become alter personalities who appear during hallucinations[50]. Putnam adds that auto-scopic hallucinations are frequently present. Some examples of auto-scopic hallucinations reported in our study are:

Elsbeth (B20): 'Sometimes I'm roaming around the house and then I meet myself every where. When I open the door, I see myself standing behind that door. I really panic when this happens'.

Grada (B23): 'In the period that my husband had this girl-friend, I had strange experiences, I really saw myself sitting next to myself. The one that was sitting next to myself, wanted to commit suicide, I didn't want to'.

Lydia (B49): 'In my dreams and also during flashbacks, I was an adult and saw myself as a child. I took myself as a child by the hand and talked to myself: 'I will take care of you'. This is why this Canadian movie[51] moved me so much'.

Other women mentioned visual hallucinations surrounding (self-) destruction. For a description of these hallucinations we refer to chapters 7 and 8.

6.5.7 Auditory hallucinations partially related to child sexual abuse

In the interview 27 women reported to have auditory hallucinations. Eight of these 27 women described auditory hallucinations partially related to child (sexual) abuse. The hallucinations of four of these women contained a mixture of

---

[50] Imaginary playmates are normal in children and are usually perceived as real, since children are not yet fully capable of distinguishing between reality and imaginary before the age of six. The imaginary playmates that a child creates and perceives as real, are experienced as hallucinations by adults with a diagnosis of 'Multiple Personality Disorder' (Bliss 1986, p.126-128). Putnam (1989) describes that visual and/or auto-scopic hallucinations have special characteristics in persons with an extreme dissociative disorder. The following hallucinations are frequently present: hallucinations that change body-perception, hallucinations that involve a different view of one's own face, hallucinations of alter personalities as separate people, seeing yourself from outside or looking down at yourself from above.

[51] This movie included shots of flashbacks with these double images of the sexually abused women.

flash-back elements and more symbolic representations. Illustrative is the account of Lieneke (B50) presented in the introduction of this chapter.

Four other women told that they do not remember the incest in a direct way, they heard voices informing them about their childhood.

> Hanna (B31) was sexually abused by her father, as far as she could remember until her eleventh year. He raped her brutally and threatened to kill her. She told she feels as if she only has a few memories of her 'self'. Most memories are of 'a small child'. She explains that as child she used to talk to herself and that she can't accept those memories. When she gets flashbacks this small child says, " 'you know that this has happened'. She (the small child) tells me what has happened and then I say: 'this really is terrible what you tell me'." What the voices are saying is not limited to the child abuse. She has periods in which she hears many voices. She recognises amongst others the voice of her mother.

As a child Hanna used to talk to herself in the third person to prevent being flooded by her memories. She attributed these memories to a small child and still experiences them as ego-dystonic[52].

6.5.8 General characteristics of auditory hallucinations

The poor data gathered about auditory hallucinations in the interview do not permit a thorough analysis. However, some general impressions can be reported concerning the difference between 'hysteric' or 'dissociative' hallucinations and 'psychotic' or 'schizophrenic' hallucinations, (see section 6-2-2).

Most auditory hallucinations reported met the Schneiderian criteria, specified for schizophrenic auditory hallucinations (23 of the 27).

Although we inquired about 'voices inside the head', the reports of auditory hallucinations showed these voices to be located inside the head (N=18), inside and outside the head (N=5) and outside the head (N=4). As we described in section 6-2-2, a similar proportion of 'male schizophrenics' located the voices externally.

Our respondents with auditory hallucinations were not heavily influenced sub-culturally. None were members of a sect and few were interested in para-normal phenomena. When women had dialogues with the voices, this occurred on instigation of a therapist (N=8).

Only a small fraction of women reported 'reactive psychosis'; hallucinations lasting a short period and following immediately after dramatic life-events.

---

[52] The experience to receive indirect information about child sexual abuse is not restricted to the communication given by voices. Some women report to find notes with reports of abusive experiences, while they can't remember to have written these notes. Ego-dystonic 'memories' are reported rather frequently, but women often doubt the validity of these communications. For instance, we find a rather strong correlation between finding notes made during time-gaps (item 26 of the DES) and doubting the validity of childhood memories (item 3 of the structured questionnaire), (r=.47, p=.0001).

Especially women with auditory hallucinations stated to hear voices for all ready many years.

6.5.9 Hallucinations and multiple identity-feelings

Some women with auto-scopic experiences or with voices communicating childhood incidents reported feelings of 'having two or more personalities'. Multiple identity-feelings were deduced from auto-scopic hallucinations especially when conflicting emotions were attributed to the different visual perceptions of the 'self'. Most women who hear voices arguing or discussing deduced a multiple identity too (N=15).

> Barbara (B5) told she used to be daydreaming alone in her room for long periods of time. During these periods she heard voices. When asked to give some more specific information she said: 'When I hear discussions, it is just like if there are many people in my head and that is disturbing. I can not stop it. They used to say terrible things, that I should be punished and so on. Fortunately these voices come less frequently now, it is not so frightening any more. It is just like if you are discussing with more people, you can learn new things from it (ironical)! The voices decreased, when I started to note things down in a diary. When I reread those notes, I think: what a chaos!'.

> Cynthia (B11) heard a lot of voices arguing with each other. She told that before she was in therapy 'she disappeared when the voices were quarrelling', but in therapy she learned to start a dialogue with these voices. She feels much better because 'now I'm in control. I'm the one who says what is gonna happen'.

These self-reports show that immediate perceptions, such as auditory and auto-scopic hallucinations constitute the person's sense of identity, in this case the person's sense of multiple identity[53].

6.5.10 Hallucinations and time-gaps

As we described before time-gaps were often preceded by flashbacks, (see 5-4-4). Statements of some women suggest that a similar connection exists between visual/auditory hallucinations and time-gaps (N=8).

> Lieneke (B50): 'When I go home from my therapy, I'm sitting in the bus and then the voices come. They're all talking together at the same time. I can't hear what they are saying, when I'm concentrating on one voice, I feel I'm gliding into nowhere land. When I wake up I don't know were I am, how long I have been travelling and were I have been'.

---

[53] Support for this observation is given by the findings of the principal component analysis reported in appendix 5-2. As demonstrated in appendix 5-2, auditory hallucinations and multiple identity-feelings are closely interrelated.

Certain statements suggest a gradual difference in 'disturbance of consciousness' between hallucinations and time-gaps. For instance, Elsbeth reports:

> Elsbeth (B20): 'Then I do not know were I am. I'm a very small child again, that is really creepy, I hear him (father) shouting again and feel her (mother) beating me. I'm glad that I'm conscious now of what was going on. Before, I used to roam around, walking, biking. I still go biking, but I keep conscious of what is happening. Now I can keep in mind that there are people, who care for me'.

This statement suggests that time-gaps represent a more severe degree of disturbance of consciousness than hallucinatory experiences.

A person who is hallucinating has a sufficient degree of consciousness to notice hallucinations, but a person (or a personality?) who experiences time-gaps has lost the ability to record such perceptions as hallucinations[54].

6.6 Childhood trauma and hallucinations, statistical analyses

In section 6.3 we discussed several ways in which (childhood) traumata are supposed to be related to hallucinations. The formulated assumptions will be examined in this section. But, first we will give information about the prevalence of hallucinatory experiences. As already described, hallucinatory phenomena are subdivided in flashbacks with a hallucinatory character, visual hallucinations, and auditory hallucinations.

6.6.1. Prevalence of hallucinatory experiences

Table 6-1 gives the prevalences of hallucinatory flashbacks, visual and auditory hallucinations.

Table 6-1: Prevalence of hallucinatory flashbacks, visual, and auditory hallucinations, (percentages)

N=97	hallucinatory experiences	
	n	%
Hallucinatory flashbacks	33	34
Visual hallucinations	41	42
Auditory hallucinations [a]	37	43

[a] N=86

---

[54] Statistical analysis does give some support to this conceptualization. An analysis of variance (one-way ANOVA) shows that the mean cumulative trauma-score of the 16 women with hallucinatory flash-backs is 9.06 (s.d.=6.07) and the mean trauma-score of the 11 women with time-gaps is 12.64 (s.d.= 8.03). The differences in mean cumulative trauma-scores are in the expected direction, but do not reach a 95% level of significance (F=1.74, p=.19).

As is shown in table 6-1 a third of the women experienced hallucinatory flashbacks. Women with visual hallucinations (42%) often reported more than one kind of visual hallucination: 70% (N=29) of those women described three or more different types of visual hallucinations. Auditory hallucinations were recently heard by almost half of the women (43% of the women indicated it on the D.E.S), whereby 38% (N=14) heard those hallucinations sometimes and 63% (N=23) heard voices a considerable amount of time (a score 50 or more on the D.E.S.). In total, 64% of the women indicated at least one hallucinatory experience.

Women with hallucinatory flashbacks tend to report visual hallucinations as well (χ^2 with continuity correction=14.33, df=1, p<.001). A somewhat less strong association exists between hallucinatory flashbacks and auditory hallucinations (χ^2= 7.13, df=1, p<.01). The association between visual and auditory hallucinations is significant (χ^2=9.07, df=1, p<.01). A rather large number of women, namely 27, reported visual as well as auditory hallucinations.

It is difficult to evaluate the prevalence rate of hallucinations found in our study. Prevalence of hallucinations reported in community studies ranges from 8% to 71%, (for a review see Slade and Bentall, 1988). Occurrence of hallucinations in 'normal' populations seems to be more common than is usually thought. Although the women participating in our study do report psychiatric symptoms only a fraction (24%) of them has been admitted to psychiatric institutions[55].

6.6.2 Cumulation of childhood trauma and hallucinatory flashbacks

One may wonder whether the intensity of emotions evoked by the original trauma or by the flash-back is related to the experience of hallucinatory flashbacks. As described in section 2-5-1 we constructed a cumulative trauma-score (C.T.S.). We examined whether there was a significant difference in cumulative trauma-score between two groups of women, with and without hallucinatory flashbacks. Findings are presented in table 6-2.

Analysis of variance (one-way ANOVA) shows an association between the cumulative trauma-score and presence or absence of hallucinatory flashbacks, (F=28.96, p<.0001).

---

[55] For respondents reporting hallucinations the admission to psychiatric institutions is slightly higher: 40% of the women with visual hallucinations, 30% of the women with perceptual disturbances during flashbacks and 27% of the women hearing voices.

Table 6-2: Cumulative trauma-score of women with and without
hallucinatory flashbacks, (one-way ANOVA)

<u>N</u>=97		cumulative trauma-score	
	<u>n</u>	<u>M</u>	<u>s.d</u>
No hallucinatory flashbacks	64	4.62	3.5
Hallucinatory flashbacks	27	10.5	7.0
F=28.96, p<.0001			

The group of women with hallucinatory flashbacks includes women who experienced a time-gap after the intrusion by flashbacks. As was shown in section 5.6 the cumulative trauma-score was rather strongly related to the experience of time-gaps, therefore we excluded the women with time-gaps after flash-backs. When those women are excluded we still find a significant difference in cumulative trauma-score between women with and without hallucinatory flash-backs, (F=14.87, p<.001).

In section 6-5-10 we expressed the thought that time-gaps associated with hallucinatory flash-backs may indicate a more extreme disturbance in consciousness than hallucinatory flashbacks. We constructed a factor called 'intensity of flash-backs', which distinguished between no or hardly any flashbacks (33%), flashbacks (38%), hallucinatory flashbacks (17%) and flashbacks preceding time-gaps (12%). The correlation between cumulative trauma-score and intensity of flashbacks is rather strong, (r=.49, p<.0001).

6.6.3 Cumulation of childhood trauma and visual hallucinations

One may wonder whether severely traumatized women more frequently report visual hallucinations than less severely traumatized women. In order to investigate this question we examined whether there was a significant difference in cumulative trauma-score between two groups of women with and without visual hallucinations. In table 6-3 findings are presented.

Analysis of variance shows that women with visual hallucinations have a significantly higher cumulative trauma-score than women without such hallucinations, (F=10.4, p<.01).

Table 6-3: Cumulative trauma-score of women with and without visual hallucinations, (one-way ANOVA)

N=97		cumulative trauma-score	
	n	M	s.d
No visual hallucinations	56	4.75	4.2
Visual hallucinations	41	8.17	6.2
F=10.40, p<.01			

We described the construction of a sum-score of visual hallucinations in section 2-4-3, (different kinds of visual hallucinations simply added). The cumulative trauma-score and the sum-score of visual hallucinations are correlated, (r=.37, p<.001).

6.6.4 Cumulation of childhood trauma and auditory hallucinations

The same question can be raised with regard to auditory hallucinations. Table 6-4 gives data about the difference in cumulative trauma-score between women with and without auditory hallucinations.

Table 6-4: Cumulative trauma-score of women with and without auditory hallucinations, (one-way ANOVA)

N=86		cumulative trauma-score	
	n	M	s.d
No auditory hallucinations	49	4.92	4.5
Auditory hallucinations	37	6.20	1.0
F=6.70, p<.01			

Women with auditory hallucinations have a significantly higher cumulative trauma-score than women without auditory hallucinations, (F=6.70, p<.01). However, when the frequency of auditory hallucinations is taken into account, we find no correlation between cumulative trauma-score and auditory hallucinations, (r=.13, p=n.s.).

This last finding calls for a closer look at the data. In general, six characteristics of child sexual abuse are considered to be indicators for the severity of child sexual abuse, (see chapter 4-7). Only one of these six characteristics of child sexual abuse, father (-figure) being the perpetrator, was found to be associated with the occurrence of auditory hallucinations, (χ^2 with continuity correction=4.06, df=1, p<.05).

As reported in section 2-5-1, we constructed the cumulative trauma-score by dividing childhood into three age periods, young child (0-6 years), child (7-12 years), and adolescent (13 years or older) and each woman got scored for experiences with sexual abuse, physical aggression by perpetrator, and for abuses by others in the family. This procedure resulted in one general cumulative trauma-score and 9 sub trauma-scores. We examined whether women with and without auditory hallucinations differ with respect to (sub-) trauma-scores. These findings are presented in table 6-5.

Table 6-5: Sub trauma-scores in two groups of women with and without auditory hallucinations, (one-way ANOVA)

N=86		sexual child abuse (0-6 yrs)		physical aggres. perp (0-6 yrs)		other family abuse (0-6 yrs)	
	n	M.	s.d.	M.	s.d.	M.	s.d.
No auditory hall.	49	.306	.55	.14	.35	.25	.43
Auditory hall.	37	.703	.1	.41	.6	.62	.64
		F= 5.6, p< .05		F= 6.4, p<.01		F=10.6, p<.001	

N=86		sexual child abuse (7-12 yrs)		physical aggres. perp. (7-12 yrs)		other family abuse (7-12 yrs)	
	n	M.	s.d.	M.	s.d.	M.	s.d.
No auditory hall.	49	2.19	1.82	.98	1.2	.37	.52
Auditory hall.	37	2.54	2.18	1.43	1.64	.65	.59
		F=.7, p=n.s.		F=2.19, p=n.s.		F=7.29, p<.01	

N=86		sexual child abuse (≥13 yrs)		physical aggres perp. (≥13 yrs)		other family abuse (≥13 yrs)	
	n	M.	s.d.	M.	s.d.	M.	s.d.
No auditory hall.	49	1.67	1.94	.83	1.2	.41	.54
Auditory hall.	37	2.32	2.24	1.35	1.55	.62	.55
		F=2.08, p=n.s.		F=3.02, p=n.s.		F=3.29, p=n.s.	

The results of an analysis of variance, (table 6-5) show that women with auditory hallucinations differ significantly from women without hallucinations in degree of traumatization before the age of 7. Women with auditory hallucinations have experienced before the age of 7 more aggression by the perpetrator, (F=6.4, p<.01) and more neglect by 'other family members', (F=10.6, p<.001) than women without auditory hallucinations. Of course we must be careful to interpret retrospective accounts of abusive situations before the age of seven: the only conclusion that can be drawn is that these women can not remember a period in which the perpetrator or the mother did not abuse or neglect them.

Another striking finding is, that 'abuse by other family-members' is more strongly associated with auditory hallucinations than abuses at the hands of the perpetrator. 'Other family-members' predominantly concerns the mother of the child. Women with auditory hallucination are more frequently neglected or abused by the mother before the age of seven, (F=10.6, p<.001), and between the age of seven and twelve, (F=7.29, p<.01) than women without auditory hallucinations.

6.6.5 Childhood trauma, dissociation, repression, and hallucinations

In 6-3-6 we formulated several assumptions about the ways traumata in childhood may influence cognitive psychological styles of functioning and how these styles of cognitive functioning may be related to hallucinatory experiences. Several of these assumptions have been investigated in our study. Extreme attentional strategies may be deployed to prevent being overwhelmed by intense emotions evoked by traumata or memories of traumata. These strategies may result in the experience of time-gaps. Time-gaps are examples of extremely impaired monitoring of environmental and internal processes, (see chapter 3 and 5). In general, thoughts about trauma are often repressed, (see section 2-2-1). Of the women who participated in our study 28% reported to have had intervals in which they hardly gave any thought to their history of sexual abuse, and 29% have had intervals in which they had completely forgotten it.

Emotions evoked by traumata may be devoid of a 'self-reference', they are subsumed under the concept of repression of feelings. We asked about several kinds of depersonalization feelings, such as out-of-body-feelings, not recognising one's own face in the mirror, and being withdrawn behind an imaginary emotional wall, (see appendix 2.2.V). We examined the relation between hallucination and disturbances in reality monitoring. Two items of the D.E.S. (items 8 and 24) refer in a rather direct way to disturbances in reality monitoring. These two questions concern difficulties in distinguishing thought processes from real acts, and difficulties in distinguishing dreams from real events.

In table 6-6 the relations are presented between dissociative and repressive cognitive styles, and hallucinatory phenomena. The analyses of variance (one-way ANOVA) concern repressive and dissociative cognitive styles and presence versus absence of hallucinatory experiences. Correlations are calculated between on the one hand dissociation or repression, and on the other hand frequency of visual hallucinations, frequency of auditory hallucinations, and intensity of hallucinatory flashbacks. As is demonstrated in table 6-6 repression of feelings and time-gaps are consistently associated with hallucinatory experiences.

Repression of memories and impaired monitoring are less consistently correlated with hallucinatory experiences[56].

Table 6-6: Repression of memories and emotional feelings, dissociative cognitive styles and hallucinatory experiences, (ANOVA and Pearson correlations)

N=97	hall.flash-back		visual hall.		auditory hall.	
	F	r	F	r	F	r
Repression of memories	4.62*	.20	12.07***	.38	1.20	.06
Repression of feelings	9.56***	.35	12.48***	.42	10.58****	.48
Impaired monitoring a)	4.2*	.29	4.04*	.35	1.60	.10
Time-gaps b)	14.92***	.40	15.2***	.48	14.77****	.40

a) Two items of the D.E.S. (items 15 and 24) refer in a rather direct way to disturbances in reality monitoring. b) The frequencies of self-reported time-gap symptoms included in the D.E.S. (items 3, 4, 5, 6, 8) are summed in order to create a time-gap-score.

* p<.05, **p<.01, ***p<.001,****p<.0001

To investigate whether repressive and dissociative cognitive styles play an important mediating role between childhood trauma and hallucinatory experiences, three stepwise regression analyses have been performed. In these analyses, the cumulative trauma-score (C.T.S), repression of memories, repression of feelings, impaired monitoring and time-gaps are considered to be factors predicting intensity of flashbacks, visual hallucinations and auditory hallucinations.

Findings of the stepwise regression analysis on intensity of flash-backs are presented in table 6-7.

The analysis shows two factors contributing significantly and independently to intensity of flashbacks: cumulative traumatic childhood incidents and repression of emotional feelings. Of those two factors, the cumulative trauma-score contributes most, (see Std. Coefficient or F removed). The multiple correlation of these two factors with intensity of flash-backs is R=.54, p<.0001, the explained variance is 29%.

---

[56] There is no significant correlation between repression of memories and experiences of time-gaps (r=.14). Repression of feelings however correlates strongly with time-gaps (F=33.75, r=.53) as well as with repression of memories, (F=11.40, r=.24).

Table 6-7: Repressive and dissociative cognitive styles and intensity of flashbacks, (stepwise regression analysis, 2 steps removed)

N=97	ß-Coeff.	Std.Coeff.	F to remove
C.T.S. a)	.08	.43	18.19
Repression of feelings	.04	.21	4.06

	Part. Corr	F to enter
Repression of memories	.15	1.79
Impaired monitoring	.14	1.56
Time-gaps	.08	.43

a) C.T.S. is cumulative trauma-score

Findings of the stepwise regression analysis on visual hallucinations (sum-score) are presented in table 6-8.

Table 6-8: Repressive and dissociative cognitive styles and visual hallucinations (sum-score), (stepwise regression analysis, 2 steps removed)

N=97	ß-Coeff.	Std.Coeff.	F to remove
Time-gaps	.33	.33	10.6
repression of memories	.49	.33	10.7

	Part. Corr	F to enter
C.T.S. a)	.18	2.66
Repression of feelings	.09	.65
Impaired monitoring	.05	.18

a) C.T.S. is cumulative trauma-score

The analysis shows two factors contributing significantly and independently to visual hallucinations: time-gaps and repression of memories. Both factors contribute equally to visual hallucinations, (see Std. Coefficient or F removed). The multiple correlation of these two factors with visual hallucinations is R=.55, p<.0001, the explained variance is 29%.

Findings of the stepwise regression analysis on frequency of auditory hallucinations are presented in table 6-9. The findings shown in table 6-9 indicate that also two factors contribute significantly and independently to auditory hallucinations: repression of feelings and time-gaps. Repression of feelings contributes most to auditory hallucinations, (see Std. Coefficient or F removed). The multiple correlation of these factors with visual hallucinations is R=.56, p<.0001, the explained variance is 30%.

Table 6-9: Repressive and dissociative cognitive styles and frequency of auditory hallucinations, (stepwise regression analysis, 2 steps removed)

N=97	ß-Coeff.	Std.Coeff.	F to remove
Repression of feelings	.23	.41	13.90
Time-gaps	.57	.22	4.01

	Part. Corr	F to enter
Impaired monitoring	-.18	2.62
C.T.S. a)	-.15	1.83
Repression of memory	-.10	.73

a) C.T.S. is cumulative trauma-score

Together, these findings indicate that the cumulative trauma-score is the most important factor to account for intensity of flashbacks. Extreme dissociative and repressive cognitive styles are both important factors to account for visual hallucinations, and depersonalization feelings are the most important factor accounting for auditory hallucinations. Findings suggest that both cognitive psychological styles, repression and dissociation, play a mediating role between childhood trauma and visual and auditory hallucinations. For the experience of hallucinatory flashbacks, the mediating role of repression and dissociation is less important.

6.7 Summary and discussion

We departed from the point of view that studying hallucinations in their own right is more fruitful than considering hallucinations as a part of psychiatric syndromes. Three kinds of hallucinations are distinguished: hallucinatory flashbacks, visual hallucinations and auditory hallucinations. Theory and research on hallucinatory phenomena show several factors that are involved in the etiology of hallucinations. In our study, 64% of the women report hallucinatory phenomena. It is difficult to evaluate this prevalence rate, because the prevalence of hallucinations reported in community studies ranges from 8% to 71%, (for a review see Slade and Bentall, 1988).

In some women, flashbacks are associated with perceptual disturbances (hallucinatory flashbacks). West (1975) assumed that hallucinations, amongst others, emerge after an 'input overload'. We found that the cumulation of childhood trauma is associated with the experience of hallucinatory flashbacks. This suggests that the intensity of emotions elicited by flashbacks, 'jams' the perceptual system. Perceptions are based on memories of the past (Edelman,

1989). If memories of the past invoke very intense emotions, perceptual disturbances (hallucinations) may result.

After traumatic experiences, persons may suffer from chronic nightmares. In some of these persons the state of consciousness that is usually manifest during dream periods (REM-sleep), can be found during waking periods. Women in this study not only report post-traumatic nightmares, but other kinds of nightmares and night-terrors as well. Some women described that nightmares (not identified as post-traumatic nightmares) are also experienced during day-time and these daymares imply a difficulty in reality-discrimination.

Of the women in our study, 57% have had intervals during which they never thought about, or had completely forgotten child sexual abuse. Some women reported that initially they didn't recognise that the flashbacks contained memories. Most women who had initially forgotten their history of sexual abuse, and later experienced images of that abuse, started extensive verification processes. They discussed details of the images, more accessible to public verification than the sexual abuse as such, with sisters, aunts, grandmothers, brothers etc. Uncertainty about the provenance of their 'unbidden images' made some women refuse to participate in our study, because they had not yet verified well enough whether their images were based on real memories. We found that repression of memories significantly and independently contributes to the occurrence of visual hallucinations. Women repressing memories of child sexual abuse are more inclined to attribute a hallucinatory quality to 'unbidden images' than women who are not repressing memories.

Some women who participated in our study said that during flashbacks they could not get rid of the feeling 'this has not been happening to me', even when they had ample information that the flashbacks consisted of real memories. In trauma theory such feelings are described as 'depersonalization feelings' and are thought to refer to repression of overwhelming emotions, (Horowitz, 1986). We made the assumption that a general coping strategy of 'repressing emotions', learned by repeated traumatization, may increase the risk of hallucinatory experiences. We ascertained that consistent and rather strong relations exist between disturbances in self-reference and hallucinatory flashbacks, visual and auditory hallucinations. Disturbance in self-reference is the main factor contributing to auditory hallucinations. These findings suggest that 'not recognising feelings as belonging to the self' facilitates the attribution of emotions and associated thoughts and images to ego-dystonic sources. This attribution process is especially important in the etiology of auditory hallucinations.

Time-gaps are examples of extremely inadequate monitoring of internal and external processes. Such inadequate monitoring is thought to be the result of excessive deployment of attention. We assumed that during trauma a person uses extreme attentional strategies to exclude overwhelming emotions from consciousness. If a person persistently deploys extreme attentional strategies, she will not monitor what is going on in her own mind. She will be less familiar with her own thoughts, and the impaired recognition of her own thoughts increases the probability of (auditory) hallucinations. We found that the frequency of time-gaps correlates with intensity of hallucinatory flashbacks, frequency of visual hallucinations and auditory hallucinations. These correlations are stronger than those between cumulative childhood trauma, and visual and auditory hallucinations. These findings suggest that extreme deployment of attentional strategies plays a mediating role between severe (childhood) trauma and visual as well as auditory hallucinations.

A young child has to learn the difference between reality and imagery. If a child's parents are not themselves able to make this distinction, a child may have serious difficulty in learning this distinction. From literature it is known that parental incest is usually associated with a distortion of reality, (Summit, 1983). A child being abused by one or both parents from young age on, may gain certain profit from not learning the difference between reality and imagination. Learning this distinction may be too devastating for the child. We found that auditory hallucinations are predominantly associated with neglect, physical or sexual abuse by parents of children before the age of 7. Of course one should distrust reports of memories that go back to such an early age. The most distinctive feature is that these women can not remember a period in which their father or their mother did not neglect, beat or sexually abuse them. These findings suggest that women being abused or neglected from early age on may never have learned to discriminate between reality and imagination, this may be especially so for auditory perceptions.

Hallucinations and extreme dissociative disturbances can both be conceptualized as 'disturbances in the consciousness'. Certain research findings suggest that time-gaps are a more extreme form of disturbance in consciousness than hallucinations. During hallucinations the consciousness is able to notice what is going on and this is not the case during time-gaps. Hallucinations, dissociation as well as reactions on severe psychological trauma seem to involve similar psychological elements: the lack of integration of intense emotional feelings into the immediate, preconscious feelings of 'self', extreme disattentional strategies, experiences of involuntariness and changes in level of consciousness. The finding that auditory hallucinations are connected to neglect and abuse by parental figures at an early age, but not to the cumulation of childhood trauma and that time-gaps are associated with the cumulation of childhood trauma, but not with early child abuse should however warn us against too generalized a conceptualization.

Chapter 7

I shall bleed for it

child sexual abuse and self-injury[57]

Ans (B4): Her father died when she was four years old. Her stepfather abused her sexually from the age of eight until she was thirteen years old. It started in the following way. First her stepfather physically assaulted her with permission of her mother. The physical assaults were so terrible that several times she was taken to the First-Aid-Post for help, because she was injured. After these assaults her stepfather came to her to make things up again. His settlements consisted in sexual intercourse. She reports: 'When you are a child you are glad he is not angry at you any more'. Her stepfather also gave her money for having sexual contact. She feels very ashamed and guilty about this situation, although she rationally knows she should not. Ans started to injure herself before the age of 12. Several times she was admitted to a hospital because she inflicted severe bodily harm upon herself. She preferred a stay in the hospital to her presence at home. Social workers did notice she was in a bad family situation and tried to help her, but did not intervene. She is still inflicting bodily harm by cutting and hitting herself. She has no voluntary control over this kind of behaviours. She says: 'I notice somehow that I'm roaming around, looking for something and then I'm in this vacuum. I do not notice what I do. First I see the things my stepfather did and then I'm gone. Afterwards I find out I have been cutting myself'.

7.1 Introduction

This chapter starts with a discussion on self-injury and psychiatric diagnosis. A tendency exists to give persons with self-injurious behaviour the diagnosis of 'borderline personality disorder'. We choose to study self-injurious behaviour as

---

[57] Nicole Muller's literature study about self-injurious behaviour and her description of our data on self-injury have been important contributions to this chapter.

a symptom in itself (7-2). Several studies show a relationship between childhood trauma and self-injury (7-3-1). The question why this relation exists has been answered in different ways. Early parental neglect is seen as a main cause of self-injurious behaviour (7-3-2). Childhood abuse evokes rage and this rage is expressed by self-injurious behaviour (7-3-3). Especially child sexual abuse evokes shame and guilt, and these feelings direct the rage towards the 'self' (7-3-4). Flashbacks and elicited emotions may form the link between child sexual abuse and self-injurious behaviour in adulthood (7-3-5). Self-injurious behaviour may be conceived as a cry for help (7-3-6). Assumptions about the connection between child sexual abuse and self-injurious behaviour are summarised (7-3-7). In the detailed description of self-injurious behaviour several aspects of this behaviour are considered (7-4), such as the frequency (7-4-1), the form (7-4-2), the age of onset (7-4-3), the body parts injured (7-4-4), the emotional feelings (7-4-5), the state of consciousness accompanying self-injury (7-4-6), and the subjectively experienced relation between child sexual abuse and self-injury (7-4-7). The question why child sexual abuse is connected with self-injury is investigated. The relations are presented between frequency of self-injury and respectively severity of child sexual abuse (7-5-1), characteristics of child sexual abuse evoking self-blame feelings (7-5-2), the interaction between severity of child sexual abuse and self-blame feelings (7-5-3), and early parental abuse (7-5-4). The question whether the form of self-injury is related to differential characteristics of child sexual abuse is considered in (7-5-5). The chapter ends with a summary and conclusion (7-6).

7.2 Self-injury and psychiatric diagnosis

Self-injury is defined as deliberate, non-life-threatening, self-effected bodily harm or disfigurement of a socially unacceptable nature, (Walsh and Rosen 1988, p.10).

In, for instance, D.S.M.-III-R (American Psychiatric Association, 1987), self-injury is mentioned as one of the symptoms of the diagnosis borderline personality disorder. Favazza and Conterio (1989) write: 'The prevalent approach emphasizes characterological psycho-pathology and considers self-injury as a manifestation of borderline personality disorder'. Until recently this disorder was thought to be associated with early parental neglect. Recently, Herman and van der Kolk (1987) suggested that borderline symptomatology can be found in persons with a history of severe child (sexual) abuse and this abuse is not limited to early age-periods. Other authors protest against the 'almost knee-jerk response' to diagnose everyone who inflicts self-harm as having a 'borderline disorder'. For instance, Favazza and Favazza (1987) stress the symbolic value that such behaviour has in many cultures.

Favazza and Favazza (1987) and Walsh and Rosen (1988) in their recent handbooks on self-injury, plead not to focus on a single psychiatric disorder, when one is confronted with self-injury. They agree with Kahan and Pattison (1983) that self-injury should be included in the D.S.M.-IV as a distinct syndrome. Kahan and Pattison propose the term 'Deliberate Self-harm Syndrome'. This syndrome has the following features:

1. A sudden, irresistible impulse to harm oneself physically.
2. A psychological experience of existing in an intolerable, uncontrollable situation from which one cannot escape.
3. Mounting anxiety, agitation, and anger in response to the perceived situation.
4. Perceptual and cognitive constriction resulting in a narrow perspective of the situation and of alternatives of action.
5. Self-inflicted destruction or alteration of body tissue done in a private setting.
6. A rapid temporary feeling of relief following the act of self-harm.

7.3 Traumata and self-injury

7.3.1 Studies on childhood trauma and self-injury

Several studies on sexual or physical child abuse show that women with a sexual or physical child abuse history are frequently inclined to self-destructive or, more specifically, to self-injurious behaviour, (Carroll, Schaffer, Spensley & Abramowitz, 1980; Simpson and Porter, 1981; DeYoung, 1982; Adams-Tucker, 1982; Carmen, Rieker, & Mills, 1984; Brière, 1984; Shapiro, 1987; Draijer, 1988; Favazza and Conterio, 1989; Herman, Perry, & van der Kolk, 1989; van der Kolk, 1989; Goodwin, Cheeves, & Connell, 1990).

For a detailed review of the studies mentioned above we refer to appendix 7-1. Most of these studies are performed on groups of in- or out patients. When the study incorporates a control group, self-injurious behaviour is more frequently found in women with a sexual/physical child abuse history than in the comparable control group, (Brière, Carmen et al., Herman et al., Simpson and Porter).

There are two studies about self-injury done with groups comparable to women in our study. DeYoung (1982) reported that 58% (26 of the 45) of her clinical sample of women with a history of paternal incest self-inflicted bodily harm for 3 months or longer, and Shapiro (1987) reported that 6 out of 11 (55%) psychotherapy patients with a paternal incest history harmed themselves. In both studies, self-injurious behaviour had not been important in selecting patients for the therapy group.

Favazza and Conterio (1989) studied a large group of 'habitual self-injuring' women. They mention that 69% of these women had a history of sexual or physical child abuse. Carroll, Schaffer, Spensley & Abramowitz (1980) compared a group of self-injuring in-patients with a matched control group. They found that self-injuring patients had experienced significantly more major separations before the age of 10, more family aggression, more physical abuse and anger prohibitions, as compared with the control group.

Today a significant body of research shows a connection between sexual or physical child abuse and self-injury. A few authors discussed the question why and how child abuse is related to self-injury. Several assumptions regarding this question are formulated and these will be considered in the next sections.

7.3.2 Early parental abuse and self-injury

Persons with self-injurious behaviour are frequently found to be neglected and physically abused by their parents at an early age. The link between early abuse and self-injury is thought to consist of 'identification processes'. The young child that is abused will identify her or himself with the parents and the hostility of the parents is 'introjected', (DeYoung, 1982; Shapiro, 1987). For instance, Shapiro stressed the importance of 'primitive identifications with the intrusive, controlling and sadistic aspects of a parental figure'. She describes the childhood history of a self-injuring woman, sexually abused from early age until eighteen years of age by father, mother and brothers. The family participated in sex rings and the sexual abuses were very sadistic in character. As a result, the woman injured herself sadistically as a natural attitude towards herself. Simpson and Porter (1981) noticed that the abusive situation may have been the only situation in which the child got attention from the parent. A child may learn to physically stimulate itself and care for 'the self' by injuring 'that self'.

Van der Kolk (1989) postulated another way in which early parental neglect and self-injurious behaviour are related. He developed a complex theory about early parental neglect and self-injury. He assumed that biological processes play an important role in compulsive self-injurious behaviour. Early attachment is demonstrated to be mediated by neurophysiological systems. One of these systems is the endogenous opiate system, (Panksepp, Normansell, Herman, Bishop, & Crepeau 1988). In animals early disruption of the attachment between parent and child causes long lasting biological changes. When animals early in life are derived from parental care, they develop fewer opioid receptors. The endogenous opiates, in turn, have been demonstrated to play an important role in the formation of social attachment. A lack of endogenous opiates results in withdrawal, in diminishing social needs. Such processes, demonstrated in primates and mice, are thought to be important in humans too. Van der Kolk assumed that:

> *people who were neglected or abused as children may require much higher external stimulation of the endogenous opioid system for soothing than those whose endogenous opioids can be more easily activated by conditioned responses based on good early caregiving experiences, (van der Kolk 1989, p.401).*

According to van der Kolk, repeated self-injury can be conceived as one form of addiction to intensive stimuli. These intensive stimuli are necessary to evoke an optimum level of endogenous opiate production in the brain. The fact that many women report relaxation after self-injury supports such an assumption.

7.3.3 Rage evoked by trauma and self-injury

Simpson and Porter (1981), studying the childhood experiences of self-injuring patients, frequently found a history of physical abuse, sexual abuse and neglect. They described disruption of the attachment process as an important etiological factor for self-injurious behaviour, but next to that they stressed that repeated parental attacks towards children may have built tremendous reservoirs of partially or completely repressed anger and rage. Carmen, Rieker, and Mills (1984) stated that one of the common patterns of response to chronic (sexual/physical) victimization is the lack of acknowledgement by victims of their anger towards the perpetrator. This denial of anger is partly motivated by the perceived danger caused by the intensity and uncontrollability of the anger and partly motivated by the complex relationship between victim and perpetrator.

7.3.4 Shame and guilt evoked by trauma and self-injury

Simpson and Porter (1981) mentioned that, especially when a child has been sexually abused, an element of self-punishment is present in self-injury. For young people it is difficult to determine how responsible they are for sexual abuse. Often children are told by the (uninvolved) parent or by other family members that the events are their own fault and often they feel helpless and guilty. DeYoung (1982), in her article on self-injurious behaviour in paternal-incest victims, stated that a reason for self-punishment lays in the child's perception that her body has betrayed her. A child may not have control over her body's involuntary response to sexual stimulation. She may feel that her body is bad and that it deserves punishment. Lindberg and Distad (1985b), who studied 27 adolescents with a history of child sexual abuse, interpreted self-destructive and self-injurious behaviour as an attempt to alleviate stress or to assert some control over the helplessness created by the incest experience. Stress and helplessness are logical and predictable responses within the incest frame work. Lindberg and Distad also found adolescents with an incest history to feel responsible for 'their participation' in the incest. Shapiro (1987) exclusively focused on self-injury and self-blame in violent paternal incest victims. She stresses the importance of attitudes in the culture that 'blame the victim': the child is often seen as a seducer of the adult. The sexually abused child may feel she is responsible for the abusive behaviour. The self-destructive behaviour used by the victim is a mechanism by which she copes with the emotional pain and the, either conscious or unconscious, self-blame created by the incest. When the child does not disclose the sexual abuse, she remains powerless: her anger and her disappointment towards others are directed inward. Shapiro suggested that it is important, when treating a self-injuring woman with a history of child sexual abuse, to ascertain the level of guilt or shame this woman is struggling with, because self-blame is the psychic link between the actual incest experience and the self-injury occurring much later in life and yet the woman seems to lay no conscious connection between both incidents.

7.3.5 Trauma, flashbacks and self-injury

Persons may react to pain evoked by flashbacks with self-injury. Greenspan and Samuel (1989) reported some cases of self-cuttings. The self-cuttings were part of a post-traumatic stress disorder, in reaction to a rape experience. This rape was experienced when grown-up. A case was presented were the self-cutting of the arm provided a release for unbearable tension that had been build up as part of a rape-related flashback. Lindberg and Distad (1985b) suggested that stress and helplessness experienced in the period of self-injury are logical and predictable responses within the incest frame work. De Young (1982) found that the emotional state before and during the self-injury is one of intense feelings, of depersonalization or trance-like feelings. The sight of blood, bruises or burns after injurious behaviour may result in calm and relief.

7.3.6 Self-injury as a cry for help

Based on two case-reports of children, DeYoung (1982) stated that self-injurious behaviour can be a childish way to prevent incest. She remarked that self-injuring behaviour is rare in prepuberal children who have not been physically or sexually abused. Self-injury can also be seen as a poignant, non-verbal call for help, as noted by Simpson and Porter (1981).

7.3.7 Assumptions

It appears that self-injury is a complex multi-determined behaviour. Several notions exist about the psychic mechanism playing the intermediate role between child (sexual) abuse and self-injury. In each individual a unique constellation of factors may be found that contributes to self-injury. Below the assumptions derived from these studies discussed are summarised.

- When a woman is abused or neglected at an early age, there is an increased risk of repetitive self-injury.
- When a woman has been repetitively and severely abused as a child she will experience a tremendous rage. This rage increases the risk of repetitive self-injury.
- When a woman feels guilty or ashamed about her history of child sexual abuse there is an increased risk of repetitive self-injury.
- When a woman frequently experiences flashbacks on child sexual abuse there is an increased risk of repetitive self-injury.
- A cry for help is considered to be a main motive when children injure themselves.

7.4 Characteristics of self-injury, descriptive results

Detailed information about the research strategy is given in chapter 2. In section 2-3-2 the way of inquiring about self-injury is presented.

Of the women participating in our research (N=97), 51% (N=49) reported having ever injured themselves. Additionally four women experienced almost irresistible urges to self-injury, but they found ways of controlling these urges, and from seven women we did not obtain information on self-injury.

We used a rather conservative measure of occurrence of self-injury. If a woman did not give clear positive evidence that she had harmed herself, we did not count it. If certain common self-harming behaviour, like nail-biting or scratching, was reported, but this behaviour was not excessive, we did not count it as self-injury either.

Frequency of self-injury was scored as once, several times, or frequent; onset as before 12 years, between 12 and 18 years, and later than 18 years of age.

7.4.1 Frequency of self-injury

Frequency of self-injurious behaviour is reported in table 7-1. These percentages only concern the group of women with self-injurious behaviour. Only five women injured themselves once, the others inflicted self-injury sometimes (43%) or frequently (47%).

Table 7-1: Frequency of self-injury, (percentages)

N=49	frequency of self-injury	
Frequency	n	%
Only once	5	10
Several times	21	43
Frequently	23	47

The 5 women who injured themselves only once, were all older than eighteen years when injuring and had felt an unbearable tension.

7.4.2 Forms of self-injury

We distinguished forms of self-injury whereby tools, such as knives or fire, are used, and forms of self-injury whereby such tools are not used. In tables 7-2 and 7-3 the frequencies of different forms of self-injury are presented.

Table 7-2: Forms of self-injury with help of tools, (percentages)

N=49	forms of injury, with help of tools a)	
	n	%
Cutting	17	35
Burning	3	6
Scratch with knife	4	8
Swallow/inserting	3	6
Unknown	1	2

a) Categories are not mutually exclusive.

Table 7-3: Forms of self-injury without tools, (percentage)

N=49	forms of self-injury without tools a)	
	n	%
Head rocking	10	20
Self-hitting	9	18
Scratching excessively	13	27
Biting	6	12
Hair-pulling	2	4
Making fractures	3	6
Unknown	3	6

a) Categories are not mutually exclusive.

The most reported self-injuries are self-cutting (35%) and excessive scratching (27%). More than a third of the women (35%) injured themselves in several ways.

7.4.3 Age at onset of self-injury

In table 7-4 figures about the age of onset of self-injurious behaviour are presented. Most of the women who injured themselves (53%) started this behaviour in adulthood, after the age of eighteen, but more than a third of the self-injuring women (35%) started to harm themselves before the age of thirteen. Two of the women who inflicted self-harm before the age of thirteen started this behaviour before, and 15 during the period of sexual abuse.

Table 7-4: Starting-age of self-injury, (percentage)

N=49	age of onset	
	n	%
12 years or younger	17	35
13 to 18 years	6	12
18 years or older	26	53

In general, self-injury in children between the ages of 3 and 13 is rarely observed. DeYoung (1982) suggested that self-injury in this age period may be a signal of physical or child sexual abuse. Twelve women linked their self-injurious acts as a child directly to the sexual abuse situation. Motives mentioned were 'a cry for help' and 'to prevent sexual abuse'.

Ans (B4) told she punched her fists in her face to get a bloody nose. 'But, nobody asked what was the matter with me. I could not tell. I felt powerless. I wanted attention. I already had a wrong kind of attention'.

Another woman felt that the lower part of her body was suspect. She had put a shell into her vagina, that was completely crooked in her flesh.

In general, the onset of self-injury is during adolescence (Favazza and Favazza, 1987). In our study, a minority of the self-injuring women (12%) started to harm themselves in this period. The main motive these women mentioned was to reduce tension. They all felt tense before and relieved after their self-injury, and they all felt pain during or after their self-injurious acts.

A third of the self-injuring women (33%) can be called 'habitual self-mutilators'. These women started to harm themselves before the age of 19 (9 started before the age of 12) and continued to injure themselves during adulthood. The majority of self-injuring women started or continued self-injurious behaviour in adulthood (86%). A third of the self-injuring women (33%) still harmed themselves during the time of the interview.

A minority of the self-injuring women (12%), stopped this behaviour before their 19th year. Some of these women stopped because the gain from their self-injury became less. Others told that their reason for stopping self-injury was that it became too painful.

Babs (B9) told: 'It hurt me so much, I had to stop with it'.

Some women found other ways of coping with their griefs, fears, tension or other emotions, often with the help of psychotherapy.

7.4.4 Body parts injured

Self-injury was directed against a variety of body-parts, see table 7-5.

Table 7-5: Body parts as targets for self-injurious behaviour,
(percentage)

N=49	body parts [a)	
	n	%
Whole body	14	28
Head/face	16	33
Limbs	17	35
Vagina	7	15
Unknown	6	12

[a)Categories are not mutually exclusive.

A minority of the self-injuring women (15%) injured their genitals. In our study some women reported an immediate link between genital injury and their sexual abuse experiences.

> Erna (B20) has been abused, sexually as well as physically, by almost all family-members, from being a baby to 28 years of age. Furthermore, she has been prostituted to others. During the abusive period she started to cut herself all over her body, and to scratch her vagina extremely. She reports: 'I sometimes had the feeling I raped myself again...... It's so hard to be nice to yourself, when you're used to feeling pain'.

> Koos (B42) has been sexually abused by her father from her 9th till her 13th. Years later, in adulthood, she was violently raped again. She put broken glass pieces into her vagina because 'they can not penetrate me when I have glass pieces in, because then they would cut themselves and could not do anything any more'.

Coons, Ascher-Svanum and Bellis (1980), and Favazza and Favazza (1987) found only six English written publications, all written before 1975, about women injuring their genitals. This may indicate that genital self-injury is a form of self-injury rarely reported. In the light of the virtual non-existence of literature on genital self-injury, the reportage of genital self-injury by the women in this study is relatively high.

7.4.5 Emotions, feelings of pain and self-injury

Self-injury is described by Favazza and Favazza (1987) and others as a kind of self-healing act. Persons who injure themselves feel either very tense and anxious or have intense depersonalization and derealization feelings. The act of self-injury seems to be quite efficacious in reducing tension, anxiety or depersonalization. The emotions after the act of self-harm are described as relief from the intense emotional state felt before the act of injury. After the act they calm down. Many persons describe they do not feel pain during or after their self-injury, (Muller 1989).

In our study we have asked about the emotional and mental states during the self-injurious behaviour. Not all women who injured themselves could give a reliable description of their emotional state during the self-injury. About 80% of the women who injured themselves reported emotional feelings usually accompanying the self-injury: 16 women (33%) told they felt very tense, 10 women (20%) reported intense emotions like anxiety or rage and 14 women (27%) described they felt empty, depersonalized, distressed. Twenty women (41%) felt relief after the act of self-injury. But, other emotions are also reported, like feeling ashamed for the self-injury, feeling angry with oneself that it happened again, or feeling scared by what they had done. For a few women the act of self-harming had the meaning of self-healing.

> Door (B15) said: 'I'm quickly upset and angry towards myself. Then I have to hit my head with my fists. In the beginning I felt relief, but now I feel ashamed when it happens. I wish I would be able to prevent it'.

Twenty-two women (43%) told they didn't feel pain during the acts of self-harm and three women explained they wanted to feel pain. They went on injuring themselves until they felt pain. Half of the women who did not feel pain during self-injury also did not experience pain afterwards.

> Francine (B22) told: 'I used to scratch and cut myself everywhere and washed myself so roughly, that my skin went open. It was good to feel the physical pain, because I couldn't stand the emotional pain. It also gave me the reassurance that it was my body with which I could feel, if I wanted to'.

7.4.6 State of consciousness during self-injury

Self-injury may also occur in response to auditory or visual hallucinations on self-injury or as a result of obsessive thoughts about self-harm, (Favazza and Favazza, 1987). The experience of time-gaps (amnesia) roundabout self-injury is another disturbance of consciousness associated with self-injury, (Putnam, 1989). Persons may harm themselves without being consciously aware of performing these acts. In table 7-6 figures about difficulties with reality-discrimination connected self-injury are presented. Of the women who struggled with impulses of self-injury, whether or not they actually performed them, 44% had hallucinations, vivid dreams or intensely intrusive thoughts related to self-harm. Seven women described very vivid dreams about injuring themselves. Anna (B1) told she always had dreams about self-injury before she was cutting herself. Later, she realized these dreams could be conceived as a signal for the impulse of self-harm that would come. This realization made it possible for her to control the self-cuttings.

Table 7-6: Mental states surrounding self-injury, (percentage)

N=53	mental states surrounding self-injury [a]	
	n	%
Vivid Dreams	7	14
Auditory/visual Hall.	10	20
Obsessions	13	27
Twilight consciousness	15	30
Time-gaps	7	14

[a] Categories are not mutually exclusive.

Ten women had visual hallucinations concerning self-injury or heard voices telling them to harm themselves. Four women resisted these urges successfully, the other women had to obey the hallucinations.

> Carla (B43) told that, while sitting in a chair, she regularly experienced images in which she could see herself walking to the kitchen, picking up a knife and harming herself. When she thought she could not resist these hallucinations and would actually perform what she saw herself doing all the time, she would phone her psychotherapist.

> Lieneke (B50) was hearing the voice of her father calling her. She tried to resist that voice. Sometimes however, she found out that she had been doing what her father told her to do. She had to repeat the acts of harm that her father did to her during the sexual abuse. During these self-injurious acts she had no awareness of doing this at all.

Seven women found out afterwards they had been cutting or burning themselves, but had no memories about doing so. Others told they often were in a daze state when injuring themselves. In the literature about self-injury, no attention is paid to acts of self-injury occurring in daze states or during time-gaps.

7.4.7 Child sexual abuse and self-injury

A subjectively felt relation between their injurious behaviour and the history of childhood (sexual) abuse was reported by more than one third (39%) of the self-injuring women. For most of these women (12 of these 19), the connection between self-injury and child sexual abuse was obvious, as discussed in the previous sections. The other seven women (14%) felt an irresistible urge to harm themselves as a reaction to triggers and flashbacks. Years later, a particular smell or noise appeared to function as a trigger for self-injury. Some women reported self-injury directly after reliving the trauma.

> Ans (B4) was abused by her stepfather for a long period of time. She has been hospitalized several times as a child and as an adult, because she was/is injuring herself terribly. She reports that in such situations images of the abuse invaded her. She loses consciousness and afterwards finds herself with cuts all over her body.

Another woman said the self-injury had the function of bringing her back to reality when reliving the trauma.

> Ilse (B37) was cutting herself when she saw her husband naked, because the face of her husband changed into her father's, who had abused her for many years. She said 'Then I feel like that little girl again..... Everything is happening again..... Through cutting I can come back to reality'.

However, 61% of the women who harm or have harmed themselves felt no subjective connection between the self-injury and their childhood experiences. In the next part of this chapter, we will investigate whether self-injury is correlated with particular characteristics of child (sexual) abuse and how much variance in self-injury is explained by a history of child (sexual) abuse.

7.5 Childhood trauma and self-injury, statistical results

In section 7-3 we discussed several ways in which (childhood) trauma might be related to self-injury. The formulated assumptions will be examined in this section. As a measure for self-injury we choose the frequency of self-injurious behaviour. First, the question is investigated whether severity of child sexual abuse is associated with frequency of self-injury. Then self-blame feelings are considered, and finally age is taken into account.

7.5.1 Severity of child sexual abuse and self-injury

In general, six characteristics of child sexual abuse are considered to be indicators for the severity of child sexual abuse: sexual abuse at the hands of multiple perpetrators, severity of coercion, intrusiveness of sexual acts, duration of sexual abuse, age difference between girl and perpetrator, and father (-figure) being the perpetrator, (see chapter 4-7). Table 7-7 presents findings about relations between these six characteristics and frequency of self-injury. As the data in table 7-7 show, it is found that when a girl has been sexually abused at the hands of several perpetrators she is more inclined to self-injurious behaviour than if she has been abused by one perpetrator. None of the other characteristics of child sexual abuse correlates with frequency of self-injury at a significant level, either considered individually or in combination with the six characteristics.

No association is found between respectively severity of coercion, intrusiveness of sexual acts and frequency of self-injury. This is surprising, because in literature, as described in section 7-3, violent and intrusive incest experiences are supposed to be related to self-injurious behaviour.

Table 7-7: Severity of child sexual abuse and frequency of self-injury,
(Correlations and F-values, and multiple regression ß-coefficients,
Standard coefficients and t-values)

N=90,	frequency of self-injury				
	r	F	ß-Coeff.	std.Coeff.	t-value
Multiple perpetrators [a]	.26*	6.11*	.22	.22*	2
Intrusiveness of sexual acts	.19	3.32	.22	.13	1.2
Severity of coercion	.18	2.91	.18	.12	.88
Duration	-.02	.03	-.15	-.13	1.15
Father (-figure) as perpetrator.	.02	.04	.19	.07	.59
Age difference girl-perpetrator	-.15	2.17	-.69	-.18	1.5
Multiple R	.36*	2.10		.13	

[a] More information about the way of inquiring and coding characteristics of child sexual abuse was given in chapter 4.

* $p<.05$, **$p<.01$, ***$p<.001$,****$p<.0001$

Moreover, in literature father-daughter incest is considered to be important in explaining the psycho-dynamics of incest leading to self-injurious behaviour. For this reason the studies of Shapiro and De Young included only women who experienced father-daughter incest. The lack of any association between father-daughter incest and frequency of self-injury is puzzling and surprising. Women who injured themselves, were frequently sexually abused by their fathers (46%). However, women who did not injure themselves were abused by their fathers even more frequently (54%).

7.5.2 Self-blame and self-injury

In table 7-7 we saw a small tendency that the lower the age difference between perpetrator and girl, the higher the frequency of self-injury. In this study the perpetrators are divided into perpetrators who were at least five years older than the girl but not yet 18 years of age when the abuse started and perpetrators older than 18 years of age when the abuse started. Brothers of the girl constitute the major part of non-adult perpetrators. Further analysis shows that women sexually abused by their brothers, injured themselves more frequently than women abused by other perpetrators, (χ^2 with continuity correction= 9.56, df=3, $p<.01$). Of the 26 women who have been sexually abused by their brothers, 21 have injured themselves. Moreover, women who have been sexually abused by one brother, and not by others in or outside the family, reported the highest frequency of self-injury. A two-way analysis of variance (2-way ANOVA) showed a significant interaction effect between sexual abuse by brother and number of perpetrators, (F=3.51, $p<.05$).

An inspection of the interviews shows that women who were sexually abused by a brother blame themselves strongly for the sexual abuse. They experienced extreme guilt and shame feelings.

Ali (B3): 'My brother was tyrannizing everybody in the family. He was very aggressive and had epileptic attacks. I used to obey him in everything. The sexual abuse started when I was six and he was eleven years. I did not have words for it, but I knew it was intensely bad. I can not remember whether I resisted him. I knew it was a death sin. After he went to the catholic seminary I had the feeling I was seducing a priest of God. I was scared to death. I also felt so guilty'.

Four women who had sexual contacts with a brother mention extreme guilt feelings in relation to religious aspects, like: 'When I was twelve my menses did not come. I saw this as a punishment from God for my sins', 'I was praying in my bed all the time while waiting, if he would or would not come. I did not dare to confess to a priest. I was sexually stimulated'. None of these women however, makes a direct conscious connection between these intense self-blame feelings and the self-injurious behaviour.

In section 7-2-4 we saw that authors stressed self-blame and self-punishing feelings expressed by self-injurious behaviour. Several characteristics of child sexual abuse that might evoke self-blame feelings are included in our study. In table 7-8 findings are presented about self-blame characteristics of child sexual abuse and frequency of self-injury.

Table 7-8: Self-blame and frequency of self-injury, (correlations and F-values, and multiple regression: ß-coefficients, Standard coefficients and t-values)

N=89	frequency of self-injury				
	r	F	ß-Coeff.	Std.Coef f.	t-value
Explicitness of resistance	-.29**	7.92	-.39	-.33**	3.35
Intrusiveness of sexual acts	.19	3.32	.38	.22*	2.26
Know sexual abuse sisters	-.16	2.16	-.32	-.13	1.36
Age difference girl-perpetrator	-.15	2.17	-.71	-.19	1.89
Multiple Regression	.44***	4.84		.19	

* p<.05, **p<.01, ***p<.001,****p<.0001

As is shown in table 7-8 a negative correlation exists between explicitness of resistance and frequency of self-injury, (r=-.29, P<.01). Women who did not resist in a manifest way, but used coping mechanisms like dissociation or avoidance strategies, do harm themselves more frequently than the women who have physically defended themselves against the sexual abuse. It seems that women who resisted in a manifest way have reasons why they are 'not to blame' for the abuse. Before this conclusion can be drawn, other possible interpretations have to be explored. For instance, it is possible that explicitness of resistance is associated with the age at which the sexual abuse occurred. However, findings do not show a correlation between explicitness of resistance and age at with sexual abuse started or ended.

There is a slight tendency that if a woman knows that her sisters or girl-friends have also been sexually abused, she will tend to harm herself less frequently. It might be that if others are also abused, a woman has 'less reason to blame herself' for the sexual abuse and may be able to defend herself better when others try to blame her. Intrusiveness of sexual acts is conceived as a possible self-blame characteristic. Women who experienced sexual penetration might blame themselves for not having been able to prevent these acts whereas women who were not penetrated may say 'I have never been raped'. In the multiple regression analysis intrusiveness of sexual acts is correlated with frequency of self-injury, (see Standard Coefficient column of table 7-8).

7.5.3 Interaction self-blame, severity of child sexual abuse and self-injury

In literature, self-injury is thought to occur when enormous rage evoked by severe child sexual abuse is directed against the 'self'. Self-blame feelings are considered important in directing this rage, (see 7-3-3 and 7-3-4 and 8-2-3). These notions made us wonder whether there exists an interaction between self-blame characteristics and severity of child sexual abuse in respect of frequency of self-injury. In order to explore possible interactions we first performed a stepwise regression analysis. Findings are presented in table 7-9.

Table 7-9: Stepwise regression analysis, in the first step the variance in
frequency of self-injury due to explicitness of resistance is removed.

$\underline{N}$=89	frequency of self-injury	
	$\underline{r}$	$\underline{partial\ r}$
Explicitness of resistance	-.29	
Number of perpetrators	.25	.26
Severity of coercion	.18	.29
Intrusiveness of sexual acts	.19	.23

When the variance due to the relation between explicitness of resistance and self-injury is removed, the correlation between severity of coercion and frequency of self-injury grows from r=.18 to r=.29.

The interaction between self-blame feelings and severity of coercion in respect of frequency of self-injury is further explored by a multiple regression analysis, see table 7-10.

Table 7-10: Interaction between explicitness of resistance and severity of coercion with regard to frequency of self-injury, (multiple regression)

N=89	frequency of self-injury			
	r	ß-Coeff.	Std.Coeff.	t-value
Explicitness of resistance	-.29**	-.44	-.37***	3.55
Severity of coercion	.18	.44	.29**	2.72

* p<.05, **p<.01, ***p<.001,****p<.0001

When explicitness of resistance and severity of coercion are taken together in an analysis, the correlation of both characteristics with frequency of self-injury is higher (see standard coefficient column of table 7-10) than when they are considered separately, (see r in column of table 7-10). The explicitness of resistance interferes with the relation between severity of coercion and self-injury and vice versa[58]. Exploration of the data shows that there are 12 women who experienced life-threatening actions at the hands of the perpetrator and physically resisted him. On the other hand there are 14 women who experienced life-threatening actions by the perpetrator, but these women did not explicitly resist the perpetrator, they mainly tried to avoid him. The 12 women who physically resisted the perpetrator in life-threatening situations hardly tend to injure themselves, (their average score lay between no self-injury and having injured themselves once). In contrast, the 14 women who did not explicitly resist the perpetrator almost all injured themselves, (their average score lay between occasional and frequent self-injury).

An interpretation of these findings is that violent and repeated sexual abuse may evoke a reservoir of suppressed rage. This suppressed aggression needs not be directed against oneself. Only if a woman blames herself (about the way she resisted the abuse), this (suppressed) rage is directed against herself. Women who have physically resisted the perpetrator (even in life-threatening situations) may have a reason to say to themselves or to others 'I did what I could to prevent the abuse'. Some women were clearly proud they had dared to resist the perpetrator. This pride may have prevented them from directing the rage evoked by the serious abuse situation against themselves. The women who did not explicitly resist may be vulnerable to accusations by the environment or by themselves of not having defended themselves. In this context it is good to realize we are discussing children who have been sexually abused and subjected to life-threats by perpetrators who were at least five years older.

---

[58] Severity of coercion and the explicitness of resistance are negatively correlated r=-.27. But, when a perpetrator doesn't use coercion, the woman reports no resistance (sic!).

7.5.4 Early parental neglect and self-injury

In 7-3-1 and 7-3-2 we saw that several studies report a relation between early parental neglect or early trauma and self-injury, (Carroll et al., 1980; Herman, Perry & van der Kolk, 1989; van der Kolk, 1989)[59]. In our study a cumulative trauma-score is composed in a similar way as reported by Herman, Perry and van der Kolk (1989). In section 2-5-1 we reported that this score is constructed by dividing childhood into three age periods, young child (0-6 years), child (7-12 years), and adolescent (thirteen years or older) and each woman got scored for experiences with sexual abuse, physical aggression by perpetrator, and for abuses by others in the family. This procedure resulted in one general cumulative trauma-score and 9 sub trauma-scores. We assumed that self-injurious behaviour can especially be found in women who were traumatized early in life.

When we consider the correlations between age period of traumatization and self-injurious behaviour, we find correlations between frequency of self-injury and self-injurious behaviour that are not restricted to particular age-periods, (correlations between self-injury and physical aggression of the perpetrator before the age of seven, between seven and twelve, and after the age of twelve are respectively r=.26, r=.20, r=.23 and correlations between frequency of self-injury and sexual abuse in the period seven to twelve years, and after the age of twelve are respectively r=.27, r=.21).

However, when we consider the differences in cumulation of traumatization in four different groups of self-harming women another picture emerges. As the figures presented in table 7-11 show, we find that women who regularly inflicted self-injury, experienced more physical aggression from the perpetrator before the age of seven, than the women who injured themselves less frequently, (F=3.92, p<.01). No significant differences in sub trauma-scores were found between several groups of women with or without self-injury. Especially women who frequently inflict self-injury have been subjected to physical aggression by the perpetrator before the age of seven.

---

[59] A problem is that researchers define early youth in different ways (e.g. Herman et al. describe trauma experiences before the age of 6 and Carroll et al. describe major separation before the age of 10).

Table 7-11: Sub trauma-scores and frequency of self-injury, (one-way ANOVA)

N=89		sexual child abuse (0-6 yrs)		physical aggres. perp (0-6 yrs)		other family abuse (0-6 yrs)	
	n	M.	s.d.	M.	s.d.	M.	s.d.
No self-injury	42	.57	.74	.21	.47	.41	.54
Self-injury once	5	.57	.78	.14	.38	-	-
Self-injury irregul.	21	.66	1.23	.17	.38	.5	.71
Self-injury regular	23	.39	.66	.61*	.66	.48	.51
		F=.39, p=n.s.		F=3.92, p<.01		F=1.56, p= n.s.	

N=89		sexual child abuse (7-12 yrs)		physical aggres. perp. (7-12 yrs)		other family abuse (7-12 yrs)	
	n	M.	s.d.	M.	s.d.	M.	s.d.
No self-injury	42	1.9	1.45	1	1.04	.5	.55
Self-injury once	5	2.29	.76	.57	.98	-	-
Self-injury irregul.	21	2.89	2.97	1.22	1.96	.5	.5
Self-injury regular	23	3.13	2.38	1.70	1.49	.52	.51
		F=2.37, p=n.s.		F=1.77, p=n.s.		F=1.78, p=n.s.	

N=89		sexual child abuse (≥13 yrs)		physical aggres perp. (≥13 yrs)		other family abuse (≥13 yrs)	
	n	M.	s.d.	M.	s.d.	M.	s.d.
No self-injury	42	1.57	1.25	.79	.90	.5	.51
Self-injury once	5	1.71	2.50	.74	1.25	-	-
Self-injury irregul.	21	2.17	2.99	1.22	1.93	.56	.62
Self-injury regular	23	2.70	2.87	1.57	1.73	.57	.59
		F=1.31, p=n.s.		F=1.73, p= n.s.		F=2.21, p=n.s.	

*p<.01

7.5.5 Characteristics of childhood trauma and form of self-injury

Until now we have considered the relation between characteristics of child sexual abuse and frequency of self-injury. A remark should be made with regard to the form of self-injury. The finding that self-injurious behaviour is not typically associated with early child sexual abuse might be explained by the fact that we incorporated several forms of self-injury. Is cutting or burning oneself a qualitatively different form of self-injury than scratching or head banging? Scratching and head banging is often considered as a more neurotic form of behaviour, whereas self-cutting is often considered as a sign of a borderline personality disorder. An exploration of the data shows that two characteristics of child sexual abuse discriminate between the persons who scratch and those who injure themselves by cutting.

Self-injuring women who cut themselves differ from self-injuring women who scratch or bang in respect to explicitness of resistance (Mann-Whitney test, Z corrected for ties= -2.68, p<.01) and physical aggression by the perpetrator before the age of 7 (Mann-Whitney test, Z corrected for ties = -1.77, p=.07). Women who did not explicitly resist the perpetrator are more inclined to cut themselves than to scratch themselves. The same is found for women who have been physically assaulted by the perpetrator before the age of 7 [60].

This makes it plausible that two different factors play a role in cutting/burning: early parental neglect and self-blame feelings. The cuttings of the women who blame themselves (for not explicitly having resisted the sexual abuse) may have a symbolic meaning, they express conscious or unconsciously '*I have to bleed for it*'.

7.5.6 Level of education and frequency of self-injury

A further exploration of the data showed that there is a significant negative correlation between level of education and frequency of self-injury (r=-.21, p<.05). A higher level of education seems to decrease the risk of self-injurious behaviour.

7.5.7 Multiple regression analysis characteristics of child sexual abuse and self-injury

One may wonder how much variance in frequency of self-injury is explained by characteristics of child sexual abuse presented above and which of these characteristics contribute independently to frequency of self-injury. To answer this question a multiple regression analysis was performed. The results of this multiple regression analysis is presented in appendix 7-2 [61]. The multiple regression analysis shows that physical aggression by the perpetrator before the age of 7, explicitness of resistance, age difference between girl and perpetrator, severe coercion applied by three or more perpetrators, being abused by stepfather and age of onset of sexual abuse all contribute independently at a 10% level of significance to frequency of self-injury.

The multiple correlation was found to be R=.55, p<.0001, explaining 31% of the variance in frequency of self-injury. Moreover, level of education (not incorporated in appendix 7-2, because it is not a characteristic of child sexual

---

[60] There is no correlation between explicitness of resistance and violent sexual abuse or being beaten up by the perpetrator before the age of 7.

[61] Only independent and significantly contributing characteristics were incorporated. As level of significance we chose p≤.1.

abuse) contributed independently at an 10% level of significance to frequency of self-injury.

7.6 Summary and discussion

Half of the women in this study have injured themselves during their life. Self-injury is frequently reported as one of the problems connected with child sexual abuse. The frequency of self-injurious behaviour in our study is in line with findings of other studies. One third of the women who injure themselves start this behaviour at a young age. Self-injury of children in this age group may function as a signal to the environment, indicating sexual or physical child abuse, because self-injury done by these children is otherwise rare.

The majority of the women report emotions before, during and after their self-injurious acts, as described in the literature on the 'Deliberate Self-Harm Syndrome'. Besides these feelings, we found that a considerable number of women struggling with self-harm impulses had hallucinations, vivid dreams or intensely intrusive thoughts connected with these impulses. These features are not described in the 'Deliberate Self-Harm Syndrome'.

More than a third of the women who injured themselves experienced a direct connection between child sexual abuse and self-injury. Self-injury is conceived to be: a way of preventing sexual abuse, a manner to give to others a signal for help, or part of the post-traumatic stress syndrome when reliving the trauma. However, almost two third of the women do not express a subjectively experienced connection between their child sexual abuse and self-injury.

Our findings show self-injury to be a multi-determined behaviour. The factors correlating with self-injury can be grouped around three main etiologies: (a) self-blame feelings evoked by particular characteristics of child sexual abuse, (b) rage feelings evoked by severe coercion applied by the perpetrator of sexual abuse, (c) early childhood experiences of physical aggression by the perpetrator.

Our findings support the following theoretical model about the relation between child sexual abuse and self-injurious behaviour: The more severe child sexual abuse experiences are, the more overwhelming complex and confusing emotions they may evoke. Whether a woman injures herself when re-experiencing these complex and overwhelming emotions, partly depends on her self-blame feelings.

In the literature about child sexual abuse, self-blame and guilt are described as nearly always present. However, some women find reasons why they are not to blame, like 'I have done the best I could to resist him', 'He was grown-up, so I'm not responsible for it' or 'He also abused others'. Summit (1983) explains how guilt and self-blame feelings of women who have been sexually abused are a way of getting control over a situation, in which a girl felt herself completely helpless. It is more devastating to be completely helpless against persons that should take care of you, than to blame yourself. Blaming yourself gives the illusion that you would have been able to control the situation. This interpretation suggests that intra-psychic processes produce self-blame feelings. But, we do not know whether self-blame exists only in the minds of the women, or whether it reflects the attitude towards child sexual abuse in the family or even in the general culture. Physical resistance by women has always been an important issue in rape crimes. In the criminal justice system, questions about the resistance of women dominate(d) the proceedings, (Abarbanel, 1986). The self-blame attitude seems to be in line with the general attitude towards rape. Guilt and self-blame feelings of our respondents were rather striking, for instance to even put the question how did you resist' during the interview was often very 'touchy'. The more visible forms of self-injury like cuttings and burnings are highly correlated with self-blame feelings, and may have the symbolic value, 'I have to bleed for it'.

Of course it is intolerable that young girls, mostly between seven and twelve years old, who are sexually abused and subjected to severe aggression, by persons who are at least five years older, would meet an attitude that holds them responsible for these abuses. The idea that these girls are to blame if they have not physically resisted the perpetrator is unjustified.

In this study it appears that self-injury is partly based on cognitive appraisals of the sexual abuse situation. Support for this point of view is provided by the negative correlation between level of education and frequency of self-injury. The higher the education, the more a woman is able to obtain information, the more she is confronted with the attitude that the perpetrator, and not the girl, is responsible for sexual abuse. This gives hope for therapeutic processes. To lay the responsibility for child sexual abuse where it belongs, on the shoulders of the perpetrator, may reduce self-injurious behaviour. For a group of women self-injurious behaviour may be prevented by a change in opinions in our culture about the responsibilities of girls and women with regard to rape and child sexual abuse.

Our finding that women who frequently injure themselves are predominantly subjected to early physical aggression by the father, suggests that a 'borderline character disorder' is another cause of regular self-injury. However, parental neglect at an early age was not related to self-injury. Our findings primarily indicate that women who have been physically assaulted at an early age may have learnt to punish themselves, the way they have been punished by the perpetrator.

Chapter 8

I don't care if I die

child sexual abuse and suicidality

Anja (B27) came from a family with 9 children. When she was young she had a special relation with her aunt and uncle who had no children. Aunt and uncle owned a farm with horses. She often visited them, because they gave her the attention she missed at home. She used to help her uncle in the stables with horses. She takes herself to be ten years old when her uncle started the sexual abuse. At a certain moment he placed her in a rain barrel in such a way that she couldn't escape. She can't remember exactly what happened, she has images that he went with his hand in her trousers. She remembers another moment of terrible pain. As a child she didn't understand what was going on, now she knows she was deflowered at that moment. When her uncle tried to rape her she resisted, 'I have always been fighting when he approached me, but he was much stronger than I was'. Her uncle gave her rewards and blackmailed her. She was fond of one of his horses, she was the only one who was allowed to ride that horse. If she resisted sexual contact by fighting, he threatened to sell that horse. She completely avoided the farm of her aunt and uncle at age 16/17, after he sold that horse. She left her family and went to live with the parents of her girlfriend. She had a sexual relationship with the father of this girlfriend. This relationship was kept secret from her friend and the mother. When she was 20 years, she wanted to stop the relation with the father of the girlfriend. The father didn't want this to happen. He threatened with suicide, if she would leave. At a certain moment, she actually left this family and he committed suicide. He left a letter in which he explained that he committed suicide, because she stopped the relation. After his death she had a few meetings with her girlfriend and the mother and then the contact was broken. Persons to whom she once told this history with the father of the girlfriend, held her responsible. She was supposed to be responsible for her own acts at that age. She said: 'I feel responsible for it, but it never would have taken place, if I hadn't had this previous history with my uncle'. Now she has problems in sustaining relations with men. She made a serious suicide attempt after one boyfriend finished a relation with her.

8.1 Introduction

Several studies indicate a connection between childhood trauma and suicidality (8-2-1). The question why this connection exists has been answered in several ways. Early parental neglect is thought to be important in the etiology of depression and suicidality (8-2-2). Child sexual abuse is thought to evoke rage and shame and these feelings are directed towards the self (8-2-3). Repeated experience of trauma causes a learned helplessness and this learned helplessness increases the risk of suicidal behaviour (8-2-4). Traumata evoke hardly controllable chronic arousal, and a high level of chronic arousal may increase the risk of suicidality (8-2-5). The different assumptions deduced from these theories are summarised (8-2-6). Before the results of the study are discussed certain aspects of suicidality are described, such as prevalence of suicidal ideation and suicidal behaviour (8-3-1), the age at onset of suicidality, (8-3-2) the emotional state surrounding suicidal behaviour (8-3-3), state of consciousness surrounding suicidal behaviour (8-3-4) and the subjectively experienced connection between child sexual abuse and suicidality (8-3-5). Several assumptions are investigated concerning the relation between child sexual abuse and suicidality. The following assumptions about the etiology of suicidality are considered: the severity/rage assumption (8-4-1), the learned helplessness theory (8-4-2), the chronic arousal assumption (8-4-3), the self-blame assumption (8-4-4) and the early parental neglect assumption (8-4-5). The chapter ends with a summary and conclusion.

8.2 Traumata and suicidality

8.2.1 Studies on childhood trauma and suicidality

Suicidality includes suicidal ideation as well as suicide attempts. The rate of suicide attempts in the Dutch population is 5% (Kerkhof and Diekstra, 1982). Women more often than men attempt suicide, this means that more than 5% of women performs such an attempt at least once in their life (van Egmond, 1988). Suicidal ideation is much more common than suicidal behaviour, Draijer (1990) reports that 46% of women in a study on a representative sample of women experienced suicidal ideation.

Several studies show that in women with a history of child sexual abuse the rate of suicidality is higher than in comparable control-groups. These studies have been performed in samples of the general population, in samples of women asking psychotherapy, and in samples of the psychiatric patient population.

In 1986 two reviews on studies about child sexual abuse and suicidality were published, (Browne and Finkelhor, 1986; Coons, 1986). After 1986, several other studies on child sexual abuse and suicidality have been reported, (Brière and

Runtz, 1987; Goodwin, Cheeves & Connell, 1987; Conte and Schuerman, 1987; Bryer, Nelson, Miller & Krol, 1987; Cavaiola and Schiff, 1988; Egmond and Jonker, 1988; Draijer; 1988, 1990; Egmond, Garnefski & Jonker, 1990).

We refer to appendix 8-1 for a systematic review of the main studies about child sexual abuse and suicidality published after 1986. Although the connection between child sexual abuse and suicidality is well established, such findings do not immediately provide an explanation for this connection. Different theories are proposed. In the next section these theories are presented.

8.2.2 Early parental neglect and suicidality

Child sexual abuse is often associated with a general climate of emotional neglect and parental dysfunctioning (Finkelhor, 1986; Draijer, 1990). A child experiencing parental neglect at an early age may be inclined to pathologically disturbed behaviour during adolescence and adulthood. This disturbed behaviour is ascribed to a borderline character disorder. Suicidality may be conceived as a behavioural symptom of a borderline character disorder. Herman, Perry and van der Kolk (1989) recently found relations between early childhood trauma and the diagnosis borderline personality disorder. Suicidality was one of the symptoms of the borderline pathology.

8.2.3 Rage and shame evoked by trauma, and suicidality

In the literature about the psycho-dynamic notion it is frequently stated that child sexual abuse evokes rage that is directed against the 'self', resulting in suicidal behaviour. For instance, Carmen, Rieker and Mills (1984) state that child sexual abuse elicits a chronic experience of rage, that is directed towards the 'self'. Persons with a history of child (sexual) abuse have:

> Extreme difficulties with anger and aggression, self-image and trust. In contrast
> to the outrage and disgust experienced by others hearing of the abuse, victims do
> not usually acknowledge their anger towards their perpetrator, in part because of
> the complex relationship between victim and abuser. After years of abuse, victims
> blame themselves as they come to believe that the abuse can be explained only by
> their essential 'badness', (Carmen, Rieker, and Mills, 1984, p.382).

8.2.4 Trauma, learned helplessness and suicidality

The most elaborated theory about trauma and suicidality is the learned helplessness theory. The theory of learned helplessness was developed by Seligman in the period 1965-1969, (Seligman, 1975). He reported that dogs, cats and other animals who received repeated inescapable shocks learn that shocks are unavoidable. These animals do not try to escape new shocks, even if these could be prevented. In new aversive, but controllable, situations the dogs remain passive. Seligman ascribes three effects of repeated exposure to uncontrollable aversive situations: (a) a decreased motivation to take initiatives, (b) a general expectation that one can not avoid or stop aversive situations, (c) feelings of depression; aversive situations initially produce anxiety, but depression will result if aversive situations are repeated and uncontrollable. Seligman stressed that after repeated unescapable trauma a general expectation will develop, that the environment is uncontrollable. In contrast, shocks that can be avoided by subjects produce neither cognitions about uncontrollability of the environment nor depressed and passive behaviours.

In 1978 Abrahamson, Seligman and Teasdale introduced a 'revised learned helplessness theory'. In this revision, the accent changed from inescapable shocks to cognitive attitudes: not the inescapable shocks but cognitive dysfunctional attributions play an important role in humans. Events are not uncontrollable 'per se', but it is the person who perceives these events as uncontrollable. The accent changed from 'stimulus based' feelings of helplessness to 'response-based' feelings of helplessness. In the revised learned helplessness theory a person feels depressed because the person, (a) blames her/him self for the cause of negative events (internality), (b) thinks that these events will manifest themselves in the future (stability) and (c) has similar self-blame feelings in other situations (globality). These cognitions are denoted with the term 'dysfunctional attribution style'. The revised learned helplessness theory predicts that persons with a general stable, global, internal dysfunctional attribution style will be more vulnerable to react with depression in 'aversive' situations than persons without such a dysfunctional attribution style[62]. These attributions make persons more vulnerable to react with depression in stressful life-events.

Studies on child abuse and suicidality systematically report that child (sexual) abuse is related to suicidal behaviour. These findings have caused a renewed interest in the original 'learned helplessness' theory. For instance, van der Kolk (1987) writes:

> The animal model of inescapable shock is especially helpful for studying the behavioural and physiological effects of traumatization. This is the only biological model for a major psychiatric disorder: surprisingly, it has been applied principally to depression rather than traumatization, (van der Kolk, 1987, p.67).

In chapter 4 we reported that many women in our study as a child lived in a situation from which they couldn't escape and in which they were repeatedly

---

[62]   Many studies have been performed to test the role of these dysfunctional attitudes in relation to depression. De Heus (1989) gives a detailed review of these studies. The main conclusions of De Heus are: The results of several studies show that 'dysfunctional attitudes', as described in the revised learned helplessness theory are present during depressive periods, but they are not necessarily present when depression is over. De Heus concludes that no sufficient empirical evidence exists to support the assumption that the cognitive dysfunctional attitudes cause a depression, when a person is confronted with stressful life events. The dysfunctional attitudes should be conceived as one of the characteristics of depression.

traumatized. Especially in case of long-lasting sexual abuse, girls tried to stop this abuse, but were confronted with massive oppression.

The 'learned helplessness' theory predicts that women who experienced inescapable 'aversive' situations will, when compared with women who experienced controllable 'aversive' situations, have a reduced ability to recognise signals of new 'aversive' situations and moreover, have difficulties in taking the right actions to prevent those situations. When confronted with new aversive situations these women will feel depressed. Suicidality is the manifestation of dominant depressive feelings.

8.2.5 Trauma, hyperarousal and suicidality

A different aspect of 'learned helplessness' concerns the inability to modulate arousal. Especially van der Kolk (1987) states that the most important post-traumatic stress symptom is the loss of ability to modulate arousal.

In many traumatized people this adaptive mechanism has been disturbed by the trauma: they continue to respond even to minor stimuli with an intensity appropriate only to emergency situations. This interferes with their ability to assess situations calmly and appropriately and to achieve the psychological distance necessary for a measured response. Autonomic arousal, no longer a preparation to meet external threat, becomes itself a precipitance of fear and emergency responses, (van der Kolk, 1988, p.66).

The relation between traumatization, hyperarousal and suicidality has not yet been elaborated. However, van Egmond, Garnefski and Jonker (1990) report that 45% of the women in their study, gave as a main motive for their suicide attempt 'to get rest for a while, to stop thinking, to be able to sleep again'. The suicide attempt did not have the purpose to stop living, but to get rest. These women took an overdose of pills in order to stop an otherwise uncontrollable hyperarousal.

8.2.6 Suicidality as a cry for help

A suicide attempt may have the meaning of a 'cry for help'. It is a way of getting attention of important others. Women with a child sexual abuse history often have a 'disguised presentation' of their problems, (Gelinas, 1983). For a long time they have kept the sexual abuse secret. They need attention for their problems, but know no way of asking it. Brière and Runtz (1987) state that a suicide attempt of a woman with a history of child sexual abuse history may be a 'relative dramatic call for help, based on the belief that extraordinary measures are required to gain the caring attention of others'.

Egmond et al. (1990) asked for the main motive after suicide attempts. They found only a small fraction (13%) of adult women indicating that gain of caring attention[63] was a main motive. After a suicide attempt women almost never spontaneously disclosed child sexual abuse or related problems. Only when the researchers asked explicitly about physical or sexual abuse, these 'stressful life-events' were mentioned.

8.2.7 Assumptions on relations between trauma and suicidality

From the literature and research reviewed above, several assumptions emerged about how trauma may increase the risk of suicidal behaviour. These assumptions will be summarised:

- When a woman is abused or neglected at an early age the risk of severe suicidality is increased.
- When a woman has been repetitively and severely abused as a child she will experience a tremendous rage. This rage increases the risk of severe suicidality.
- When a woman feels guilty or ashamed about her history of child sexual abuse this increases the risk of severe suicidality.
- When a woman has repeatedly been sexually abused in such a way that she had no possibilities to escape from that situation, she develops a learned helplessness, she will be less able to avoid new traumatizations. The feelings of helplessness experienced during new traumatizations increase the risk of severe suicidality.
- When a woman is severely traumatized she may develop an inability to modulate arousal. Continuing feelings of hyperarousal may increase the risk of severe suicidality.
- Some women with a history of child sexual abuse have a 'disguised presentation' of this history. A suicide attempt may signal a dramatic 'cry for help'.

8.3 Characteristics of suicidality, descriptive results

Detailed information about the research strategy is given in chapter 2. In section 2-3-2 the way of inquiring about suicidality is presented. The main questions about suicidality are similar to the questions used by Egmond (1988).

A suicide attempt was made by 41 women (45%). Of 6 women we did not obtain information about suicidality. Suicidality includes suicidal ideation and suicidal behaviour. Suicidality was scored as suicidal ideation, one suicide attempt and several suicide attempts.

---

[63]   The data of van Egmond's et al. about main motives for suicide attempts do not refer exclusively to women with a child abuse history, but 53% of the women who did a suicide attempt had such a history. This means that a 'cry for help' can impossibly be the main motive for a most women who have been sexually abused as a child.

8.3.1 Frequency of suicidal ideation and behaviour

The frequency of suicidal ideation and behaviour is presented in table 8-1.

Table 8-1: Prevalence of suicidality, (percentages)

N=91	prevalence of suicidality	
	n	%
no suicidal ideation	14	15
suicidal ideation a)	36	40
one suicide attempt	23	25
more suicide attempts	18	20

a) The categories have been made mutually exclusive, all women who made a suicide attempt had suicidal ideation.

Only a small fraction of the women (15%) who participated in our study have never in their lives given a thought to the possibility of suicide. A quarter of the women (25%) made once in their lives a suicide attempt, and one fifth of the women made several attempts.

In appendix 8-1 and in section 8-2-1 we have reported the prevalence of suicidality found in other studies. When we compare our findings with those reported in studies using a sample of the general population, we find that the prevalence of suicidality in our group is considerably higher. When we match our findings with studies using comparable samples, we notice similar or somewhat lower percentages of suicidal behaviour. For instance, Brière and Runtz (1987) report that 51% of the women with a history of child sexual abuse, soliciting for therapeutic help, made at least one suicide attempt and in a sample of drug-addicted adolescents it is found that 46% of the adolescents with such a history attempted suicide, (Cavaiola and Schiff, 1988).

Twenty-four women (59% of all the attempts) made a suicidal attempt by pill ingestion and 5 women (12% of all the suicide attempts) used other means. Of 12 women no valid data were obtained about the means used at the attempt. Other studies about suicidal behaviour also report that the majority of attempts were by the ingestion of a drug overdose (Paykel et. al., 1975; Egmond, 1988).

8.3.2 Age at onset of suicidality

In table 8-2 the figures about the age at onset of suicidality are presented. We did not explicitly ask when suicidal ideation started. But, when asking about suicide attempts, most women spontaneously reported suicidal ideation and the age it began, (only positive reports are counted).

Table 8-2: Age at onset suicidality, (percentages)

N=91	age at onset suicidality	
	n	%
Suicidal ideation <19 years	34	37
Suicide attempt 8-12 years	5	13
Suicide attempt 12-18 years	5	13
Suicidal ideation ≥19 years	2	2
Suicide attempts ≥19 years [a]	31	34

[a] Women who made a suicide attempt as an adult might have had suicidal ideation before the age of 19 years.

Ten women (24% of all attempters) made a suicide attempt before the age of nineteen. Three of these women did not repeat a suicide attempt when they were grown-up. Five women were girls between eight and twelve years old, when they made their first attempt.

> Mirthe (F44) lived in a children's home until she was eight. Then she went to live with her parents. Her father had no job and was in prison several times, her mother was 'apathetic' and used sedatives. The sexual abuse started as soon as she went to live with her parents, her mother knew about it, but didn't intervene. Her father was a tyrant, she had to obey him in everything. She didn't want to obey him, she describes herself as being obstinate. She tells: "I used to scream to my father, you can beat me until I die, I don't care. He always threatened me; I will kill you if you tell it to anybody, I'll kill your mother too. At a certain moment my father thought 'this is going wrong'. When I was ten years old I stole sedatives from my mother and ate them all. When I awoke in the hospital the first thing my mother said was 'you wretch'. I also jumped from a bridge and so on". At the age of eighteen she was living on her own, following an education and was working at night in a disco to earn money. She attempted suicide, because she couldn't stand 'the milieu' in the disco. It was an impulsive act, she had many discussions with her self, but she couldn't 'keep her wits together'.

Almost all women with suicidal ideation but without suicidal behaviour told that this ideation started before the age of nineteen. For instance Door (B15) said: 'From the age of fifteen every day it is in my mind that I want to die'. Five women mentioned that they had only suicidal ideation during childhood.

8.3.3 Emotional states during suicidal behaviour

Suicidality is an expression of severe depressive feelings. Feelings of depression and emptiness are also the most dominant feelings described by the women in this study.

In a previous section we saw that taking an overdose of pills may be a means to control states of hyperarousal. For 10 women in our study a main motive for suicidality is to get rest[64], they told that their thoughts went like mad and they couldn't sleep any more.

Marieke (F16) gave herself injections with insulin. Her mother was a diabetic, so she could easily get this medicine. She administered insulin because she could not sleep any more, she felt very tense. 'After the administration of insulin I felt rather musty and uninterested. I wanted to tune out'. In hospital they considered it a suicide attempt. 'I hardly realized that an overdose of insulin could be fatal'.

Feelings of numbness, chilliness or indifference were mentioned by five women as main reason for suicidality.

For instance Rie (F23) said: 'I had plenty of friends and in my job everything was all right, but at night I took pills. I felt desperately lonely. In the months preceding my suicide attempt I have been writing in my diary that I felt so numb and alone'.

8.3.4 State of consciousness during suicidal behaviour

Some women described hallucinations, twilight states of consciousness or time-gaps connected with suicidality. Table 8-3 gives the number of women who had difficulties with reality-discrimination during suicidality. Twenty women (26% of the women who reported suicidal ideation or behaviour) experienced difficulties with reality-discrimination connected with suicidality.

Table 8-3: States of consciousness surrounding suicidality, (percentages)
a)

N=91	state of consciousness	
Mental State	n	%
Vivid dreams	3	4
Auditory/visual hall.	9	12
Twilight consciousness	9	12
Time-gaps	5	6

a) Suicidal ideation as well as suicide attempts. The mental states are not mutually exclusive.

---

[64] It is a question of debate whether a woman who takes an overdoses of pills with as main motive to get rest is a 'suicide attempter'. However, suicidal intention is considered to be a difficult topic in literature about suicide. Diekstra (1981) suggests that not 'the intention' but 'the changes in environment that a person wants to get' are important in defining a suicide attempt, (Diekstra 1981).

Nine women told that 'suicidal ideation' was expressed as a visual or auditory hallucination. Some heard voices commanding them to commit suicide. Others told about visual hallucinations in which they were put up to commit suicide.

Sandra (F36) frequently dreamt that 'they are coming to take me away and then my father orders me to commit suicide'. In certain periods these dreams took the form of hallucinations in which her father was commanding her to die.

Elsbeth (B21) reports: 'I frequently saw that I was crossing the railroad while a train was coming and I felt calm, the train will come and then ....smash! At the same time I realized I do not want this to happen. I got afraid and I have avoided railroads for a long time. I have the feeling I can not trust myself'.

The experience of time-gaps is another disturbance of consciousness connected with suicidality, (Putnam, 1989). Persons may prepare or made a suicide attempt without being consciously aware of these acts. Five women reported that they made at least one suicide attempt without having memories of planning or performing this attempt.

Jans (B41) describes that she did not want to die, but in the period preceding her suicide attempt she found letters with elaborated plans for her funeral. She knew she herself had written these letters, but she could not remember doing it.

8.3.5 Child (sexual) abuse and suicidality

In table 8-4 one finds for different age periods the percentage of women mentioning a connection between child abuse and suicidality. The suicide attempts were related to child abuse by all women who did an attempt before the age of twelve years and by three of the women who did so between twelve and eighteen years of age.

Table 8-4: Experienced connection between child abuse and suicidality in different age periods, (percentages)

N=77	connection child abuse and suicidality		
	N with suicidality	N connecting suicidality to C.S.A.[a]	% connecting suicidality to C.S.A.
Suicidal attempts <19 yrs	10	8	80
Suicidal ideation <19 yrs	34	20	60
Suicidal attempts ≥19 yrs	31	6	19

[a] C.S.A. means child sexual abuse

Their suicide attempt was a cry for help, a protest against a situation of no affection, life threat and gross sexual exploitation. It was an effort to get out of the actual situation. Only a small fraction of the suicidal women older than eighteen (19%) reported a subjectively experienced connection between suicidal behaviour and child (sexual) abuse. Two women older than eighteen mention the suicide attempt to have as its main purpose the escape from actual sexual and physical abuse by their fathers. After the suicide attempt these women were admitted to a psychiatric institution. One woman made a suicide attempt when intense flashbacks concerning child sexual abuse intruded upon her. One woman made an attempt when confronted with emotional indifference of her family after the disclosure of child sexual abuse. Two women told that their suicide attempts were triggered by the sexual abuse they experienced as a child.

> Ali (B3) who was sexually abused by her brother and as a child felt guilty about it, said: 'Two times I made a suicide attempt. Exactly one and two years after the death of my brother, on the day of his funeral'.

Sometimes the suicidal ideation was explicitly present during sexual abuse.

> Ina (B35): My grandfather used to bring me to the rabbits, I was fond of rabbits. He kept rabbits on his balcony. He used to rape me on this balcony, which was very rickety, and I was afraid it would break and we would tumble down. At the same time I thought: 'I don't care if I die. It is alright if I die now'.

Suicidal ideation was sometimes evoked in adulthood by flashbacks.

> Gea (B26): 'I had completely forgotten the incest (with her brother and his friends). However, I had sexual problems and my therapist was wondering why. I got some exercises to do and then suddenly I got flashbacks, suddenly I exactly knew what happened. When these memories intruded I couldn't stand it any more. I wanted to commit suicide. I wanted to crash my car into a tree. I wanted to walk into the water, but my husband prevented it. He locked me inside the room and he did not allow me to go out alone. He tried to force me to disclose what was on my mind, but I could not. I thought it better to die then to tell what was on my mind'.

8.3.6 Suicidality and renewed traumatization

Three women mention suicide attempts in relation to spouse assaults and four women describe how unwanted sexual contacts with men triggered feelings of helplessness and suicidality.

> Door (B15) has been sexually abused by her father from the age of eight to fifteen. Her father gave her a lot of attention. He treated her as if they were married. The sexual abuse stopped because she felt ill and tired all the time. She thought she was ill 'as a punishment for the relation with my father'. When her father died, all the memories about the abuse returned. When 30 years old she went to visit a former ballet teacher. That man had been really important to her. He approached her sexually and she had no defense against him. 'I really can defend myself against men who are unknown to me, but not against somebody

who is an authority for me. He didn't actually rape me, but I was completely in
panic. I got depressed'. This experience evoked the same feelings as she had as
an adolescent and in the period after the death of her father. 'I could not have
sexual contact with my friend for a year. Later the director of the psychiatric
institution, where I received psychotherapy, seduced me into a situation I really
found disgusting. Then I started planning a suicide'.

8.4 Child sexual abuse and suicidality, statistical analyses

We choose to construct a single measure 'severity of suicidality' consisting of
four categories; 'no suicidal ideation', 'suicidal ideation', 'one suicide attempt'
and 'more than one suicide attempt'[65].

8.4.1 Severity of child sexual abuse and suicidality

In general, six characteristics of child sexual abuse are considered to be
indicators for the severity of child sexual abuse: sexual abuse at the hands of
multiple perpetrators, severity of coercion, severity of sexual acts, duration of
sexual abuse, age difference between girl and perpetrator, and father (-figure)
being the perpetrator, (see chapter 4-7). In table 8-5 findings are presented about
the relations between these six characteristics of child sexual abuse and severity
of suicidality.

For special reasons, to be discussed in next section, we give only
characteristics of sexual abuse experienced at the hands of the first perpetrator.
As table 8-5 demonstrates correlations exist between respectively intrusiveness
of sexual acts, severity of coercion applied by the first perpetrator, and severity
of suicidality. The correlations between severity of coercion, duration and
severity of suicidality, although roundabout level of significance, are rather low.
Women who, as a child, experienced more intrusive forms of sexuality are more
inclined to perform a suicide attempt than women who experienced less intrusive
forms of sexuality.

---

[65] It may be a question whether one should construct two measures of suicidality, namely suicidal
ideation and suicidal behaviour or construct one measure 'severity of suicidality'. Our decision
to construct one measure is based on several considerations. The study of van Egmond et al.
(1988) shows that the more suicide attempts women have made, the more frequently they
struggle with suicidal ideation. Moreover the study of Draijer (1990) shows the severity of
suicidal ideation and frequency of suicidal attempts to be correlated in a similar way to
characteristics of child abuse. These results suggest that it is possible to construct one measure
of suicidality.

Table 8-5: Severity of child sexual abuse by the first perpetrator and severity of suicidality, (correlations and F-values)

N=91	severity of suicidality	
	r	F
Intrusiveness of sexual acts [a]	.30**	8.57
Severity of coercion	.21*	4.12
Duration	.20	3.51
Father(-fig) as perpetrator.	.05	.18
Multiple perpetrators	.09	.65
Age difference girl-perpetrator	-.06	.03

* p<.05, **p<.01

[a] More information about the way of inquiring and coding characteristics of child sexual abuse was given in chapter 4.

In 8-3-1 we saw that only a minority of the women (15%) participating in our study have never given a thought to the possibility of suicide. Close examination of the data shows that this fraction even decreases when the severity of child sexual abuse is taken into account. When women are selected who as a girl were subjected to sexual penetration for one year or more with any form of coercion[66], only five of these women (7%) never experienced suicidal ideation. A history of severe childhood trauma seems to be almost universally associated with experiencing suicidal ideation.

8.4.2 Learned helplessness and suicidality

We assumed that when a woman has repeatedly been sexually abused in such a way that she had no possibilities to escape from that situation, she develops a 'learned helplessness' and she will be less able to avoid new traumatizations. These new traumatizations will evoke suicidality.

As we described in the previous section, almost all women who were sexually abused as a child for one year or more experienced suicidal ideation. The awareness that sexual abuse is inescapable mostly develops after the age of twelve, when girls become aware of the meaning of sexuality, and actively try to resist or avoid the abuse. We find a correlation between age at which child sexual abuse stopped and severity of suicidality, (r=.26, p<.01). This correlation seems to increase when we select women who experienced sexual intercourse as a child, (r=.38, p<.01).

The learned helplessness theory states that new traumatizations evoke suicidality, (see section 8-2-4 and 8-2-6). One form of new traumatization

---

[66] N=72 minus 3 missing, N=69.

concerns physical assaults by spouses. In this study, 19% of the women were married to a spouse who regularly beat them, and another 8% are irregularly beaten by their spouse[67]. When women who are married or living alone (mostly divorced) are selected, a quarter (25%) of these women have been regularly beaten by their spouses. One may wonder whether those renewed traumatizations increase the risk of severe suicidality. In table 8-6 findings about spouse-beatings and severity of suicidality are presented.

Table 8-6: Spouse-beatings and severity of suicidality, (one-way ANOVA)

N=87		severity of suicidality	
	n	M	s.d.
No spouse-beatings	63	2.38	.99
Irregular spouse-beatings	7	2.14	.69
Regular spouse-beatings	17	3	.94
		F=3.24, p<.05	

As is shown in table 8-6 women who are regularly beaten by their spouse differ from the others in severity of suicidality. Of the 17 women who were regularly beaten by their spouses, twelve women made one or more suicide attempts. The finding presented indicates that this kind of renewed traumatization increases the risk of severe suicidality.

However, certain other findings seem to indicate that renewed traumatization does not increase the risk of severe suicidality. For instance, table 8-5 shows no correlation between number of perpetrators having sexually abused the girl and severity of suicidality. Neither did we find a correlation between cumulation of childhood trauma and severity of suicidality, (see table 5-8). On the contrary, a closer look at the data shows an opposite tendency. Most characteristics of child sexual abuse experienced at the hands of a first perpetrator correlate somewhat higher with severity of suicidality than similar characteristics of child sexual abuse by a second or third perpetrator.

When the correlation between severity of suicidality and characteristics of child sexual abuse of a second perpetrator and a third perpetrator are considered, we find that severity of coercion applied by a second or a third perpetrator is negatively correlated with severity of suicidality, (respectively r= -.39 and r= -.25). These correlations do not reach a 5% level of significance, because the number of women having experienced sexual abuses by a second or a third perpetrator are rather small, (respectively N= 21 and N=16). These findings should therefore be considered with caution, they may however have a heuristic

---

[67] In a sample of a normal population it was found that resp. 11% and 9% of the women are regularly or incidentally physically assaulted by their spouses, Romkes (1989).

value. Further exploration shows a significant interaction between intrusiveness of sexual acts, severity of coercion and severity of suicidality. Findings are presented in table 8-7.

Table 8-7: Interaction between intrusiveness of sexual acts and severity of coercion by a second perpetrator and severity of suicidality, (Multiple regression analysis)

n=21	severity of suicidality			
	r	p	partial r	p
Intrusiveness of sexual acts second perpetrator	.21	n.s.	.42	.06
Severity of coercion second perpetrator	-.39	.08	-.55	.02
Multiple correlation	.55		.31	.04

Data in table 8-7 show an increased risk of severe suicidality for a girl sexually abused by a second perpetrator who hardly used any coercion, while nevertheless intercourse has taken place, (R=.55, p<.05). A closer look at the verbal statements of women about revictimization shows that some women experiencing non-coercive, but intrusive sexual abuse by a second or third perpetrator become keenly aware of their inability to prevent these sexual contacts, [see the case history of Anja (B27) in the introduction of this chapter and the case history of Door (B15) in section 8-4-6]. These findings indicate that after the severe traumatization of a first perpetrator, non-coercive but unwanted intercourse by a second perpetrator may result in the development of cognitions that 'one is unable to cope with situations, that one should be able to prevent'. Such situations become especially 'aversive' and elicit suicidality.

In heterosexual relationships, many women sometimes have intercourse while they do not want to have it, (Vennix, 1989 [68]; Beelen, 1989). It may be that unwanted, but non-coercive intercourse in partner-relationships evokes suicidality in women who as a child were subjected to sexual intercourse from which they could not escape. When we select the group of women who have never been living as an adult in a heterosexual partner-relationship (N=21), no correlation exists between intrusiveness of sexual acts experienced as a child at the hands of a perpetrator and severity of suicidality, (r=.11, p=n.s). For all women participating in our study, intrusiveness of sexual acts experienced as a child is correlated with severity of suicidality, (r=.30, p<.01, see table 8-5). When we select the group of married women (N=39), the correlation between

---

[68] Vennix (1989) reports that in heterosexual partner-relationships 5% of the women frequently have intercourse while they do not want to have it and 39% sometimes have intercourse while they do not want.

intrusiveness of sexual acts and severity of suicidality becomes rather strong, (r=.40, p<.01).

8.4.3 Hyper-arousal and severity of suicidality

In general, trauma may result in an increased arousal of the autonomic nervous system, (van der Kolk, 1987). This increased arousal itself may become something to be feared. We did not measure level of autonomic arousal, but we incorporated several measures that indirectly may indicate a high level of arousal, such as post-traumatic stress symptoms, level of dissociation and hallucinations. We have investigated the question whether respectively severity of post-traumatic stress symptoms, level of dissociation and hallucinations are correlated to severity of suicidality[69]. Findings are presented in table 8-8.

Table 8-8: Post traumatic stress, level of dissociation, and hallucinations and severity of suicidality, (correlations and F-values)

N=91	severity of suicidality	
	r	F
Post Traumatic Stress	.30**	8.52**
Dissociative Experience Scale	.25*	5.27*
Auditory hallucinations	.24*	4.58*
Visual hallucinations	.31***	9.81***

* p<.05, **p<.01, ***p<.001

As is demonstrated in table 8-8, severity of post-traumatic stress symptoms, level of dissociation, visual and auditory hallucinations are indeed related to severity of suicidality. The highest correlations are found between respectively: severity of post-traumatic stress symptoms, visual hallucinations, and severity of suicidality.

A stepwise regression analysis shows that level of post-traumatic stress and visual hallucinations both contribute in an independent way to severity of suicidality.

8.4.4 Self-blame and suicidality

We assumed that self-blame directs rage provoked by traumatization against the 'self' and that this may increase the risk of severe suicidality. In section 7-2-4 we saw that authors describe several characteristics of child sexual abuse that might evoke self-blame feelings. Other characteristics are found to counteract self-blame, such as explicitness of resistance, being abused by an adult

---

[69] I refer to appendix 2-2 for information about the post-traumatic stress list, to chapter 5 and appendix 5-2 for information about level of dissociation and to chapter 6 for information about hallucinations.

perpetrator, and knowledge about sexual abuse of others. In table 8-9 the data are presented about 'self-blame' characteristics and severity of suicidality,

Table 8-9: Self-blame characteristics and severity of suicidality, (correlations and F-values)

N=91	severity of suicidality	
	r	F
Explicitness of resistance	-.05	.19
Age difference girl-perpetrator	.04	.15
Knowing sexual abuse sisters	.02	.04

* p<.05, **p<.01, ***p<.001,****p<.0001

As table 8-9 shows no correlation exists between self-blame characteristics and severity of suicidality. No indication exists that self-blame feelings are associated with severity of suicidal behaviour.

8.4.5 Early parental neglect and suicidality

Persons who were neglected at an early age are frequently diagnosed as having a 'borderline character disorder'. One symptom of borderline character disorder is suicidality. We assumed that persons who were neglected or abused at an early age will exhibit an increased risk of suicidal behaviour. In our study a cumulative trauma-score is constructed. As reported in section 2-5-1 this score is constructed by dividing childhood into three age periods, young child (0-6 years), child (7-12 years), and adolescent (13 years or older) and each woman got scored for experiences with sexual abuse, physical aggression by perpetrator, and for abuses by others in the family. This procedure resulted in a cumulative trauma-score and 9 sub trauma-scores. To investigate the relation between early parental neglect and suicidality the cumulative trauma-score was subdivided into three age-periods and different traumata experienced in early childhood.

Table 8-10: Sub trauma-scores and severity of suicidality, (correlations and F-values)

N=90	severity of suicidality	
	r	F
Sexual Child Abuse (0-6yrs)	.08	.55
Physical Aggression Perpetrator (0-6y)	.08	.55
Other family Abuse (0-6yrs)	.13	1.44
Cumulation trauma (0-6 yrs)	.14	1.5
Cumulation trauma (7-12 yrs)	.07	.37
Cumulation trauma (≥13 yrs)	.16	2.2
Cumulative trauma-score	.13	1.97

* p<.05, **p<.01

As data presented in table 8-10 show women who were neglected, physically or sexually abused at an early age do not experience more severe suicidality than women not abused at such an early age.

8.4.6 Multiple regression analysis characteristics of child sexual abuse and severity of suicidality

One may wonder which of the characteristics presented above contributes to severity of suicidality and how much variance in severity of suicidality is explained by characteristics of child sexual abuse. To answer this question a multiple regression analysis is presented in appendix 8-2. As shown in this appendix physical assaults by spouses, age at with sexual abuse stopped, experiencing visual hallucinations and intrusiveness of sexual acts by the first perpetrator contribute independently at a 5% level of significance to severity of suicidality. The multiple correlation was found to be R=.45, p<.001, explaining 21% of the variance of severity of suicidality.

8.5 Summary and discussion

A history of severe childhood trauma seems to be almost universally associated with experiencing suicidal ideation. Only a small fraction of the women (7%) who were subjected to sexual intercourse as a child for more than a year never experienced suicidal ideation. Almost half of the women participating in our study (45%) attempted suicide one or several times. This prevalence of suicidality is in line with suicidality reported in comparable groups of women with a history of child sexual abuse who solicit for therapeutic help and much higher than the prevalence of suicidality found in samples of general populations.

Different explanations are offered for consistent research findings that women who have been sexually abused as a child are inclined to make a suicide attempt. One of these explanations concerns the idea that a suicide attempt is 'a cry for help'. Children are found to differ in this respect from adult women. Eight out of ten women who attempted suicide below the age of 18 said that this attempt was meant as 'a cry for help', a protest against a situation of no affection, life threats and gross sexual exploitation. A similar motive is mentioned by a small fraction of suicide attempters who were older than eighteen years (15%) when they made an attempt. Almost a fifth of the women who participated in this study was trapped in an incest-situation after the age of eighteen and for some of these women the suicide attempt was the only means of escaping from this situation. For some other women, who were locked in a relation with a spouse who regularly beat them, the suicide attempt also had the meaning of 'a cry for help'. After the suicide attempt most women were admitted to a hospital or psychiatric institution and this admission is one way of stopping an unbearable incest or spouse-beating situation. A suicide attempt that has as its main motive 'a cry for help' is often understood as a means to get caring attention from others and manipulative aspects are stressed. However, such a suicide attempt is also a way to escape from direct exploitation.

The learned helplessness theory was developed after studying animals exposed to repeated unescapable trauma. These animals, in later situations, did show passive behaviour with respect to trauma that could be avoided. They did not respond to signs preceding traumatization, did not take initiatives to avoid it and looked 'depressive'. Later the learned helplessness theory has been revised. In human beings the cognitive dysfunctional attitudes are predominantly related to depression and suicidality. The consistent findings that child (sexual) abuse is connected with childhood traumatization compels to a revaluation of the original learned helplessness theory. In our study many women reported that they actively started to resist child sexual abuse when they reached adolescence. Some were successful in stopping the abuse, others experienced the inability to exert control over unwanted sexual acts. These women find themselves to be in a situation with repeated unescapable traumatization. The age at which sexual abuse ended is found to be related to severity of suicidality and this is especially so when women were subjected to sexual intercourse. Suicidal ideation almost always started in childhood and waxed and waned throughout life.

The learned helplessness theory predicts that women who are severely traumatized will more often than others experience revictimization, because they have a reduced ability to respond to signals of traumatization and will not take initiatives to prevent it. We found that a quarter of the women who had a heterosexual relationship were regularly beaten by their spouses, (twice as high as found in a sample of the normal female population). Women who were sexually abused as a child and moreover, were regularly beaten by their spouses are more inclined to attempt suicide than sexually abused women who did not experience such maltreatments.

According to the learned helplessness theory a person who has been repeatedly traumatized will feel helpless and depressed when she or he is confronted with a new traumatic situation. These reactions can be conceived as conditioned (emotional) responses. A question is which new situations should be considered as 'traumatic', triggering depressive feelings. Our findings indicate that unwanted but non-coercive intercourse later in life constitutes a 'traumatic' situation for women with a history of child sexual abuse. First of all, we find that women who as a child experienced sexual intercourse will have more severe suicidal behaviour than women sexually abused in other ways. This relation is rather strong in the group of women who have heterosexual partner relationships later in life. Moreover, we find that a woman who was severely traumatized by a first perpetrator and experienced sexual intercourse by a second perpetrator who did not or hardly use coercion is more inclined to attempt suicide. For the majority of women, intercourse is the most common sexual experience in adult life. Sexual intercourse in heterosexual partner relationships takes place at least one time a week. Other sexual acts than intercourse can more easily be avoided by heterosexual women. In partner relationships most women sometimes have intercourse while they do not 'really' want. Verbal reports of women show that intercourse with a male partner later in life evokes in some women similar feelings as child sexual abuse. Some women do tell their husbands about their associations and together they find ways to prevent the triggering of memories and associated feelings. However, other women find themselves unable to tell their husband what they feel. They think their husband will perceive their feelings as embarrassing, denigrating or insulting. Some women who told their husbands that intercourse evoked similar feelings they experienced during child sexual abuse, reported that their husbands indeed felt insulted. These findings lead to the conclusion that depression and suicidality may constitute a conditioned response triggered by situations resembling the original trauma. The 'traumatic' character of these situations is not necessarily 'traumatic' for the majority of the people. On the contrary, helplessness is perhaps experienced most keenly in situations that other people can cope with, but the person with a history of severe trauma feels unable to.

Findings lead to the following theoretical notions; non-coercive but unwanted sexual intercourse may trigger feelings of depression and helplessness. Moreover, a woman may experience extreme helplessness, because she feels unable to prevent the triggering of these feelings. And finally she may be keenly aware of the 'strangeness' of her helplessness. This combination increases the risk of suicidal behaviour.

In a multiple regression analysis we found that especially women with visual hallucinations are inclined to suicidal behaviour. A closer inspection of the contents of visual hallucinations reveals that many visual hallucinations are about either the fear to be killed or the intent to commit suicide. Some people are very anxious to act or experience acts such as the ones they see during the hallucinations. This study shows that these anxieties should be taken very seriously.

Sexual abuse is thought to evoke rage and through self-blame feelings this rage is directed against 'the self'. These psycho-dynamic processes played a role in the etiology of self-injurious behaviour, (see chapter 7). No indications are found that these psycho-dynamic processes also play a role in the etiology of suicidal behaviour.

Suicidality is often thought to be a symptom of an underlying 'borderline' character disorder. This borderline character disorder is described as resulting from a disturbance in the relationship between the child and the primary caretakers at an early age. None of the findings obtained in this study support this assumption.

Almost all women with a history of severe child abuse report suicidal ideation. This suicidal ideation may increase the vulnerability of a woman to actual suicidal behaviour. The characteristics of child abuse explain only a fraction of the suicide attempts later in life. It seems that adult life circumstances, especially social encounters with men, quality of marriage, reaction of the family of origin when child sexual abuse is revealed, etc. determine whether suicidal ideation is triggered again and again and whether, once or more often, suicide will be attempted.

Summary and Conclusions

This study has as its central question: are different characteristics of child (sexual) abuse associated with different psychiatric symptoms in adult life? Of all symptoms ascribed to child sexual abuse, four problem areas have been selected for further investigation: dissociative disturbances in consciousness, hallucinations, self-injury and suicidality. The primary practical aim of this study is to gather information useful for therapists treating women who experienced sexual abuse as a child. Women with such a history soliciting for therapy may indirectly profit from the insights gained.

Chapter 1 deals with the recent and rapid developments in the area of research on child (sexual) abuse and psychological impacts. These developments explain why our study departs from the viewpoint that connections between child (sexual) abuse and particular psychiatric symptoms have already been established to a reasonable degree. We express our opinion that not only a sound methodology and a good categorisation are needed, but especially theories that offer a better understanding of associations between characteristics of child sexual abuse and psychiatric symptoms. Such theories provide starting-points and guide-lines for therapy.

Each study on child sexual abuse and psychological impact will encounter several kinds of methodological problems. Chapter 2 presents a synopsis of these problems and the choices made in this study.

One important methodological problem concerns the retrospective character of data on child sexual abuse. The retrospective character evokes the question of reliability of these data. Studies on memory processes relating to (traumatic) childhood incidents give rise to a rather complicated picture. First of all, childhood incidents may simply have been forgotten. Secondly, memories of traumatic (childhood) incidents are often repressed or denied. Thirdly, a considerable fraction of the severely abused women will regularly experience flashbacks or post-traumatic nightmares. These traumatic incidents will be relived in a detailed way and will hardly be subjected to 'interpretative and reconstructive' activities. Finally, we may expect that a person who is in a depressive mood during the interview, will judge the childhood circumstances more negatively than when this person is not in a depressive mood during the interview. The analysis shows on the one hand that one may expect reliable memories, especially when flashbacks are concerned. Normal retrieval difficulties, and in case of severe trauma, denial and repression seem to hamper the reliability of retrospective reports on the other hand.

A second methodological issue relates to the social undesirability of child sexual abuse and psychiatric symptoms. One can only expect reliable information when women trust the study, are willing to disclose their history and symptoms, and moreover, do not repress or deny child sexual abuse. These considerations influenced our choice of respondents. We approached persons, giving emotional support to women with a history of child sexual abuse, and asked them to help us with contacting. This way of recruitment has, besides advantages, certain obvious disadvantages. For instance, we had no preliminary information on the characteristics of women who might cooperate in our study. We compensated this disadvantage by comparing the demographic and childhood characteristics of our respondents with those reported in other relevant studies. This comparison showed that our respondents have a relatively high level of education. Their characteristics of child sexual abuse can best be compared to those of women receiving poli-clinical or psychiatric help. The data obtained in this study are partly generalizable to women in such populations who have a history of child sexual abuse.

Chapter 3 presents in a condensed way the historical and theoretical reflections on the concepts of consciousness and dissociation. We argue that in the definition of dissociative disorders, 'disturbances of consciousness' deserve to be preferred to 'disturbances of memory' or 'disturbances of identity'.

Consciousness is considered to be a complex and obscure notion. Unity and continuity are not fundamental properties of consciousness. Consciousness can not be attributed to specific mental functions. However, certain agreement exists on the functions of consciousness. Consciousness has two functions: (1) Monitoring ourselves and our environment, so that sensations, percepts, memories, and thoughts come to be accurately represented in phenomenal awareness. (2) Controlling ourselves and our environment, so that we are able to voluntarily initiate and terminate behavioural and cognitive activities. Consciousness seems to be necessary for voluntary control of activities, for long-term planning as well as for communicating one's mental state to others. Certain properties are attributed to consciousness: (a) Consciousness is usually a 'personal' consciousness. (b) In general, events that are not consciously identified are not likely to be consciously recalled later on. (c) Attentional strategies are thought to play a mediating role between perception of information and conscious identification of that information.

Cognitive psychologists state that normally persons are conscious of facts, thoughts, and images that are selectively attended to. When selectively attended facts or images are not available to consciousness (temporarily or permanently), this is considered to be a special, dissociative state. When such a state is spontaneously reported and frequently experienced, it indicates multiple streams of consciousness. Such a state is conceived to be a pathological condition, indicating a severe dissociative disorder, like multiple personality disorder. The most extreme form of dissociative disturbance in consciousness concerns behaviour of a person that would normally be selectively attended, occurred outside 'operative consciousness' and voluntary control. In this study such a state is called a time-gap, in analogy to the concept used by William James to denote a similar phenomenon. Time-gaps are also denoted by other terms such as: time-loss, blackout, subconsciousness, co-consciousness.

We argue that one should make a distinction between time-gaps and repression. Repression concerns motivated forgetting. It is about emotional incidents that had been selectively attended to, and processed in short and long-term memory, but were subsequently excluded from consciousness. In retrospect, it may be difficult to differentiate between time-gaps and repression. Amnesia as a concept includes both time-gaps and repressions.

The characteristics of family dynamics and child sexual abuse are given in Chapter 4. Our attempt was to gain understanding in the meaning of different characteristics, and to examine several assumptions developed in other studies.

In our study, 100 women participated. These women were, as a child, predominantly sexually abused at the hands of their father or stepfather for a period of four or more years. Most women were subjected by the perpetrator(s) to physical aggression (more than a third) and/or threats to be killed (a quarter). Severe means of coercion are not so much used to accomplish sexual contact, but are primarily applied when sexual abuse lasts for a long period of time. Under such conditions, most girls try to stop the abuse, they attempt to disclose the situation, behave rebelliously and run away from home. In such escalating situations a considerable proportion of the perpetrators resorts to massive oppression in order to keep control over what is happening. The application of severe coercion by a sexual abusive father appears to be unrelated to the socio-economic class of the family. This finding is rather exceptional, because for instance physical aggression against a child, not associated with sexual abuse, is predominantly found in lower socio-economic classes. It seems plausible that the use of severe means of coercion by the father is inherently related to long-lasting sexual abuse.

Only a quarter of the women had an 'exclusive' relation with the perpetrator. Most women told that the perpetrator sexually abused other children too, or they themselves were abused at the hands of multiple perpetrators.

Most perpetrators and girls try to hide sexual abuse from the mother. This appears to be the case especially when a woman reports to have had a normal or good relation with her mother as long as she can remember. When sexual abuse lasts longer, attempts to hide become less rigid. Multiple sexual abusive experiences are seldom hidden from mother. Mother either is involved in the abuse or she is considered to be too powerless to intervene.

Child sexual abuse is found to occur in families with many children. In these families, elder brothers are predominantly the perpetrators.

We find that parentification does increase the risk of child sexual abuse by father (-figures).

Findings of our study can partly be generalized to women in poli-clinical or psychiatric settings. This means that therapists engaged with women who were sexually abused as a child, in majority are confronted with rather severe traumata. Women with such histories frequently have several different therapeutic contacts before they find a satisfying therapeutic relation. A good understanding by therapists of the different conditions in which child sexual abuse may occur, is the starting-point for more satisfying help.

Chapter 5 starts with theories concerning the relation between child sexual abuse and dissociative disturbances. Several assumptions have been deduced from these theories and from observations by leading psychiatrists. We expected a high level of dissociation in persons who, as a child, experienced overwhelming trauma that repeatedly took place in a family context characterized by neglect and ambivalent attitudes.

In general, people are inclined to react with depersonalization or dissociation when confronted with overwhelming trauma, e.g. life-threatening dangers. Dissociative reactions have the function to provide protection from immediate, overwhelming emotions. Such reactions are thought to have a transient character. In persons with a dissociative disturbance, depersonalization and dissociative symptoms are frequently experienced over a long period of time. Most of these persons, as psychiatrists and researchers in this field emphasize, were as a child severely traumatized.

We asked about disturbances in consciousness in the recent past in two different ways: with the Dissociative Experience Scale (D.E.S.), a structured questionnaire that predominantly contains questions on disturbances in consciousness, and in a semi-structured interview. Studies on the D.E.S. provide scorings-intervals for patients in the United States. In our study more than a third of the women (38%) would have received a diagnosis of multiple personality disorder, if they had been living in the United States and had been treated by a therapist willing to give this diagnosis.

In the interview, a third of the women reports to experience time-gaps. Certain important authors, like William James, wonder whether consciousness has the capacity to identify time-gaps. Statements about time-gaps made by some women indicate that complex learning processes precede this identification. First, a person may notice that things have changed, while they themselves are the only ones being capable of doing so (indirect registration). Moreover, important others in the direct environment may inform the person that she did seem to be fully aware of some acts that she can not herself remember having done. By combining information, a person learns to recognise that a certain inner state of feeling, such as 'being in a vacuum, being nowhere', precedes the experience of a time-gap (direct registration). The presence of important others, giving feedback on the behaviour of the person, may be crucial in this respect.

We find that a high level of dissociation tends to be reported by: (a) women having a childhood history in which they feared to be killed during sexual abuse, (b) women who, as a child, were subjected to group-rapes in which unknown perpetrators were involved, (c) women who, as a child, were physically assaulted by the perpetrator before sexual abuse started, (d) women who, as a child, were sexually abused at the hands of multiple perpetrators, (e) women who, as a child, experienced physical aggression associated with sexual abuse for a considerable time, (f) women whose mother was involved in the sexual abuse.

A multiple regression analysis shows four characteristics significantly and independently contributing to level of dissociation: cumulation of childhood trauma, age at onset of sexual abuse, physical aggression preceding sexual abuse, and being forced to have sexual contacts with unknown perpetrators. The anxiety experienced by a child when repetitively being severely beaten, tied or threatened with murder at an early age, seems to be so overwhelming that a permanent disturbance in conscious monitoring of the environment is likely to result.

In trauma theory it is assumed that flashbacks are accompanied by emotions evoked by the original trauma. Almost half of the women who experienced time-gaps mentions a connection between child (sexual) abuse and these (non-)experiences in adult life. For instance, the experience of a time-gap was often preceded by the intrusion of memories. This finding suggests that memories of overwhelming child abuse trigger a reoccurrence of dissociative reactions in adult life. We find that time-gaps are more strongly related with cumulation of childhood trauma than any other psychiatric symptom included in this study.

A debate is going on about the question whether or not dissociative disorders should be conceived as a special form of post-traumatic stress disorder. Our findings suggest that dissociative disturbances in consciousness result from repeated and severe traumatization, experienced as a child. One may expect that psychotherapy aiming at regaining consciousness of and voluntary control over memories of traumatic childhood incidents, will be effective in decreasing the prevalence of dissociative disturbances.

In Chapter 6, we departed from the viewpoint that studying hallucinations in their own right is more fruitful than considering them as part of a psychiatric syndrome, like schizophrenia or multiple personality disorder. In general, auditory and visual hallucinations are thought to be misrepresentations of a person's own thoughts in lexical (word) and visual (image) form, so that they are treated as perceptions. Several theories concerning the connection between (childhood) trauma and hallucinations are summarised and the assumptions, deduced from these theories, are examined.

Three kinds of hallucinations are distinguished: hallucinatory flashbacks, visual hallucinations and auditory hallucinations. In our study, 64% of the women reports hallucinatory phenomena. It is difficult to evaluate this prevalence rate, because in studies using samples of general populations this rate ranges from 8% to 71%.

A third of the women reports that flashbacks are accompanied by perceptual disturbances (hallucinatory flashbacks). Some authors assumed that hallucinations will emerge after an 'input overload'. This hypothesis is supported by our finding that the cumulation of childhood trauma is strongly associated with experiencing hallucinatory flashbacks. It seems plausible that the intensity of emotions, triggered by flashbacks, 'jams' the perceptual system and results in perceptual disturbances.

After traumatic experiences, a person may chronically suffer from nightmares. Such persons sometimes have a disturbance in wake-sleep cycles: brain waves typically accompanying dream episodes are manifest during waking states. In our study some women frequently suffering from nightmares, experienced daymares with similar contents as their nightmares (not identified as post-traumatic nightmares). These daymares imply difficulties in discriminating the reality of the 'intruding images'.

In his early works, Freud assumed that hallucinations refer to repressed memories of traumatic childhood incidents. In our study, more than half of the women (57%) have had intervals during which they never thought about, or had completely forgotten child sexual abuse. The degree to which a person has repressed her memories appears to be significantly and independently correlated to the frequency with which a person experiences visual hallucinations. This finding suggests that the more a woman is repressing her memories the more she is inclined to attribute a hallucinatory quality to 'intruding images'.

Repression does not only refer to visual memories, but also to feelings associated with traumatization. In trauma theory, it is thought that repression of overwhelming emotions results in feelings of 'depersonalization'. We find that when a woman is inclined to repress her emotions (frequently experiences feelings of depersonalization), she has an increased tendency to report hallucinatory flashbacks, visual and auditory hallucinations. These findings suggest that the depersonalization of feelings facilitates the misattribution of thoughts and images to ego-dystonic sources.

During trauma a person may use extreme attentional strategies to exclude overwhelming incidents from consciousness. Time-gaps are thought to be the successful result of this excessive deployment of attention. A person who is persistently deploying extreme attentional strategies, will be less familiar with her own thoughts. This process may increase the risk that the person misattributes her own thoughts to ego-dystonic sources. We find that women who frequently experience time-gaps are inclined to report visual as well as auditory hallucinations. Intruding memories may instigate extreme attentional strategies, which in turn increase the risk of visual and auditory hallucinations.

Hallucinations and time-gaps can both be conceptualized as 'disturbances in consciousness', as a consequence of extreme attentional strategies. Several research findings suggest that time-gaps are a more extreme form of disturbance in consciousness than hallucinations. During hallucinations the 'operative' consciousness is able to identify what is going on and this is not the case during time-gaps.

A young child has to learn the difference between reality and imagination. Most children learn to make this discrimination before the age of seven, but some children may never learn to make this distinction, because learning reality-discrimination is too devastating for these children. We find that the experience of auditory hallucinations is predominantly associated with neglect, physical or sexual abuse by their parents of children who were six years or younger. Of course one should take some reserve when considering reports of incidents that go back to such early ages. The most distinctive feature is, that these women can not remember a period in which their father or their mother did not neglect, beat or sexually abuse them. These findings make it plausible that these women have never learned to distinguish reality from imagination.

In making the distinction between reality and internal representations, most persons use the available information on the imaginary or reality character of an experience. In order to arrive at an adequate judgement, it is important that misleading information is absent. Some women told explicitly that they had images about child sexual abuse, but that they did not know whether their images concerned memories. In these cases, reality-discrimination can not be considered an easy job. Most women, who had initially forgotten their history of sexual abuse and later experienced images of that abuse, started extensive verification processes. They discussed details of the images, more accessible to public verification than the sexual abuse it self, with sisters, aunts, grandmothers, brothers etc. In that way they tried to get more clarity in the question whether the images represented real incidents or not. Uncertainty about the provenance of their 'intruding images' made some women refuse to participate in our study, or to identify some images as memories. However, it is to be expected that some women will never find others capable of confirming or denying details of their 'intruding images'. Several psychiatrists have expressed the opinion that it is not important whether images of sexual abuse reflect real childhood trauma or not. We disagree with this statement, because the therapeutic processes involved can not but be different. Our results show that hallucinations may decrease when repression of memories and associated feelings diminishes. This indicates that a therapy directed at decreasing repression of memories and associated emotional feelings and attentional strategies, will be more successful in diminishing hallucinatory experiences, than a therapy presuming that reality-discrimination is not important. Moreover, women who discover that images reflect real incidents will probably change their attitudes towards the perpetrator and their family. They will start a process to redefine their relations with their family of origin. A woman who gets support from her family-members, may find alleviation of some of her problems.

Chapter 7 describes theories on the connections between self-injurious behaviour and childhood trauma. Assumptions derived from those theories are examined in this chapter.

We find that half of the women in this study have injured themselves during their life. A quarter of all respondents have injured themselves regularly. Self-injury is considered to be a socially very undesirable activity and no reliable figures exists about self-injury in samples of general populations. The prevalence of self-injury in our study is in line with prevalences found in other studies using comparable samples. One third of the women who injure themselves start this behaviour at a young age. Self-injury of children between the age 3 to 13 may function as a signal to the environment, indicating sexual or physical child abuse, because self-injury by children is otherwise rare.

The majority of women report emotions before, during and after their self-injurious acts, as described in the literature on the 'Deliberate Self-Harm Syndrome'. Besides these feelings, we found that a considerable number of women struggling with self-harm impulses had hallucinations, vivid dreams or intensely intrusive thoughts connected with these impulses. These features are not described in the 'Deliberate Self-Harm Syndrome'.

About a third of the women who injured themselves indicated during the interview a connection between child sexual abuse and self-injury. Self-injury was found to be a direct way of preventing sexual abuse, or a manner to give to others a signal for help. Some adult women injured themselves when experiencing flashbacks concerning childhood trauma.

The theories connecting child sexual abuse and self-injury can be grouped around three main etiologies: (a) Self-blame and guilt feelings evoked by particular characteristics of child sexual abuse result in self-injury. (b) Rage feelings evoked by particular characteristics of (sexual) abuse result in self-injury. (c) Self-injury is a manifestation of the borderline personality disorder, resulting from neglect and abuse experienced as a very young child.

We find that so-called self-blame characteristics of child sexual abuse are associated with the frequency of self-injury. Especially when women had resisted the perpetrator in an explicit way, they were less inclined to self-injurious behaviour. Moreover, an interaction is found to exist between rage evoked by the severity of coercion associated with child sexual abuse and self-blame evoked by non-explicitness of resistance, resulting in an increased frequency of self-injury. These findings support the following theoretical model: The more severe child sexual abuse has been, the larger is the risk that memories on child abuse will be associated with overwhelming complex and confusing emotions. Whether a woman injures herself when re-experiencing these complex and overwhelming emotions, partly depends on the self-blame feelings also evoked by memories of child sexual abuse.

Some therapists observed that self-blame and guilt feelings are nearly always present in women who were sexually abused as a child. They suppose that these feelings of guilt and self-blame are a protection against feelings of complete helplessness. The feelings of self-blame give women the illusion that they would have been able to change the situation. This interpretation suggests that intra-psychic processes produce self-blame feelings. But, we do not know whether self-blame exists only in the minds of the women, or whether it reflects the attitude towards child sexual abuse in the family or even in our culture in general. For instance, physical resistance by women in rape crimes has always been an important issue. In the criminal justice system, questions about the resistance of women (have) dominate(d) the proceedings. For centuries rape has only been identified as such if the woman resisted the rapist physically. The self-blame attitude seems to be in line with the, until recently, general attitude towards rape. The more visible forms of self-injury like cuttings and burnings are highly correlated with self-blame feelings, and may have the symbolic value, 'I have to bleed for it'. Of course it is intolerable that young girls, mostly between seven and twelve years old, who are sexually abused and subjected to severe aggression, by persons who are at least five years older, would meet an attitude that holds them responsible for these abuses. The idea that these girls are to blame if they have not physically resisted the perpetrator is overtly unjustified.

Our findings suggest that self-injury is partly based on cognitive appraisals of the sexual abuse situation. Some women find reasons why they are not to blame, like 'I have done the best I could to resist him', 'He was grown-up, so I'm not responsible for it' or 'He also abused others'. Support for the point of view, that self-injury is partly based on cognitive appraisals, is provided by the negative correlation between level of education and frequency of self-injury. The higher the education, the more a woman has acces to information, the more she is confronted with the attitude that the perpetrator, and not the girl, is responsible for sexual abuse. This gives hope for therapeutic processes. To lay the responsibility for child sexual abuse where it belongs, on the shoulders of the perpetrator, may reduce self-injurious behaviour.

We find that self-injury is correlated with cumulation of childhood trauma independent of the age period in which the trauma took place. But, we also find that among women who frequently injured themselves, a relatively large group were subjected to early physical aggression by the father. This finding may point to a borderline character disorder, but it is more plausible that women who have been physically assaulted at an early age have learnt to punish themselves, in similar ways as they were punished by the perpetrator.

Chapter 8 deals with theories and assumptions on the connection between child sexual abuse and suicidality.

We find that only a small proportion of the women (15%) never had any suicidal ideation. When the severity of the child sexual abuse is taken into account, almost all women experienced suicidal ideation. Almost half of the women participating in our study (45%) attempted suicide one or several times. This prevalence of suicidality is in line with the suicidality reported in comparable groups of women with a history of child sexual abuse who solicit for therapeutic help, but it is much higher than the prevalence of suicidality found in samples of general populations.

Different explanations are offered for consistent research findings that women who have been sexually abused as a child are inclined to do a suicide attempt. One of these theories relates to the idea that a suicide attempt is 'a cry for help'. Women with a child sexual abuse history need attention for their problems, but know no way of asking it. A suicide attempt that has as its main motive 'a cry for help' is often understood as a means to get caring attention from others and manipulative aspects are stressed. We find that for children and adolescents the suicide attempt is predominantly 'a cry for help', a protest against a situation of no affection, life threats and gross sexual exploitation. A similar motive is mentioned by a small fraction of suicide attempters who were older than eighteen years (15%) when they made an attempt. Almost a fifth of the women who participated in this study was still trapped in an incest-situation after the age of eighteen and for some of these women their suicide attempt was the only means of escaping from this situation. For some other women, who were locked in a relation with a spouse who regularly beat them, the suicide attempt also had the meaning of 'a cry for help'. After the attempt most women were admitted to a hospital or psychiatric institution and this admission implies that a situation of unbearable incest or spouse-beating situation stops (temporarily). When therapists are confronted with a suicide attempt they should keep an open mind for the possibility that a suicide attempt appears to be (is) the woman's only way of escaping from direct exploitation and abuse.

Another explanation for the connection between childhood trauma and suicidality is offered by the learned helplessness theory. This theory has been developed after systematic observations of the behaviour of animals exposed to repeated unescapable trauma. These animals, in later situations, did show passive behaviour with respect to trauma that could be avoided. They did not respond any more to signs preceding traumatization, did not take initiatives to avoid it and looked 'depressive'. Later this learned helplessness theory has been used to explain depression in humans. Then this theory has been revised and emphasis has switched from 'uncontrollable traumata' to dysfunctional cognitions. The following notion was developed: a depressive person has not been confronted with uncontrollable traumata, but the person has the dysfunctional cognition that situations are uncontrollable. The consistent findings that child (sexual) abuse is connected with childhood traumatization compels to a revaluation of the original 'learned helplessness' theory. In our study, many women reported that they saw no possibilities to escape from sexual abuse. Some women actively started to resist child sexual abuse when they reached adolescence and were successful in stopping the abuse, but for others it appeared to be impossible to exert control over unwanted sexual acts. These women find themselves to be in a situation with repeated unescapable traumatization. We find that the age at which the sexual abuse ended is related to severity of suicidality, especially when girls were subjected to sexual intercourse.

The learned helplessness theory predicts that women who are severely traumatized will more than others experience revictimization, because they have a reduced ability to respond to signals preceding traumatization and will not take initiatives to prevent it. We find that a quarter of the women who had a heterosexual relationship were regularly beaten by their spouses, (twice as high as found in a sample of the normal female population). Women who as a child were sexually abused and moreover, were regularly beaten by their spouses are more inclined to attempt suicide than sexually abused women who did not experience such maltreatments.

According to the learned helplessness theory a person who has been repeatedly traumatized will feel helpless and depressed when she or he is confronted with a new traumatic situation. These reactions can be conceived as conditioned (emotional) responses. A question is what new situations should be considered as 'traumatic', triggering depressive feelings. Our findings indicate that a particular kind of situation constitutes a 'trauma' for women with a history of child sexual abuse, namely unwanted but non-coercive intercourse later in life. First of all, we find that women who as a child experienced sexual intercourse will have more severe suicidal behaviour than women sexually abused in other ways. This relation is particularly found in the group of women who had heterosexual relationships later in life. Moreover, we find that especially those women tend to attempt suicide, who were severely traumatized by a first perpetrator and as a child had sexual intercourse with a second perpetrator who did not or hardly use coercion. For the majority of women, intercourse is the most common sexual experience in adult life. Sexual intercourse in heterosexual partner relationships normally takes place at least one time a week. In most partner relationships, women sometimes have intercourse while they do not 'really' want. Sexual acts other than intercourse can more easily be avoided by heterosexual women.

Our findings suggest that unwanted, but non-coercive sexual intercourse with a partner triggers feelings of depression and helplessness in women who were sexually abused as a child. Women may, but need not be conscious of these associations. The learned helplessness theory predicts that women may feel helplessness to prevent the triggering of depressive feelings. Verbal reports of women in our study show that some women were keenly aware of the 'exceptional state' of her helplessness. This combination increases the risk of suicidal behaviour.

Almost all women with a history of severe child abuse report suicidal ideation. This suicidal ideation may increase the vulnerability of a woman to actual suicidal behaviour. The characteristics of child abuse explain only a fraction of the suicide attempts later in life. It seems that adult life circumstances, especially social encounters with men, quality of marriage, reaction of the family of origin when child sexual abuse is revealed, etc. determine whether suicidal ideation is triggered again and again and whether, once or more often, suicide will be attempted.

The appendices contain, among other things, summaries of previous studies on child sexual abuse and respectively level of dissociation, hallucinations, self-injury and suicidality.

Finally, some concluding remarks concerning the study as a whole have to be made. The central question of our study was whether different characteristics of child sexual abuse are associated with different kinds of psychiatric symptoms. The research findings presented show that characteristics of sexual abuse experienced as a child and family circumstances accompanying this abuse, may indicate the psychological problems women struggle with in adult life. Women who were sexually abused as a child should not be conceived as a 'homogeneous group' when considering psychiatric symptoms. For a thorough understanding of the symptomatology and an adequate therapeutic treatment of the symptoms, it is necessary to carefully assess the character of child sexual abuse and the psychological processes connecting child sexual abuse with the psychiatric symptom.

We departed from the point of view that studying psychiatric symptoms is to be preferred to studying psychiatric syndromes. Women who get into contact with psychiatrists will generally get a psychiatric diagnosis, such as a borderline character or a mood disorder. Our findings show that it is important to pay attention to the psychic processes underlying each psychiatric symptom. It should be avoided to make too generalised assumptions on psychological processes underlying groups of symptoms (syndromes). For instance, our findings show that psychological processes connecting child sexual abuse with self-injury different considerably from processes connecting child sexual abuse with suicidality. In many studies it is assumed that both symptoms are expressions of self-destruction and that similar psychological processes are involved.

In dissociative disorders, especially in multiple personality disorder, it is assumed that different and separate layers of consciousness exist, explaining all the symptoms of the women with these disorders. Hallucinations in persons with extreme dissociative disturbances are explained as the influence a dissociated layer of consciousness exerts upon the 'operative' consciousness. Although we do not exclude such an explanation, it seems to us premature to depart a priori from such an explanation. It is, to our opinion, more productive to develop theory and research, connecting for instance extreme attention deployment, disturbances in consciousness, and disturbances in irreflective self-reference, than to debate about the differences and similarities between the diagnoses schizophrenia and multiple personality disorder.

Self-evidently other studies are needed to give our results a wider perspective.

Samenvatting en Conclusies

Deze studie heeft als centrale vraagstelling: 'Hangen verschillende vormen van seksuele kindermishandeling samen met verschillende psychiatrische symptomen op volwassen leeftijd?' Van alle psychische symptomen, die zijn toegeschreven aan seksuele kindermishandeling, hebben we vier probleemgebieden geselecteerd voor nader onderzoek: dissociatieve stoornissen in het bewustzijn, hallucinaties, zelf-beschadiging en suicidaliteit. Het primaire praktische doel van deze studie is het verzamelen van informatie bruikbaar voor therapeuten die vrouwen met een seksueel misbruik verleden behandelen. Vrouwen met een dergelijk verleden die met de hulpverlening in aanraking komen kunnen indirekt voordeel hebben van de verkregen inzichten.

Hoofdstuk 1 behandelt de recente en snelle ontwikkelingen op het gebied van onderzoek naar seksuele kindermishandeling en psychologische implicaties. Deze ontwikkelingen verklaren waarom onze studie vertrekt vanuit het gezichtspunt dat verbanden tussen (seksuele) kindermishandeling en een aantal psychiatrische symptomen in redelijke mate zijn aangetoond. We zijn van mening dat er niet alleen behoefte is aan een goede onderzoeksmethode, en een goede kategorisatie, maar vooral aan theorieën, die inzicht verschaffen in de processen waarop de relaties tussen seksuele kindermishandeling en psychiatrische symptomen berusten. Dergelijke theorieën bieden aanknopingspunten voor therapie.

Ieder onderzoek naar seksuele kindermishandeling en de psychologische implicaties ontmoet verschillende problemen van methodologische aard. Hoofdstuk 2 bevat een beknopte samenvatting van deze problemen en de keuzes die in dit onderzoek zijn gemaakt.
Een van de belangrijkste methodologische problemen betreft het retrospectieve karakter van de gegevens over seksuele kindermishandeling. Bestudering van geheugenprocessen, die betrekking hebben op (seksuele) incidenten in de kindertijd, levert een vrij complex beeld op. Ten eerste kunnen incidenten uit de kindertijd gewoon vergeten zijn. Ten tweede worden herinneringen aan traumatische gebeurtenissen vaak verdrongen of ontkend. Ten derde kan men verwachten dat een deel van de vrouwen, die als kind seksueel zijn misbruikt, regelmatig flashbacks of post-traumatische nachtmerries ervaren. Traumatische incidenten worden tijdens flashbacks meestal gedetailleerd herbeleefd en blijken nauwelijks onderhevig te zijn aan allerlei 'interpretatie en herstructurerings' processen. Ten slotte valt te verwachten dat bij een depressieve

stemming ten tijde van het interview het oordeel van de vrouw over de voorvallen in de kindertijd negatiever uitvalt dan bij een andere stemming tijdens van het interview. Deze analyse laat zien dat men aan de ene kant zeer betrouwbare herinneringen kan verwachten vooral wanneer het flashbacks betreft. Aan de andere kant kan men verwachten dat normale vergeet- en, in geval van ernstige trauma's, verdringingsprocessen de betrouwbaarheid van de retrospectieve verslagen kunnen aantasten.

Een tweede methodologische probleem heeft betrekking op de sociale onwenselijkheid van seksuele kindermishandeling en psychiatrische symptomen. Men kan alleen dan betrouwbare informatie verwachten als respondentes een onderzoeksproject vertrouwen, persoonlijke informatie wensen te verstrekken en bovendien in staat zijn om het verleden tot zich door te laten dringen. Deze overwegingen hebben een invloed gehad op onze keuze van respondentes. We hebben contact gezocht met personen die emotionele ondersteuning geven aan vrouwen die als kind seksueel misbruikt zijn en hen gevraagd ons te helpen bij het leggen van contacten. Deze manier van benaderen heeft naast de genoemde voordelen, enkele duidelijke nadelen. Een van deze nadelen betreft het gebrek aan informatie vooraf over de kenmerken van de vrouwen die aan het onderzoek zouden willen meewerken. We hebben dit nadeel gecompenseerd door achteraf de demografische kenmerken en de aard van de kindermishandeling van onze respondentes te vergelijken met soortgelijke gegevens uit ander relevant onderzoek. Het blijkt dat de vrouwen die aan ons onderzoek meewerkten een relatief gezien hoge opleiding hebben genoten en dat zij het best te vergelijken zijn met de groep seksueel misbruikte vrouwen die met de psychologische of psychiatrische hulpverlening in aanraking is gekomen. De in dit onderzoek verkregen gegevens kunnen gedeeltelijk worden gegeneraliseerd naar alle vrouwen met een dergelijk verleden die een therapeutische behandeling vragen.

Hoofdstuk 3 behandelt op een beknopte manier de historische en theoretische overdenkingen van de concepten 'bewustzijn' en 'dissociatie'. We beargumenteren dat bij definiëring van dissociatieve stoornissen de voorkeur dient te worden gegeven aan 'verstoringen in het bewustzijn' boven 'verstoringen in het geheugen' of 'verstoringen in de identiteit'.

Er bestaat een zekere overeenstemming over de functies van het bewustzijn, alhoewel bewustzijn wordt beschouwd als een complex en obscuur begrip, waarbij pluriformiteit en discontinuiteit normale condities zijn. Deze functies worden als volgt omschreven: (1) Het registreren van onszelf en de omgeving, op zodanige manier dat sensaties, percepties, herinneringen en gedachten nauwkeurig gerepresenteerd worden in ons fenomenologisch bewustzijn. (2) Het beheersen van onszelf en onze omgeving, zodat we in staat zijn vrijwillig gedragingen en cognitieve aktiviteiten te beginnen en te beeindigen. Het bewustzijn lijkt vooral noodzakelijk voor de vrijwillige beheersing van het gedrag, het plannen maken voor langere termijn en het elkaar vertellen van wat er in je omgaat. Er zijn zekere eigenschappen die aan het bewustzijn worden toegeschreven: (a) Het bewustzijn is als regel een 'persoonlijk' bewustzijn. (b) Over het algemeen zullen gebeurtenissen die niet bewust worden geregistreerd, ook later niet bewust worden herinnerd. (c) Aandachtsprocessen worden geacht een mediërende rol te vervullen tussen het ontvangen van informatie en het bewustworden daarvan.

Cognitieve psychologen beweren dat, in normale omstandigheden, personen zich bewust worden van feiten, gedachten en beelden als de persoon selectief haar/zijn aandacht daarop richt. Als feiten of beelden waaraan de persoon selectief aandacht besteedt, toch niet doordringen tot het bewustzijn (tijdelijk of blijvend), dan wordt dit beschouwd als een dissociatief verschijnsel. Als een dergelijke toestand spontaan wordt vermeld en regelmatig wordt ervaren, dan wijst dit op het bestaan van meerdere lagen van bewustzijn. Dit wordt als een pathologische toestand beschouwd en is indicatief voor ernstige dissociatieve stoornissen, zoals de meervoudige persoonlijkheids stoornis. De meest extreme vorm van bewustzijnsverstoring treedt op, als een persoon meldt dat er regelmatig gedachten, gevoelens, houdingen en gedragingen plaats hebben waaraan wel aandacht is besteed, maar die toch buiten het 'vigerende bewustzijn' en de vrijwillige beheersing omgaan. In dit onderzoek noemen we een dergelijke ervaring een 'tijd-sprong' analoog aan het begrip 'time-gap' dat William James introduceerde voor soortgelijke verschijnselen. Een tijd-sprong wordt ook wel aangeduid met begrippen als 'black-out', 'tijd-verlies', onbewuste processen of co-consciousness. We beargumenteren dat er onderscheid gemaakt dient te worden tussen repressie en dissociatie. Repressie of verdringing heeft te maken met gemotiveerd vergeten, met emotionele gebeurtenissen waarop selectief de aandacht gericht is geweest, die opgenomen zijn geweest in het kortdurende en langdurende geheugen, maar vervolgens (aktief) uit het bewustzijn zijn gebannen. In geval van retrospectie kan het moeilijk zijn om tijd-sprongen te onderscheiden van verdringing. Het begrip amnesie (iets niet kunnen herinneren) kan betrekking hebben op beide verschijnselen.

Hoofdstuk 4 bevat pogingen de betekenis te begrijpen van de verschillende vormen van seksueel misbruik en de gezinssituaties waarin dit voorkomt. De 100 vrouwen die aan ons onderzoek meededen werden als kind merendeels langer dan vier jaar seksueel misbruikt door hun (stief- of pleeg-)vader. Meer dan een derde deel van de vrouwen werd door een dader geconfronteerd met fysiek geweld en daarnaast werd een kwart van de vrouwen door een dader van het seksueel misbruik met de dood bedreigd. We vinden dat zware dwangmiddelen niet zozeer worden aangewend om seksueel contact te bewerkstellingen, maar vooral worden toegepast bij langdurig seksueel misbruik. In een dergelijke situatie pogen de meeste meisje het sexuele misbruik te stoppen, zij proberen erover aan anderen te vertellen, trekken zich van geen enkele regel iets aan en dreigen weg te lopen. In deze geescaleerde situatie grijpen nogal wat daders naar zware repressieve middelen om de zaak onder beheersing te houden. Het toepassen van zware dwangmiddelen door een vader die zijn dochter seksueel misbruikt blijkt niet gerelateerd te zijn aan een bepaalde sociaal economische klasse van het gezin. Deze bevinding is opvallend, omdat bijvoorbeeld fysieke aggressie tegen kinderen, die niet seksueel misbruikt worden, wel duidelijk is gerelateerd aan sociaal economische klasse. De bevinding doet vermoeden dat het gebruik van zware dwangmiddelen door de vader inherent is aan langdurig gedwongen seksueel misbruik.

Slechts een kwart van de vrouwen in ons onderzoek had een 'exclusieve' relatie met de dader. De andere vrouwen vertellen dat de dader ook andere kinderen seksueel misbruikte of dat zij als kind seksueel misbruikt zijn door meerdere daders. De meeste daders en kinderen proberen het seksuele misbruik voor de moeder te verbergen. Dit blijkt vooral het geval als het meisje van jongs af aan een normale of goede relatie met de moeder had. Hoe langer het misbuik duurt hoe minder pogingen worden gedaan door dader en meisje om het seksuele misbruik echt te verbergen. Seksueel misbruik waarbij meerdere daders betrokken zijn wordt zelden voor de moeder verborgen gehouden. De moeder is of zelf bij het misbruik betrokken of wordt als te machteloos beschouwd om het misbruik te kunnen stoppen. We vinden dat seksueel misbruik nogal eens voorkomt in grote gezinnen en dat in die situatie oudere broers voornamelijk de daders zijn. Parentificatie-processen, (het overnemen van de huishoudelijke taak van de moeder, of de oudste dochter zijn in het gezin) verhogen de kans op seksueel misbruik door de vader.

Onze onderzoeksbevindingen kunnen gedeeltelijk worden gegeneraliseerd naar vrouwen met een seksueel misbruik verleden die in aanraking komen met de hulpverlening. Dit betekent dat therapeuten, als zij een vrouw met een seksueel misbruik verleden onder behandeling krijgen, merendeels met ernstige trauma's worden geconfronteerd. Vrouwen die als kind misbruikt zijn hebben vaak verschillende kontakten voordat zij bevredigende therapeutische hulp vinden. Een goed begrip bij therapeuten voor de verschillende omstandigheden waaronder seksueel misbruik plaats kan hebben gehad, vormt het uitgangspunt voor een meer bevredigende hulpverlening.

Hoofdstuk 5 begint met theorieën over de samenhang tussen (seksuele) kindermishandeling en dissociatieve stoornissen. Verschillende hypothesen zijn afgeleid uit deze theorieën en uit de observaties van psychiaters. We verwachten dat vooral die personen een hoog niveau van dissociatie hebben, die als kind regelmatig overweldigende trauma's hebben meegemaakt in een gezinssituatie gekarakteriseerd door verwaarlozing en ambivalentie.

In het algemeen zijn mensen geneigd te reageren met dissociatie of depersonalisatie als zij geconfronteerd worden met overweldigende of levensbedreigende trauma's. Men neemt aan dat dissociatieve reacties de functie hebben bescherming te bieden tegen onmiddelijke, overweldigende emoties.

Dergelijke reacties tijdens ernstige trauma's, zo wordt beschreven, zijn van voorbijgaande aard. Personen met een ernstige dissociatieve stoornis hebben regelmatig en over lange tijdsperioden last van depersonalisatie en dissociatieve symptomen. Psychiaters en onderzoekers op dit gebied benadrukken dat de meeste personen met dergelijke stoornissen als kind ernstige trauma's hebben ervaren.

We hebben op twee verschillende manieren naar dissociatieve verschijnselen in het recente verleden gevraagd: met behulp van de Dissociatieve Ervaringen Vragenlijst (D.E.S.), die voornamelijk vragen over bewustzijnsverstoringen bevat, en in een interview. De toelichting op de D.E.S. bevat scoringsnormen, geijkt voor de Amerikaanse situatie. We vinden dat meer dan een derde van de vrouwen in ons onderzoek (38%) de diagnose meervoudige persoonlijkheids stoornis zou hebben gekregen in het geval zij contact hadden gehad met een (Amerikaanse) therapeut die bereid is een dergelijke diagnose te geven.

Tijdens het interview vertelde een derde van de vrouwen 'tijd-sprongen' te ervaren. Bepaalde belangrijke psychologen, zoals William James, vragen zich af of het bewustzijn wel in staat is om tijd-sprongen te registreren. Uit de rapportages van de vrouwen uit ons onderzoek over tijd-sprongen komt naar voren dat aan een dergelijke registratie een complex leerproces vooraf gaat. Allereerst merkt de persoon dat er van alles veranderd is, zonder dat zij zich ervan bewust is hoe die veranderingen tot stand zijn gekomen (indirecte registratie). Bovendien kunnen anderen uit de naaste omgeving vertellen dat zij het volledige bewustzijn leek te hebben in de periode waarover zij zich niets kan herinneren. Door het combineren van informatie leert de persoon dat een zekere innerlijke gevoelstoestand, zoals het gevoel in een vacuum te zitten of weg te zakken in het niets, vooraf gaat aan een tijd-sprong (directe registratie). De aanwezigheid van anderen, die informatie geven over het gedrag van de persoon tijdens de tijd-sprong, is van essentieel belang voor het directe leren registreren van en tijd-sprong

We vinden dat sommige groepen vrouwen ertoe neigen een hoog niveau van dissociatie te rapporteren: (a) Vrouwen die als kind bang waren vermoord te worden tijdens het seksuele misbruik. (b) Vrouwen die als kind gedwongen werden tot sexueel kontakt met hen onbekende mannen. (c) Vrouwen die als kind voordat het seksuele misbruik begon reeds door de dader fysiek werden mishandeld. (d) Vrouwen die als kind door meerdere daders sexueel misbruikt zijn. (e) Vrouwen die als kind gedurende een lange periode te maken hebben gehad met zowel fysiek als seksueel misbruik. (f) Vrouwen waarvan de moeder betrokken was bij het seksuele misbruik. Een multipele regressie analyse laat zien dat er vier factoren significant en onafhankelijk een bijdrage leveren aan de variantie in het niveau van dissociatie: de cumulatie van trauma's in de kindertijd, de begin leeftijd van het seksuele misbruik, fysieke agressie door de dader voorafgaand aan het seksuele misbruik en het gedwongen worden tot seksueel kontakt met onbekende mannen. De angsten die een kind op jonge leeftijd ervaart bij herhaalde ernstige fysieke aggressie, bij gedwongen seksueel contact met vreemden en bij bedreigingen met moord blijken zo overweldigend te zijn dat dit kan leiden tot een blijvende verstoring van de bewuste waarneming.

De trauma theorie beschrijft dat het zich opdringen van flashbacks meestal gepaard gaat met dezelfde emoties die ook tijdens het trauma werden opgewekt. Bijna de helft van de vrouwen meldt dat er een verband was tussen het ervaren van tijd-sprongen op volwassenen leeftijd en de (seksuele) kindermishandeling. Veelal gingen flashbacks vooraf aan de ervaring van een tijd-sprong. Dit suggereert dat als herinneringen aan de trauma's zich later opdringen, er een herbeleving optreedt van de dissociatieve reacties zoals als kind ervaren tijdens de trauma's. Het ervaren van tijd-sprongen bleek sterker gerelateerd aan cumulatie van trauma's ervaren in de kindertijd dan aan enig ander psychiatrisch symptoom opgenomen in dit onderzoek.

Er is een debat gaande over de vraag of dissociatieve stoornissen begrepen moeten worden als een speciale uitingsvorm van post-traumatische stress stoornissen. Onze resultaten suggereren dat dissociatieve verstoringen in het bewustzijn het resultaat zijn van herhaalde confrontaties met overweldigende trauma's ervaren in de kindertijd. Op basis van deze resultaten mag men verwachten, dat er een vermindering in dissociatieve bewustzijnsstoornissen optreedt, als in psychotherapie wordt nagestreefd dat de persoon het bewustzijn verkrijgt van en de beheersing over herinneringen van trauma's in de kindertijd.

In Hoofdstuk 6 vertrekken we vanuit het standpunt dat bestudering van hallucinaties als verschijnsel op zich vruchtbaarder is dan de a priori aanname dat hallucinaties een onderdeel vormen van een psychiatrische syndroom, zoals meervoudige persoonlijkheids stoornis of schizophrenie. We sluiten ons aan bij de algemeen heersende mening, dat hallucinaties betrekking hebben op misvattingen, waarbij de persoon met auditieve hallucinaties de eigen gedachten niet alszodanig herkent en de persoon met visuele hallucinatie een zelfde beoordelingsfout maakt ten aanzien van interne beeldende voorstellingen. Er bestaan verschillende theorieën over het verband tussen trauma's (in de kindertijd) en hallucinaties. Deze theorieën en de daaruit afgeleide hypothesen worden eerst besproken en zijn vervolgens onderzocht.

We onderscheiden drie soorten hallucinatoire ervaringen: hallucinatoire flashbacks, visuele en auditieve hallucinaties. We vinden dat 64% van de vrouwen in dit onderzoek hallucinatoire ervaringen vermelden. Het is moeilijk een evaluatie te geven van dit percentage, omdat onderzoeken met steekproeven uit algemene populaties zeer uiteenlopende prevalenties van hallucinaties geven, varierend tussen 8% en 71%.

Een derde van de vrouwen vertelde dat tijdens flashbacks perceptuele verstoringen optreden (hallucinatoire flashbacks). Sommige theoretici veronderstellen dat hallucinaties onder andere onstaan ten gevolge van het zich opdringen van overweldigende informatie. We vinden een sterk verband tussen de cumulatie van trauma's ervaren in de kindertijd en het last hebben van hallucinatoire flashbacks. Deze bevinding suggereert dat de intensiteit van emoties, opgewekt door de flashbacks, de perceptie van de persoon verstoort.

Na traumatische ervaringen, zo blijkt uit allerlei onderzoek, lijden personen nogal eens aan chronische nachtmerries. Sommige van deze personen blijken overdag de bewustzijnstoestand te ervaren die kenmerkend is voor de droomervaring. We vinden dat vrouwen in ons onderzoek niet alleen post-traumatische nachtmerries beschrijven, maar velen hebben chronisch last van anderssoortige nachtmerries of van 'night-terrors'. Sommige vrouwen vertellen dat zij last hebben van dagmerries met dezelfde inhoud als de nachtmerries die hen chronisch plagen. Dergelijke dagmerries impliceren moeilijkheden bij het onderkennen van het werkelijkheidsgehalte van deze zich opdringende beelden.

In zijn beginjaren veronderstelde Freud dat hallucinaties berusten op de herbeleving van verdrongen traumatische jeugdervaringen. Meer dan de helft van de vrouwen in ons onderzoek (57%) heeft perioden gekend waarin zij nauwelijks dachten aan het seksuele misbruik, dan wel het totaal vergeten waren. We vinden dat de mate van verdringing samenhangt met de frequentie van visuele hallucinaties. Dit gegeven suggereert dat vrouwen die het seksuele misbruik sterk uit hun bewustzijn hebbeb gebannen eerder geneigd zijn 'zich opdringende visuele beelden' te beschouwen als hallucinaties dan vrouwen die het seksuele misbruik niet verdringen.

Verdringen heeft niet alleen betrekking op de visuele herinnering, maar ook op gevoelens die met het trauma geassocieerd zijn. In de traumatheorie worden gevoelens van onwerkelijkheid tijdens het trauma beschreven met de term depersonalisatie en men neemt aan dat zij het gevolg zijn van het verdringen van de overweldigende emoties. We vinden dat naarmate een vrouw meer is geneigd om bepaalde emoties te verdringen (depersonalisatie-gevoelens te ervaren), zij vaker last heeft van zowel hallucinatoire flashbacks, visuele als auditieve hallucinaties. De bevindingen suggereren, dat het depersonaliseren van gevoelens het proces vergemakkelijkt waardoor gedachten en beelden worden toegeschreven aan ik-vreemde oorzaken.

Tijdens een trauma kan de persoon ertoe neigen extreme aandachtsstrategieën te gebruiken om daarmee overweldigende incidenten uit het bewustzijn te bannen. Ervaringen van 'tijd-sprongen' kunnen worden beschouwd als het resultaat van het succesvol toepassen van deze extreme aandachtstrategieën. Personen die frequent extreme aandachtstrategieën toepassen zullen in verminderde mate registreren welke gedachten er in het eigen hoofd omgaan. Een verslechterd vermogen om eigen gedachten te herkennen vermeerdert de kans op auditieve hallucinaties. We vinden dat de frequentie waarmee men tijd-sprongen ervaart, verband houdt met zowel de frequentie waarmee men visuele als waarmee men auditieve hallucinaties ervaart. Het zich opdringen van herinneringen kan resulteren in extreme aandachtsstrategieën om overspoeling door de herinneringen te voorkomen. Het regelmatig toepassen van extreme aandachtsstrategieën verhoogt het risico op zowel de ervaring van visuele als auditieve hallucinaties.

Hallucinaties en tijd-sprongen kunnen beiden begrepen worden als een 'verstoring' van het bewustzijn, als een uitvloeisel van het toepassen van extreme aandachtsstrategieën. Enkele onderzoeksresultaten geven aan dat een tijd-sprong een extremere vorm van verstoring van het bewustzijn is dan een hallucinatie. Tijdens een hallucinatie is het bewustzijn in staat op te merken wat er gaande is, tijdens de ervaring van een time-gap is 'het vigerende bewustzijn' hier niet toe in staat.

Een jong kind moet leren de werkelijkheid te onderscheiden van eigen interne voorstellingen. De meeste kinderen leren voor het zevende jaar dit onderscheid te maken, maar sommige kinderen leren het misschien nooit, omdat de werkelijkheid te pijnlijk voor hen is. We vinden dat met name auditieve hallucinaties frequenter voorkomen bij volwassenen die voor het zevende jaar door de eigen ouders emotioneel verwaarloosd, fysiek of seksueel misbruikt zijn. Vanzelfsprekend moet men een zekere reserve in acht nemen ten opzichte van rapportages van levensomstandigheden voor het zevende levensjaar. Het meest vaststaande gegeven is dat deze vrouwen zich niet kunnen herinneren als kind ooit een periode te hebben meegemaakt, waarin zij niet werden verwaarloosd of misbruikt. De bevindingen suggereren dat deze vrouwen nooit het onderscheid hebben leren maken tussen de werkelijkheid en de eigen interne voorstellingen.

Bij het maken van een onderscheid tussen werkelijkheid en interne voorstelling, verdisconteren alle mensen de aanwezige informatie over het denkbeeldigheids dan wel werkelijkheids karakter van een ervaring. Om tot een goed oordeel te komen is het belangrijk dat misleidende informatie afwezig is. Sommige vrouwen vertelden expliciet dat zij lange tijd beelden hadden van seksueel misbruik, maar niet wisten of deze beelden herinneringen aan daadwerkelijke gebeurtenissen betroffen. Het lijkt ons ook geen eenvoudige taak om in een dergelijk geval een oordeel te vormen over het werkelijkheids karakter van deze beelden. De meeste vrouwen die zich in eerste instantie niets herinnerden en beelden van seksueel misbruik kregen, startten uitgebreide zoek- en verificatie-procedures. Zij bespraken details van de beelden, die meer toegankelijk zijn voor verificatie dan het seksuele misbruik op zich, met zusters, tantes, broers, grootmoeders etc. Zo hoopten ze meer inzicht te krijgen in de vraag of deze beelden daadwerkelijke gebeurtenissen weergaven. Onzekerheid over het werkelijkskarakter van beelden van seksueel misbruik, maakte dat sommige vrouwen niet aan het onderzoek wilden meewerken of sommige beelden niet als herinneringen wilden aanmerken. Deze vrouwen moeten in de eerste plaats betrouwbare personen zien te vinden die in staat zijn bepaalde details van beelden te bevestigen of te ontkennen. Het valt te verwachten dat sommige van deze vrouwen geen betrouwbare anderen kunnen vinden om deze rol te vervullen. Verscheidene psychiaters zijn van mening dat het niet van belang is of beelden van seksuele kindermishandeling berusten op werkelijke gebeurtenissen dan wel op verbeelding. We zijn het met deze stelling niet eens, omdat de therapeutische processen in beide situaties verschillend zullen moeten zijn. Onze resultaten geven aan dat de hallucinaties zullen verminderen, naarmate de verdringing afneemt. Dit suggeert dat, in het geval de beelden werkelijke gebeurtenissen weerspiegelen, een therapie gericht op vermindering van verdringing van visuele herinneringen, geassocieerde gevoelens en aandachtsstrategieën, meer kans van slagen biedt dan een therapie waarin aangenomen wordt dat het maken van een onderscheid tussen werkelijkheid en interne voorstellingen er niet veel toe doet. Bovendien zullen vrouwen die ontdekt hebben dat hun beelden betrekking hebben op daadwerkelijke gebeurtenissen, hoogstwaarschijnlijk hun houding veranderen ten opzichte van de dader en hun (andere) familieleden. Zij zullen een proces starten waarbij de relaties met hun familieleden opnieuw worden gedefinieerd. In het geval de vrouw steun krijgt van een of meer familieleden kan dit voor haar een verlichting betekenen van een deel van de problemen die zij heeft.

Hoofdstuk 7 gaat over de samenhang tussen seksueel misbruik en zichzelfbeschadigend gedrag. Theorieën die een verklaring geven voor deze samenhang en de hypothesen die daaruit zijn afgeleid, worden systematisch behandeld.

We vinden dat de helft van de vrouwen die meededen aan ons onderzoek zichzelf ooit weleens hebben beschadigd, waarbij een kwart van alle vrouwen dit regelmatig doen of deden. Zelf-beschadiging wordt gezien als sociaal zeer onwenselijk en er zijn geen goede studies gedaan naar dit gedrag met steekproeven uit 'algemene' bevolkingsgroepen. Een derde van de vrouwen met zelf-beschadigend gedrag begon hiermee in de kindertijd. Dergelijk gedrag bij kinderen tussen 3 en 13 jaar is vrij zeldzaam en kan een signaal vormen voor de omgeving dat er sprake is van fysiek of seksueel misbruik. De meerderheid van de vrouwen die zichzelf beschadigden vertelde dat zij onbeheersbare angsten, opwinding of depersonalisatie-gevoelens hadden rondom de zelf-beschadiging. Bovendien meldde een deel van de vrouwen, die streden met de impulsen tot zelf-beschadiging, in verband hiermee hallucinaties, levendige dromen, of tijdsprongen. Ongeveer een derde van de vrouwen die zichzelf beschadigden gaf tijdens het interview een verband aan tussen de seksuele kindermishandeling en de zelf-beschadiging. Sommige vrouwen hadden zich als kind beschadigd met de bedoeling het seksuele misbruik te voorkomen, bij anderen vormde dit gedrag een signaal voor de omgeving. Sommige volwassen vrouwen voelden (onweerstaanbare) impulsen tot zelf-beschadiging opkomen naar aanleiding van flashbacks over het seksuele misbruik.

Theorieën over de gevonden verbanden tussen zelf-beschadiging en (seksueel) misbruik in de kindertijd kunnen als volgt worden gegroepeerd: (a) Schaamte en schuldgevoelens, opgewekt door het seksuele misbruik, lokken zelf-beschadiging uit. (b) Woedegevoelens, opgewekt door fysiek en seksueel misbruik, lokken zelf-beschadiging uit. (c) Zelf-beschadiging is een uitingsvorm van de 'borderline karakter stoornis' en komt voort uit verwaarlozing en misbruik door de ouders op zeer jonge leeftijd.

We vinden dat de zogenaamde 'schuldgevoelens' opwekkende karakteristieken van het seksuele misbruik samenhangen met de frequentie van zelf-beschadiging. Met name als vrouwen expliciet verzet hadden geboden tegen de dader, waren zij minder geneigd zichzelf te beschadigen. Bovendien bleek er een behoorlijke interactie te bestaan tussen de zwaarte van de gehanteerde dwangmiddelen en de expliciteit waarmee verzet was geboden, met betrekking tot de frequentie van zelf-beschadiging. Deze gegevens geven aanleiding tot het volgende model van de psychische processen die de seksuele kindermishandeling verbinden met de zelf-beschadiging: Hoe ernstiger het karakter van het seksuele misbruik is geweest, hoe groter de kans dat opdringende herinneringen gepaard gaan met complexe en overweldigende emoties. Of een vrouw zichzelf beschadigt of niet bij het ervaren van dergelijke overweldigende emoties, hangt af van de eveneens door de herinneringen opgewekte schaamte en schuld gevoelens. Dit psychologisch proces voltrekt zich niet noodzakelijkerwijs bewust.

Sommige therapeuten observeerden dat schuld- en schaamtegevoelens vrijwel altijd aanwezig zijn bij vrouwen die als kind seksueel zijn misbruikt. Zij veronderstellen dat dergelijke gevoelens een bescherming geven tegen gevoelens van totale machteloosheid. De schuldgevoelens geven de vrouwen de illusie dat zij zelf iets aan de situatie hadden kunnen veranderen. Deze interpretatie suggereert dat intra-psychische processen een oorzaak vormen voor schuldgevoelens. We weten echter niet of deze gevoelens enkel en alleen leven bij de seksueel misbruikte vrouwen. Schuldgevoelens kunnen ook het antwoord weerspiegelen op de schuldvraag zoals dit gegeven werd binnen het gezin van herkomst of zelfs een weerslag zijn van de houding ten opzichte van seksueel misbruik in de cultuur in het algemeen. Bijvoorbeeld, bij een verkrachtingsaangifte bij de politie, was (is?) het een belangrijke vraag of de vrouw fysiek weerstand had geboden tegen de verkrachter. Eeuwenlang gold dat een verkrachting slechts als verkrachting werd aangemerkt indien de vrouw zich fysiek had verzet. Dat vrouwen zich schuldig voelen over het seksuele misbruik waartegen zij zich niet expliciet hebben verzet, wijkt dus niet zo ver af van de tot voor kort algemeen geldende houding aangaande verkrachting. De duidelijk zichtbare vormen van zelf-beschadiging, zoals het zichzelf snijden, bleken gerelateerd te zijn aan de 'schuldgevoelens opwekkende' karakteristieken van het seksuele misbruik en kunnen een symbolische betekenis hebben, namelijk 'Ik zal er voor moeten bloeden'. Het is natuurlijk niet te tolereren dat jonge meisjes, die in meerderheid tussen de zeven en twaalf jaar oud waren toen zij seksueel werden misbruikt, waarbij bovendien ernstige dwangmiddelen werden toegepast door daders die ten minste 5 jaar ouder waren, met een houding worden geconfronteerd die henzelf verantwoordelijk stelt voor deze mishandeling. Het idee dat deze meisjes schuld zouden hebben, omdat zij zich niet expliciet hebben verzet, is vanzelfsprekend onhoudbaar.

Onze gegevens suggereren dat zelf-beschadiging gedeeltelijk is gebaseerd op een cognitieve beoordeling van het seksuele misbruik. Sommige vrouwen hebben redenen waarom zij zich niet direkt schuldig voelen. Bijvoorbeeld: 'Ik heb mij tot het uiterste verzet'; 'Hij was al volwassen en ik was een kind'; 'Hij heeft niet alleen mij maar ook andere meisjes seksueel misbruikt'. De indruk dat er sprake is van een cognitieve waardering van de misbruik situatie, wordt extra ondersteund door de bevinding dat de frequentie van zelf-beschadiging op een negatieve wijze samenhangt met het opleidingsniveau. Hoe hoger het opleidingsniveau van de vrouw hoe meer zij toegang heeft tot geschriften waarin staat dat de dader en niet zij verantwoordelijk is. Dit geeft hoop op resultaat bij de therapie aan sommige zichzelf beschadigende vrouwen. Als men de verantwoordelijkheid voor het seksuele misbruik daar legt waar zij hoort, namelijk op de schouders van de dader, dan is het waarschijnlijk dat dit zal bijdragen aan een vermindering in zelf-beschadiging.

We vinden dat de frequentie van zelf-beschadiging gerelateerd is aan de cumulatie van de trauma's in de kindertijd, onafhankelijk van de leeftijd van het meisje ten tijde van de traumatische ervaringen. Maar eveneens blijkt dat onder de vrouwen met chronische zelf-beschadiging zich een relatief grote groep bevindt, die voor het zevende jaar door de vader fysiek is mishandeld. Dit gegeven suggereert dat bij een deel van deze zelf-beschadigende vrouwen er sprake is van een borderline karakter stoornis. Het lijkt waarschijnlijk dat de zelf-beschadiging de weerslag is van de houding die de vrouw ten opzichte van 'zichzelf' heeft geleerd van haar vader.

Hoofdstuk 8 handelt over de samenhang tussen seksuele kindermishandeling en suicidaliteit. Theorieën, die een verklaring geven voor dit verband en de hypothesen die daaruit zijn afgeleid, worden systematisch behandeld.

We vinden dat slechts een klein gedeelte van de vrouwen (15%) nooit aan zelfmoord heeft gedacht. Betrekt men daarbij ook nog de ernst van het seksuele misbruik, dan blijken bijna alle vrouwen met een ernstig misbruikverleden gedachten over zelfmoord te hebben (gehad). Bijna de helft van de vrouwen die aan dit onderzoek meewerkten (45%) heeft een of meer keren een zelfmoordpoging ondernomen. Dit percentage is veel hoger dan het percentage vrouwen met zelfmoordpogingen in steekproeven van de algemene vrouwelijke bevolking, en stemt overeen met de bevindingen uit onderzoeken naar vrouwen met een seksueel misbruik verleden, die met de hulpverlening in aanmerking komen.

Een regelmatig geopperde verklaring voor met name de zelfmoordpoging heeft betrekking op het 'aandacht vragen'. Door middel van de zelfmoordpoging geeft de vrouw een 'hulpkreet'. Hierbij worden vaak de manipulatieve aspecten van de zelfmoordpoging benadrukt. We vinden dat met name bij kinderen de zelfmoordpoging een hulpkreet is. Het vormt een poging om te onsnappen aan liefdeloze ouders, aan levensbedreigende ervaringen en seksuele exploitatie. We vinden dat eenzelfde motief speelt bij een klein deel van de vrouwen boven de 18 jaar (15%). Bijna eenvijfde deel van de vrouwen in ons onderzoek werd na het 18-de jaar nog seksueel misbruikt en sommigen daarvan deden een zelfmoordpoging, omdat zij geen andere manier zagen om aan deze situatie te ontkomen. Andere vrouwen zaten opgesloten in een huwelijk waarin zij regelmatig werden geslagen en ook voor sommigen van hen was de zelfmoordpoging een middel om deze situatie te doen stoppen. Na een dergelijke poging werden zij opgenomen in een algemeen ziekenhuis of in een psychiatrische inrichting. Een langdurige opname impliceert dat het seksuele misbruik of de vrouwenmishandeling (tijdelijk) ophoudt. Als de hulpverlening te maken krijgt met een zelfmoordpoging moet zij erop bedacht zijn dat dit voor een poogster de enige manier is (lijkt) om te ontsnappen aan een situatie van directe mishandeling en exploitatie.

De 'geleerde hulpeloosheid' theorie levert een andere mogelijke verklaring voor het verband tussen seksuele kindermishandeling en suicidaliteit. Deze theorie is ontwikkeld aan de hand van observaties van het gedrag van dieren die onderworpen werden aan onbeheersbare elektrische schokken. Deze dieren bleven geheel passief als zij later opnieuw werden geconfronteerd met schokken, die wel beheerst konden worden. Zij bleken niet meer te reageren op signalen die aan de schokken voorafgingen, zij ondernamen tijdens de schokken geen vluchtpogingen, ook als de schokken konden worden vermeden, en zij zagen er 'depressief' uit. Later is de 'geleerde hulpeloosheid' theorie meer en meer gebruikt ter verklaring van depressief gedrag bij mensen. Deze theorie is toen herzien en hierbij verschoof de aandacht van de 'onbeheersbare' trauma's naar de 'dysfunctionele' denkbeelden. De volgende opvatting vatte post: een depressief persoon is niet geconfronteerd geweest met onbeheersbare trauma's, maar heeft foutieve denkbeelden aangeleerd, n.l. dat situaties niet beheersbaar zijn. De konsistente onderzoeksbevinding dat (seksuele) kindermishandeling gerelateerd is aan suicidaal gedrag geeft dwingend aanleiding tot een herevaluatie van de oorspronkelijke 'geleerde hulpeloosheid' theorie. In ons onderzoek geven vele vrouwen aan dat zij geen mogelijkheid zagen om aan het seksuele misbruik te ontkomen. Sommigen begonnen zich tijdens de puberteit te verzetten en hadden succes, maar voor de anderen bleek het onmogelijk enige invloed uit te oefenen op het ervaren van ongewenste seksuele handelingen. Deze vrouwen zijn als kind herhaaldelijk aan onbeheersbare trauma's onderworpen. We vinden dat de leeftijd waarop het seksuele misbruik ophield verband houdt met de ernst van de suicidaliteit en dat dit verband vooral sterk is als het seksuele misbruik bestond uit geslachtsgemeenschap.

De 'geleerde hulpeloosheid' theorie voorspelt dat vrouwen die onbeheersbaar seksueel misbruik hebben meegemaakt vaker dan anderen het slachtoffer zullen worden van mishandeling, omdat zij een verminderd vermogen hebben om op signalen van eventueel misbruik te anticiperen en minder geneigd zijn daadwerkelijke acties te ondernemen. We vinden dat een kwart van de vrouwen, die een heteroseksuele partner-relatie heeft of heeft gehad, door die partner regelmatig is geslagen. Dit is twee keer zo vaak als de prevalentie van regelmatige vrouwenmishandeling gemeld in een steekproef van de algemene vrouwelijke bevolking. Vrouwen die als kind seksueel zijn misbruikt en daarbij door hun echtgenoot regelmatig worden geslagen, doen vaker een zelfmoordpoging dan vrouwen met een sexueel misbruik verleden, die als volwassene dergelijke mishandelingen niet meemaken.

Volgens de 'geleerde hulpeloosheid' theorie zal een persoon die regelmatig is getraumatiseerd, zich hulpeloos en depressief voelen in geval van confrontaties met nieuwe trauma's. Deze reacties kunnen opgevat worden als een geconditioneerde (emotionele) respons. Een belangrijke vraag is welke nieuwe situaties 'traumatisch' zijn, d.w.z. depressies opwekken. Veelal wordt onderzoek verricht naar de samenhang tussen allerlei soorten stressvolle levensgebeurtenissen en depressiviteit. Onze gegevens suggereren dat een speciaal soort situaties een 'traumatisch' karakter hebben voor vrouwen met een seksueel misbruik verleden, n.l. door de vrouw ongewenste maar niet met geweld afgedwongen geslachtsgemeenschap. Allereerst vinden we dat vrouwen die als kind geslachtsgemeenschap hebben ervaren meer geneigd zijn tot het doen van zelfmoordpogingen dan de vrouwen die andere sexuele handelingen hebben meegemaakt. En deze relatie wordt vooral geconstateerd bij vrouwen, die getrouwd zijn of samenwonen met een man. Bovendien vinden we dat vooral die vrouwen geneigd zijn een zelfmoordpoging te doen, die ernstig seksueel misbruikt zijn door een eerste dader en daarna als kind met een tweede dader geslachtsgemeenschap hadden zonder dat deze zware dwang daartoe uitgeoefende. In het algemeen geldt voor de meeste vrouwen dat geslachtsgemeenschap de meest frekwent voorkomende seksuele ervaring is. Andere seksuele handelingen dan gemeenschap kunnen indien gewenst door vrouwen gemakkelijker worden vermeden. In veel relaties hebben vrouwen soms gemeenschap terwijl zij er niet echt zin in hebben.

Onze gegevens suggereren dat door vrouwen niet gewenste geslachtsgemeenschap in heteroseksuele partner-relaties, gevoelens van depressie en hulpeloosheid opwekken bij vrouwen die als kind seksueel misbruikt zijn. Van deze associaties kan, maar hoeft de vrouw zich niet bewust te zijn. Op basis van de 'geleerde hulpeloosheid' theorie valt te verwachten dat de vrouw zich bovendien hulpeloos kan voelen, omdat ze niet weet hoe zij de opwekking van depressieve gevoelens moet voorkomen. Verbale verslagen van vrouwen in ons onderzoek geven aan dat sommigen zich scherp bewust zijn van de 'uitzonderlijkheid' van hun gevoelens van machteloosheid. Deze combinatie van factoren lijkt bij te dragen aan het risico op suicidaal gedrag.

Bijna alle vrouwen die als kind seksueel zijn misbruikt melden dat zij aan zelfmoord hebben gedacht. Dergelijke gedachten kunnen iemand kwetsbaarder maken voor het daadwerkelijk doen van een zelfmoordpoging. De aard van het seksuele misbruik verklaart slechts een klein deel van de variantie in ernst van suicidaliteit. Het lijkt erop dat de omstandigheden waarin men zich als volwassene bevindt, en dan met name de kwaliteit van het huwelijk en de aard van de sociale ontmoetingen met mannen, bepalen of depressieve gevoelens en zelfmoordgedachten steeds weer worden opgewekt en resulteren in een of meer zelfmoordpogingen.

De appendices bevatten onder andere samenvattingen van eerder onderzoek naar seksuele kindermishandeling en respectievelijk niveau van dissociatie, hallucinaties, zelf-beschadiging en suicidaliteit.

Tot slot willen we nog enkele algemene opmerkingen maken die het gehele onderzoek betreffen. Wij stelden ons de vraag of verschillende vormen van seksuele kindermishandeling gerelateerd zijn aan verschillende soorten psychiatrische symptomen. De besproken onderzoeksresultaten laten zien dat de aard van het seksuele misbruik en de gezinssituatie waarin dit plaatsvond, het soort psychologische problemen indiceren waar vrouwen op volwassen leeftijd mee te kampen krijgen. Vrouwen die als kind seksueel zijn misbruikt vormen geen 'homogene groep' als men kijkt naar de problemen op latere leeftijd. Voor een goed begrip van de symptomatologie en voor een goede therapeutische behandeling is het noodzakelijk zorgvuldig te kijken naar de aard van de seksuele kindermishandeling en de onderliggende psychische processen die de mishandeling verbinden met het psychiatrische symptoom.

We zijn in deze studie uitgegaan van psychiatrische symptomen en niet van psychiatrische syndromen. Over het algemeen zullen vrouwen die met de psychiatrie in aanraking komen een diagnose krijgen, zoals 'borderline karakter stoornis', of 'affectieve stoornis'. Onze bevindingen laten zien dat het belangrijk is om apart aandacht te besteden aan de psychische processen achter ieder symptoom en niet te snel op generaliserende en algemene concepten terug te grijpen. Zo geven onze onderzoeksresultaten aan dat de psychische processen achter suicidaliteit en zelf-beschading bij vrouwen die als kind seksueel zijn misbruikt van elkaar verschillen, terwijl suicidaliteit en zelf-beschadiging vaak worden opgevat als 'uitingen van zelf-destructie', waarbij men aanneemt dat gelijksoortige psychische processen een rol spelen.

Bij dissociatieve stoornissen, zoals de meervoudige persoonlijkheids stoornis, veronderstelt men dat verschillende lagen van bewustzijn, de symptomen van de vrouw verklaren. Hallucinatoire ervaringen bij personen met ernstige dissociatieve stoornissen worden in deze visie opgevat als het binnen dringen van de inhoud van een afgescheiden bewustzijnslaag in het 'vigerende bewustzijn'. Hoewel wij deze verklaringswijze niet willen uitsluiten, zijn we er niet a priori van uitgegaan. We menen dat het zinvoller is op fundamenteel niveau aandacht te besteden aan theorie-vorming over en onderzoek naar bijvoorbeeld extreme aandachtsstrategieën, verstoringen in het bewust zijn, en verstoringen in irreflectieve 'self-reference' processen, dan zich te werpen op de vraag of bepaalde verschijnselen behoren tot de dissociatieve, affectieve of schizophrene stoornissen.

Vanzelfsprekend is verder onderzoek nodig om onze resultaten in een breder perspectief te plaatsen.

References

Abarbanel G. (1986). Rape and resistance. *Journal of Interpersonal Violence*, I, 1, 100-105.

Adams-Tucker C. (1982). Proximate effects of sexual abuse in childhood: A report on 28 children. *American Journal of Psychiatry*, 139, 10, 1252-1257.

Albach F. (1986). Incest als trauma: de verleidingstheorie van Freud en de gevolgen van sexuele kindermishandeling. *De Psycholoog*, 21, 557-564.

Albach F. (1991). Amnesie en herbeleving. *Maandblad voor de geestelijke Volksgezondheid*, 2, 134-153.

Albach F. (in press). Incest, trauma en hysterie, Department of psychology, University of Amsterdam, (Thesis).

Aldridge-Morris (1989). *Multiple Personality; an exercise in deception*. Lawrence Erlbaum and associates, Hove and London (UK)/Hillsdale (USA).

American Psychiatric Association (1987). *Diagnostic and statistical manual of mental disorders* . (D.S.M.-III-R, revised third edition), Washington, D.C. Author.

Andrade C. (1988). True hallucinations as a culturally sanctioned experience, *British Journal of Psychiatry*, 152, 838-839.

Arensman E. (1990) Zelfbeschadiging en suicidaal gedrag bij vrouwen: zijn er verschillen, vakgroep klinische & gezondheidspsychologie, R.U.Leiden, doctoraalscriptie.

Arkin A.M. (1981). *Sleep-talking; psychology and psychophysiology*. Hillsdale, N.J., L. Erlbaum & Associates.

Armstrong L. (1978). *Kiss Daddy goodnight*. New York: Hawthorn Press.

Asaad G. & Shapiro B. (1986). Hallucinations: Theoretical and clinical overview, *Am. J. Psychiatry*, 143, 9, 1088-1097.

Association of Sleep Disorders Centres (1979). *Diagnostic Classification of sleep and arousal disorders*, 2, 1.

Bailly L.C. (1990). *Psychotic symptoms in PTSD?*, Association pour les victimes de la repression en Exil, Paper presented at the Second European Conference on Traumatic Stress, Sept 23-27, Noordwijkerhout, The Netherlands.

Bateson G., Jackson D.D., Haley J. & Weakland J. (1956). Towards a theory of schizophrenia, Behavioral Science, 1, 251-264.

Beck J.C. & Kolk van der B A. (1987). Reports of childhood incest and current behaviour of chronically hospitalized psychotic women. *Am J Psychiatr*, 144, 11, 1474-1476.

Beelen J. (1989). *Tussen verleiden en verkrachten*. Uitgeverij An Dekker, Amsterdam.

Bennebroek Evertsz F. (1989). *Meervoudige Persoonlijkheid: een 'folie a deux'?* Department of psychology, University of Amsterdam, (internal publication).

Bentall R.P. & Slade P.D. (1985). Reality testing and auditory hallucinations: A signal detection analysis, *British Journal of Clinical Psychology,* 24, 159-169.

Bentall R.P. (1990). The illusion of reality: a review and integration of psychological research on hallucinations, *Psychological Bulletin,* 107, 1, 82-95.

Bentall R.P. (1991). The syndromes and symptoms of psychosis, in: Bentall (ed) *Reconstructing schizophrenia.* London: Methuen.

Bernstein E.M. & Putnam F.W. (1986). Development, reliability, and validity of a dissociation scale, *Journal of Nervous and Mental Disease,* 174, 727-735.

Bleuler E. (1911/1950). *Dementia praecox or the group of schizophrenias,* International University Press, monograph series on schizophrenia no.1, New York.

Bleuler M. (1978). *The schizophrenic disorders: long term patient and family studies.* New Haven: Yale University Press.

Bliss E.L. (1980). Multiple Personalities. *Arch Gen Psychiatry,* 37, 1388-1397.

Bliss E.L. (1986). *Multiple Personality, allied disorders and hypnosis.* Oxford University Press, New York, Oxford.

Boon S. & Drayer N. (1991) Diagnosing dissociative disorders in The Netherlands: A pilot study with the structured clinical interview for DSM-III-R Dissociative disorders. *Am J Psychiatry,* 148, 4, 458-462.

Boon S. & van der Hart O. (1988). Dissocieren als overlevingsstrategie bij fysiek en seksueel geweld: Trauma en dissociatie 1. *Maandblad van Geestelijke Volksgezondheid,* 11, 1197-1207.

Boon S. & van der Hart O. (1988). Het herkennen van dissociatieve stoornissen, in het bijzonder de multiple persoonlijkheid: Trauma en Dissociatie 2 *Maandblad van Geestelijke Volksgezondheid,* 11, 1208-1225.

Bowers K.S. (1984). On being unconsciously influenced and informed. In: Bowers K.S., Meichenbaum (ed.) *The unconscious reconsidered,* John Wiley & Sons, New York, Chichester, Brisbane, Toronto, Singapore.

Braun B. G. (1986). *Treatment of multiple personality disorder.* American Psychiatric Press, Washington D.C.

Braun B.G. & Sachs R.G. (1985). The development of multiple personality disorder; predisposing, precipitating and perpetrating factors, in Kluft R.P. (ed) *Childhood antecedents of multiple personality.* American Psychiatric Press.

Braun B.G. (1988). The Bask model of dissociation. *Dissociation,* 1, 1, 4-23.

Breuer J. & Freud S. (1893-1895[1974]). *Studies on hysteria.* The Pelican Freud Library, vol.3, Penguin Books.

Brière J. & Conte J. (1990). *Amnesia in adults molested as children, testing theories of repression.* Paper presented at the annual meeting of the American Psychological association, New Orleans, L.A. August 1989.

Brière J. & Runtz M. (1987). Post sexual abuse trauma. *Journal of Interpersonal Violence,* vol. 2, 4, 367-379.

Brière J. & Zaidi (1989). Sexual abuse histories and sequelae in female psychiatric emergency room patients. *Am J Psychiatry,* 146, 1606-1609.

Brière J. (1984). *The effects of childhood sexual abuse on later psychological functioning: defining a post-sexual abuse syndrome,* paper presented at the Third National Conference on Sexual Victimization of Children, Children Hospital National Medical Centre, Washington D.C.

Browne A. & Finkelhor D. (1986a). Impact of child sexual abuse: A review of the research. *Psychological Bulletin,* 99, 1, 66-77.

Browne A. & Finkelhor D. (1986b). Initial and long term effects: A review of the research. In Finkelhor D. (Ed.) *A sourcebook on child sexual abuse.* Sage publications, London.

Bryer J.B., Nelson B.A., Miller J.B. & Krol P.A. (1987). Childhood sexual and physical abuse as factors in adult psychiatric illness. *Am J Psychiatry,* 144, 1426-1430.

Buchsbaum M.S., Ingvar D.H., Kessler R. et al (1982) Cerebral glucography with positron tomography. *Arch Gen Psychiatry,* 39, 251-259.

Burgess A.W., Groth N. & McCausland M. (1981). Child sex rings. *Amer. J. Orthopsychiatry.* 51 (1), 110-119.

Burns R.B. (1979). *The self concept: theory, measurement, development and behaviour.* Long Group Limited.

Butler S. (1978). *Conspiration of silence: The trauma of incest.* San Francisco, New Glide Publications.

Cappon D. (1969). Orientational perception: III. Orientational percept distortions in depersonalization. *Amer. J. Psychiatry,* 125, 8, 1048-1055.

Carmen (Hilberman) E., Rieker P.P. & Mills T. (1984). Victims of violence and psychiatric Illness. *Am J Psychiatry* 141; 378-383.

Carroll J., Schaffer C., Spensley J., & Abramowitz S.I. (1980). Family Experiences of self-mutilating patients. *American Journal of Psychiatry,* 137-7, 852-853.

Cavaiola A.A., Schiff M. (1988). Behavioral sequelae of physical and/or sexual abuse in adolescents. *Child Abuse & Neglect,* vol. 12, 181-188.

Christianson S. & Nilsson L. (1984). Functional amnesia as induced by a psychological trauma. *Memory and Cognition,* 12, 2, 142-155.

Chu J.A. & Dill L.D. (1990). *Dissociative symptoms in relation to childhood physical and sexual abuse,* Am J Psychiatry, 147, 7, 887-892.

Cohen D. (1990). Dissociative symptoms in Jewish first and second generation. Paper presented at the *Second European Conference on Traumatic Stress,* Noordwijkerhout, The Netherlands.

Cole C.H. & Barney E.E. (1987). Safeguards and the therapeutic window. *Amer. J. Orthopsychiatry,* 57 (4), 601-609.

Conte J., Brière J. & Sexton D. (1989). *Mediators of long term symptomatology in women molested as child.* Paper presented at the 97th convention of the American Psychological Association, New Orleans.

Conte J.R. (1985). The effects of child sexual abuse on children: A critique and suggestions for future research. *Victomology: An International Journal*, 10, 110-130.

Coons P.H., Ascher-Svanum H., & Bellis K. (1986). Self-amputation of the female breast. *Psychosomatics*, 27, 667-668.

Coons P.M. & Milstein V. (1986). Psychosexual disturbances in multiple personality; characteristics, etiology and treatment. *J Clin Psychiatry*, 47, 106-110.

Courtois C.A. (1988). *Healing the incest wound*. W.W. Norton & Company, New York, London.

De Young M. (1982). Self-injurious behaviour in incest victims: a research note. *Child Welfare*, vol. LXIII, 8, 576-583.

Diekstra R.F.W. (1981). *Over suicide*. Samson, Alphen aan den Rijn.

Draijer N. (1985). De omvang van seksueel misbruik van kinderen in het gezin. *Maandblad Geestelijke Volksgezondheid*, 40, 6, 587-608.

Draijer N. (1988). *Seksueel misbruik door verwanten*. Ministerie van Sociale Zaken en Werkgelegenheid, Den Haag.

Draijer N. (1990). *Sexuele traumatisering in de jeugd; gevolgen op lange termijn van seksueel misbruik van meisjes door verwanten*, SUA, Amsterdam.

Edelman G.M. (1989). *The remembered present*, Basic Books Inc., New York.

Eeland K. & Woelinga H. (1991) Praktische richtlijnen voor de hulpverlening bij seksueel misbruik van kinderen, *VU University Press*.

Egmond M. van (1988) *De beoordeling van suiciderisico door de huisarts*. Department of psychology, University of Leiden, (Thesis).

Egmond M. van, Garnefski N., Jonker D.J.L., & Diekstra R.F.W. (1990). *Predictie van recidiverend suicidaal gedrag bij vrouwen*, Department of Psychology, Rijks Universiteit Leiden (internal publication).

Egmond M. van, Jonker D.J.L. (1988). Seksueel misbruik en lichamelijke mishandeling: risicofactoren voor (recidiverend) suicidaal gedrag bij vrouwen? *Tijdschrift voor Psychiatrie*, 30, (1), 21-38.

Ellenberger H.F. (1970). *The discovery of the unconscious*, Basic Books Inc., New York.

Ensink B.J. & Albach F. (1983). *Angst voor sexueel geweld; van overdreven angst naar gerechtvaardigde woede*. Werkgroep Vrouwenstudies van de F.S.W., D.S.W.O. publicatie, Rijks Universiteit Leiden.

Ensink B.J. & van Buuren E.T. (1987). Van overdreven angst naar gerechtvaardigde woede. In: Bruinsma, Leuw, Lissenberg and van Vliet (ed.) *Vrouw en Criminaliteit*, Boom Meppel, Amsterdam.

Ensink B.J. (1987) Enkele langdurige emotionele verschijnselen van sexuele kindermishandeling, in: *Incest- Cursusboek Boerhave Commissie*, Faculteit der Geneeskunde, Rijks Universiteit Leiden.

Ensink B.J. (1990) Child sexual abuse, dissociation and mental health care for women, in: (ed) Foeken I. *On love and violence*, Stichting De Maan, Amsterdam.

Ensink B.J. (1990) Dissociatieve verschijnselen bij sexueel misbruikte vrouwen, in: Baartman, Burgess & Rümke (Eds) *Incest en hulpverlening*, Acco, Amersfoort/Leuven.

Ensink B.J. and Otterloo D.van (1989). A validation study of the D.E.S. in the Netherlands. *Dissociation*, 2, 4, 221-223.

Escher A.D.M.A.C. & Romme M.A.J. (1989). Stemmen horen. *TVZ; het vakblad voor verpleging*, 14, 784-777.

Fahy T.A. (1988). The diagnosis of multiple Personality Disorder: a critical review. *British Journal of Psychiatry*, 153, 597-606.

Favazza A.R. and Conterio K. (1989). Female habitual self-mutilators. *Acta Psychiatr Scand.*, 79, 283-289.

Favazza A.R. and Favazza B. (1987). *Bodies under siege*. The Johns Hopkins University, Baltimore and London.

Finkelhor D. & Browne A. (1986). Initial and long term effects: A conceptual framework. In Finkelhor D. (ed.) *A sourcebook on child sexual abuse*. Sage publications, London.

Finkelhor D. (1979). *Sexually victimized children*. New York: Free Press.

Finkelhor D. (1979). What's wrong with sex between adults and children? *Amer J Orthopsychiatry*, 49 (4), 692-697.

Finkelhor D. (1986). *A sourcebook on child sexual abuse*. Sage Publications, Beverly Hills, London, New Delhi.

Finkelhor D. (1986). Designing new studies" In: Finkelhor D, (Ed) *A sourcebook on child sexual abuse*, Sage Publications, Beverly Hills, London, New Delhi.

Finkelhor D. (1987). The trauma of child sexual abuse: two models. *Journal of Interpersonal violence*, .2, 4, 348-366.

Fleiss J.L., Cohen J. & Everitt B.S. (1969). Large sample standard errors of kappa and weighted kappa. *Psychol Bull*, 72, 323-327.

Foeken I. (1987). Incestconfrontaties. *Maandblad voor de Geestelijke Volksgezondheid*, 11, 1221-1228.

Frankel F.H. (1990). Hypnotizability and dissociation. *Am J Psychiatry*, 147, 823-829.

Frenken J. & van Stolk B. (1987). *Hulpverleners en incestslachtoffers*. Van Loghum Slaterus, Deventer.

Freud S. (1896). *Zur Aetiologie der Hysterie*, Gesammelte Werke, Band 1, Fisher Verlag.

Freud S. (1905) My views on the part played by sexuality in the aetiology of neuroses In: *Freud, Sexuality and the psychology of love*, Collier Books, New York, 1963.

Freud S. (1923[1960]). *The ego and the id*, revised and newly edited by James Strachey, W.W.Norton& Company, Inc., New York.

Freud S. (1933[1960]). *Vorlesungen zur Einführung in die Psychoanalyse und neue Folge*, studienausgabe, S.Fischer Verlag.

Friedrich W.N., Urquiza A.J. & Beilke R.L. (1986). Behaviour problems in sexually abused young children. *Journal of Pediatric Psychology*, 2, 1, 47-57.

Frijda N.H. (1986). *The emotions*. Cambridge University Press, Cambridge.

Frischholz E.J. (1985). The relationship among dissociation, hypnosis, and child abuse in the development of multiple personality disorder, in (ed) Kluft R.P., *Childhood antecedents of multiple personality*, American Press Association, Washington D.C.

Fromuth M.E. (1986). The relationship of childhood sexual abuse with later psychological and sexual adjustment in a sample of college women. *Child Abuse & Neglect*, 10, 5-15.

Garber J., Seligman M.E.P. (1980). *Human helplessness; theory and applications*. Academic Press, New York, London, Toronto, Sydney, San Francisco.

Gelinas D.J. (1981). Identification and treatment of incest victims, in: Howel E. and Bayes M. (Ed.) *Women and mental health*. Basic Books, New York.

Gelinas D.J. (1983). The persisting negative effects of incest, *Psychiatry*, 46, 312-332.

Gergen K.J. (1971). *The self-concept*. Holt, Rinehart & Winston.

Glaser B.G. and Strauss (1971). *The discovery of grounded theory: strategies for qualitative research*. Aldine Publishing Company, Chicago.

Goodwin J. (1982). *Sexual abuse/incest victims and their families*. Boston, John Wright-PSG.

Goodwin J. (1985). Post-traumatic symptoms in incest victims, in: Pynoos R. (ed.) *Post-traumatic syndromes in children*. Washington: American Psychiatric Press, 155-168.

Goodwin J., Cheeves K. & Connell V. (1987). *Defining a syndrome of severe symptoms in survivors of extreme incestuous abuse*. Paper presented at the Fourth Annual Meeting of the International Society for the study of Multiple Personality and Dissociative Disorders, Chicago, Illino.is.

Goodwin J., McCarthy T. & DiVasto P. (1981). Prior incest in mothers of abused children. *International Journal of Child Abuse and Neglect.*, 5, 87-95.

Goodwin J.M., Cheeves K. & Connell V. (1988). *Borderline and other severe symptoms in adult survivors of incestuous abuse* (internal publication).

Gordon L. & O'Kleefe P. (1984). Incest as a form of family violence: Evidence from historical case records. *Journal of marriage and the family*, 27-33.

Greenspan G.S. and Samuel S.E. (1989). Self-cutting after rape. *American Journal of Psychiatry*, 146, 6, 789-790.

Groot A.D. de (1961). *Methodologie: grondslagen van onderzoek en denken in de gedragswetenschappen*. Mounton & Co. s' Gravenhage.

Goozen S. van (1987) *Desorientatie en depersonalizatie*, Department of Psychology, University of Amsterdam, (doktoraal scriptie).

Hart O. van der & Boon S. (1990). Contemporary interest in multiple personality and child abuse in the Netherlands. *Dissociation*, 3, 34-37.

Hart O. van der (Ed.) (1987). *Workshop Diagnosis and treatment of dissociative and post-traumatic stress disorders*. Post Academisch Onderwijs Geneeskunde, Vrije Universiteit, Amsterdam (internal publication).

Hartmann E. (1984). *The nightmare*, Basic Books, Inc. Publishers, New York.

Haugaard J.J. (1988). *The sexual child abuse of children*. Jossey-Bass Publishers, San Francisco, London.

Heerden J. van (1982). *De zorgelijke staat van het onbewuste*. Boom Meppel, Amsterdam.

Heilbrun A.B. (1980). Impaired recognition of self-expressed thought in patients with auditory hallucinations, *Journal of Abnormal psychology*, 89, 6, 728-736.

Heilbrun A.B., Blum N. & Haas M. (1983). Cognitive vulnerability to auditory hallucinations; preferred imagery mode and spatial location of sounds, *Brit. J. Psychiatry*. 143, 294-299.

Heilbrun A.B., Diller R., Fleming R.& Slade L. (1986). Strategies of disattention and auditory hallucinations in schizophrenics. *The Journal of nervous and mental disease,* 174, 5, 265-273.

Herman J.L. & Hirschman L. (1977). Father-daughter incest. *Signs,* 2, 4, 735-756.

Herman J.L. (1981). *Father-daughter incest*. Harvard University Press, Cambridge, Massachusetts and London, England.

Herman J.L.& van der Kolk (1987). Traumatic antecedents of borderline personality, in: Kolk B.A. van der (ed.), *Psychological trauma*. American Psychiatric Press, inc., Washington, D.C.

Herman J.L., Perry C. & van der Kolk B.A. (1989). Childhood trauma in borderline personality disorder, *Am J Psychiatr,* 146:4, 490-495.

Herman J.L., Russell D. & Trocki K. (1986). Long term effects of Incestuous Abuse in childhood. *Am J Psychiatr, 143:10,* 1293-1296.

Heus P. de (1989). *Kognitie en depressie; studies naar de aangeleerde hulpeloosheidtheorie en Beck's kognitieve theorie over depressie*. Department of Psychology, University of Leiden, Thesis, (internal publication).

Heus P. de, Beer Y. de, Egmond M. van, Roode Y. (1989). Attributiestijl, stressvolle gebeurtenissen en depressie, *Nederlands Tijdschrift voor de Psychologie,* 44, 318-328.

Heus P. de, Roode Y. de, Egmond M. van (1987). Attributiestijl en depressie, *Gedrag & gezondheid,* 15, 4, 165-173.

Heus P. de, Rooijackers B. (1990). Disfunctionele attitudes, stressvolle gebeurtenissen en depressie, *Gedrag & Gezondheid,* 18 (2), 62-67.

Hilgard E.R. (1986). *Divided consciousness: Multiple controls in human thought and action*. Expanded edition, John Wiley & Sons, New York.

Hofstadter D.R. and Dennett D.C. (1981). *The mind's I*. Penguin Books, Middlesex, New York.

Hollender M.H., Hirsch S.J. (1964). Hysterical psychosis. *Am J Psychiatry,* 120, 1066-1074.

Horowitz M.J. (1975). Hallucinations: an information-processing-approach, in: Siegel and West (Eds.), *Hallucinations: behaviour, experience and theory*. Wiley, New York.

Horowitz M.J. (1976[1986]). *Stress response syndromes*. Jason Aronson Inc, Northvale, New Jersey, London.

Imbens A. & Jonker I. (1985). *Godsdienst en incest*. De Horstink, Amersfoort.

James W. (1842-1910[1983]). *The works of William James: Talks to teachers on psychology*. Harvard University Press, Cambridge, Mass.

James W. (1890[1950]). *The principles of psychology, vol.1*. Dover Publications, Inc. New York.

Janet P. (1911). *L'etat mentale des hysteriques*. Felix Alcan, Paris.

Jaynes J. (1976). *The origin of consciousness in the breakdown of the bicameral man*, Houghton Mifflin Company, Boston.

Jehu D., Klassen C. & Gazan M. (1986). Cognitive restructuring of distorted beliefs associated with child sexual abuse. *Social work practice in sexual problems*, 49-69.

Jones D.P.H. (1986). Individual therapy for the sexually abused child. *Child abuse and Neglect*, 10, 377-385

Jonker-de Putter I. (1986). *Incest, een stem, een aanklacht*. Alphen aan de Rijn, (internal publication).

Jonker-de Putter I. (1991) Als je kind misbruikt is: Moeders van seksueel mishandelde kinderen, University of Amsterdam, (Thesis).

Justice B. & Justice R. (1976) *The broken taboo*. Human Sciences Press, New York.

Kahan J. & Pattison E.M. (1984). Proposal for a distinctive diagnosis; the deliberate self-harm syndrome. *Suicide Life Threat Behav*, 14, 17-35.

Kempe R. & Kempe H. (1984). *The common secret*. New York: W.H. Freeman.

Kendall-Tackett K.A. (1987). Perpetrators and their acts: Data from 365 adults molested as children. *Child Abuse and Neglect*, vol 11, 237-245.

Kerkhof A J.F.M.& Diekstra R.F.W. (1982). *Publieke houdingen tegenover suicide* . Leiden, vakgroep Klinische Psychologie, (internal publication).

Kerkhof A.J.F.M. (1985). *Suicide en geestelijke gezondheidszorg*, Swets & Zeitlinger, Lisse.

Keyes D. (1981). *The minds of Billy Milligan*, Bantam Books, Toronto.

Kihlstrom J.F. (1984). Conscious, subconscious, unconscious: A cognitive perspective, in Bowers K.S. & Meichenbaum (Eds), *The unconscious reconsidered*. John Wiley & Sons, New York.

Kihlstrom J.F. (1985). Hypnosis, *Ann Rev.Psychol.*, 36, 385-418.

Kihlstrom J.F. (1987). *The uncognitive unconscious*, Science, 1,144-152.

Kleber R.J. (1986). *Traumatische ervaringen, gevolgen en verwerking*, Universiteit van Amsterdam, (Thesis).

Klerman G.L. and Weissman M.M. (1980). Depressions among women: their nature and causes, in: Guttentag M., Salasin S. & Belle D. (eds.) *The mental health of women.* Academic Press, New York, London, Toronto, Sydney, San Francisco.

Kluft R.P. (1985). *Childhood antecedents of multiple personality,* American Press Association. Washington D.C.

Kluft R.P. (1987). First-Rank symptoms as a diagnostic cue to multiple personality disorder, *Am J Psychiatry* 144, 3, 293-298.

Kluft R.P., Braun B.G. & Sachs R. (1984). Multiple Personality, Intrafamilial Abuse, and Family Psychiatry. *J. Fam. Psychiatry,* l.5, 4, 283-301.

Kluft R.P., Steinberg M. & Spitzer R.L. (1988). DSM III-R revisions in the dissociative disorders: an exploration of their derivation and rationale, *Dissociation,* 1 (1), 39-46.

Kolk B. van & Hart O. van der (1989). Pierre Janet and the breakdown of adaption in psychological trauma. *Am J. Psychiatry,* 146;12, 1530-1540.

Kolk B. van der & Kadish W. (1987). Amnesia, dissociation and the return of the repressed, in: Kolk B.A. van der (ed.) *Psychological trauma,* American Psychiatric Press, Inc., Washington, D.C.

Kolk B. van der (1989). The compulsion to repeat the trauma, *Psychiatric Clinics of North America,* 12, 2, 389-411.

Kolk B.A. van der (1987). *Psychological Trauma* American Psychiatric Press, Washington D.C.

Kolk B.A. van der (1987). The psychological consequences of overwhelming life experiences, in: Kolk B.A. van der (ed) *Psychological trauma,* American Psychiatric Press Inc., Washington, D.C.

Kroon R. (1986). *De wereld op zijn kop; een literatuurstudie naar parentificatie en incest,* Department of Psychology, University of Amsterdam (doktoraal scriptie).

Kuiper P.C. (1973). *Hoofdsom der psychiatrie.* Bijleveld, Utrecht.

Laing R.D. & Esterson A. (1964). *Sanity, madness and the family: families of schizophrenia,* A Pelican Book.

Landis J. (1956). Experiences of 500 children with adult sexual deviants, *Psychiatric Quarterly supplement,* 30, 91-109.

Lewinsohn P.M. & Rosenbaum M. (1987). Recall of parental behaviour by acute depressives, remitted depressives and nondepressives. *Journal of Personality and Social Psychology,* 52, 611-619.

Lichtenburcht C., Bezemer W. & Gianotten W. (1986). *Verder na incest; hulpverlening bij het verwerken van incestervaringen.* Ambo/Baarn.

Lindberg F.H. & Distad L.J. (1985a). Post-traumatic stress disorders in women who experienced childhood incest. *Child Abuse and Neglect,* 9, 329-334.

Lindberg F.H. & Distad L.J. (1985b). Survival responses to incest: Adolescents in crisis. *Child Abuse and Neglect,* vol.9, 521-526.

Loftus E.F. & Burns T.E. (1982). Mental shock can produce retrograde amnesia. *Memory and Cognition*, 10 (4), 318-323.

Ludwig A.M. (1983). The psychobiological functions of dissociation. *American Journal of clinical hypnosis*, 26, 2, 93-99.

MacFarlene, K. & Korbin J. (1983). Confronting the incest secret long after the fact: a family study of multiple victimization with strategies for intervention. *Child abuse and neglect*, 7, 225-240.

MacNab B.I.E. (1987) *Perception of phobia and phobics*, Department of psychology, University of Amsterdam, (Thesis).

Mannarino A.P. & Cohen J.A. (1986). A clinical-demographic study of sexually abused children. *Child Abuse and Neglect*, 10, 17-23.

Meiselman K.C. (1980). Personality Characteristics of Incest history psychotherapy patients: A research note. *Archives of Sexual Behavior*, 9, 3., 195-197.

Mellor C.S. (1970). First rank symptoms of schizophrenia. *Brit.J.Psychiatry*, 117, 15-23.

Mintz S. & Alpert M. (1972). Imagery vividness, reality testing, and schizophrenic hallucinations. *Journal of Abnormal psychology,* 79, 3, 310-316.

Moffaert M.van (1989). De psychiatrische betekenis van de lokalisatie van cutane artifacten *Tijdschrift voor Psychiatrie*, 31, 7, 430-444.

Mrazek P.B. & Mrazek D.A. (1981). The effects of child sexual experiences: a review and synthesis of research. In: Constantine L.L. & Martinson F.M. (eds.) *Children and sex, New Findings New Perspectives*. Boston: Little, Brown & Co.

Mrazek P.J., Lynch M.A. & Bentovim A. (1983). Sexual abuse of children in the United Kingdom. *Child Abuse & Neglect*, 7, 147-153.

Muller N. (1989). *Ik bloed dus ik leef!*. Departement of Psychology, University of Amsterdam, (dotoraal scriptie).

Nederhof A.J. (1981). *Some sources of artifact in social science research; non-response, volunteering, and research experience of subjects*, DSWO-press, Rijks Universiteit Leiden, (Thesis,).

Nicolai N. (1991) Incest als trauma: Implicaties en consequenties voor de behandeling. *Tijdschrift voor psychotherapie*, 17, 1, 12-30.

Noordenbos G. (1987). *Onbegrensd lijnen; een onderzoek naar culturele en sexespecifieke factoren in de ontwikkeling van anorexia nervosa*. DSWO Press, Rijks Universiteit Leiden (Thesis).

Noyes R., Hoenk P.R. & Kupperman (1977). Depersonalization in accident victims and psychiatric patients. *Journal of nervous and Mental disease*, 164, 6, 401-407.

Otterloo D.van (1987). *Onderzoek naar de validiteit en de betrouwbaarheid van een dissociatie vragenlijst*. Department of Psychology, University of Amsterdam, (doktoraal scriptie).

Panksepp J., Normansell L., Herman B., Bishop P. & Crepeau (1988). Neural and neurochemical control of the separation distress call, in: Newman J.D. (ed.) *The physiological control of mammalian vocalization.* Plenum Press, New York, 263-299.

Parkin A.J. (1987). *Memory and Amnesia.* Basil Blackwell, Oxford.

Paykel E.S., Prusoff B.A.& Myers (1975). Suicide attempts and recent life events; a controlled comparisation. *Arch Gen Psychiatry,* 32, 327-333.

Pennebaker J.W. (1983). *The psychology of physical symptoms.* Springer Verlag, New York.

Pennebaker J.W., Hughes C.F. & O'Heeron (1987). The psychophysiology of confession: Linking inhibitory and psychosomatic processes. *Journal of Personality and Social Psychology,* 52, 4, 781-793.

Piaget J. (1974). *The child and reality.* Muller, London.

Pilowsky D. & Chambers W. (1986). *Hallucinations in children.* American Psychiatric Press, Washington D.C.

Pitman R.K., van der Kolk B.A., Orr S.P., Greenberg M.S. (1990). Naloxone-reversible analgesic response to combat-related stimuli in posttraumatic stress disorder. *Arch Gen Psychiatry,* 47, 541-544.

Prince M. (1906[1968])). *The dissociation of a personality.* Johnson Reprint Corporation, New York.

Putnam F.W. (1984). The psychophysiologic investigation of multiple personality disorder; a review. *Psychiatric Clinics of North America,* 7, 31-39.

Putnam F.W. (1985). Dissociation as response to extreme trauma, in: Kluft R.P. (ed) *Childhood antecedents of multiple personality,* American Press Association, Washington D.C.

Putnam F.W. (1989). *Diagnosis & Treatment of Multiple Personality Disorder.* The Guilford Press, New York London.

Putnam F.W. Guroff J.J., Silberman E.K., Barbaran L & Post R.M. (1986). The clinical phenomenology of Multiple Personality Disorder: review of 100 recent cases. *Journal of Clinical Psychiatry,* 47, 285-293.

Rappard M. van (1988). *Tot hier en niet verder; verzet van mishandelde vrouwen.* Ambo/Baarn.

Remell S.A. (in press). *Adult females sexually molested as children and youth: differential effects to sexual functioning, level of dissociation, and relationship satisfaction.* University of Texas at Tyler (internal publication).

Ribberink M.L. & Slurink G.E. (1988). *Seksueel geweld en gynaecologische klachten,* vakgroep clinische psychologie, Rijks Universiteit Utrecht, (doktoraal scriptie).

Rijnaarts J. (1987). *Dochters van Lot.* Rainbow Pocketboeken, Amsterdam.

Robert P., Ellul E., Vernet J.P., Desportes J., Lecleire C., Mollo E. & Darcourt G. (1989). Differenciation des psychoses hallucinatoires chroniques et des psychoses dissociatives a partir du test de Rorschach. *Psychiatry & Psychobiology,* 4, 2, 91-99.

Romkes R. (1989). *Geweld tegen vrouwen in heterosexuele relaties: een landelijk onderzoek naar de omvang, de aard, de gevolgen en de achtergronden.* SUA, Amsterdam.

Romme M.A.J. and Escher A.D.M.A.C. (1989). Hearing voices, *Schizophrenia bulletin,* vol.15, no.2, 209-216.

Romme M.A.J. and Escher A.D.M.A.C. (1990). *Stemmen horen accepteren, internal publication,* Vakgroep Sociale Psychiatrie, Rijks Universiteit Limburg, (interne publicatie).

Rosenbaum M. (1980). The role of the term schizophrenia in the decline of diagnoses of multiple personality. *Arch Gen Psychiatry,* 37, 1383-1385.

Ross C.A & Norton G.R. (1988). Multiple personality disorder patients with a prior diagnosis of schizophrenia. *Dissociation,* 1, 2, 39-42.

Ross C.A., Heber S.R.N., Norton N., & Anderson G. (1989). Differences between multiple personality disorder and other diagnostic groups on structured interview. *The Journal of Nervous and Mental Disease,* 177, 8, 487-491.

Ross C.A., Miller S.D., Reagor P., Bjornson L., Frase G.A. & Anderson G. (1990). *Multicenter structured interview data on 102 cases of multiple personality disorder,* (internal publication).

Ross C.A., Norton G.R. & Wozney K. (1989). Multiple Personality Disorder: An analysis of 236 cases. *Can. J. Psychiatry,* 34, 413-418.

Ross C.A., Ryan L., Anderson G., Ross D. & Hardy L. (1989). Dissociative Experiences in adolescents and college students, *Dissociation,* 2,.4, 240-243.

Russell D.E.H. (1984). The prevalence and seriousness of incestuous abuse: stepfathers versus biological fathers, *Child Abuse & Neglect,* 8, 15-22.

Russell D.E.H. (1986). *The secret trauma.* Basic Books Inc. Publishers, New York.

Sacks M.H., Carpenter W.T., Strauss J.S. & Bethesda (1974). Recovery from delusions, *Arch Gen Psychiatry,* 30, 117-120.

Saltman V and Solomon R.S. (1982). Incest and the multiple personality *Psychological Reports,* 50, 1127-1141.

Sandfort Th. (1982). *Retrospectie als methode van dataverzameling; een overzicht van literatuur met betrekking tot de vraag of retrospectie valide en betrouwbare data op kan leveren.* Rijks Universiteit Utrecht: IKPP, (internal publication).

Sandfort Th. (1988). *Het belang van de ervaring.* Homostudies, Rijks Universiteit Utrecht, (Thesis).

Schatzman M. (1973). *Soul murder: persecution in the family,* Penguin Books, Middlesex.

Scheppele K.L. and Bart P.B. (1983). Through women's eyes: defining danger in the wake of sexual assault, *Journal of social issues,* 39, 2, 163-81.

Schneider K. (1959). *Clinical psychology.* Grune & Stratton, New York.

Schreiber F.R. (1973[1980]). *Sybil.* Bruna & Zoon (ned. vertaling), Utrecht/Antwerpen.

Seligman M.E.P (1975). *Helplessness; on depression, development and death*, Freeman and Company, San Francisco.

Sgroi S.M., Blick L.C. & Porter F.S. (1982). A conceptual framework for child sexual abuse, in Sgroi S.M. (ed.) *Handbook of clinical intervention in child sexual abuse.* Lexington, MA: D.C.Health.

Shapiro S. (1987). Self-mutilation and self-blame in incest victims. *American Journal of Psychotherapy*, XLI, 1, 47-54.

Shean G. (1982). Cognition, emotion, and schizophrenia, in: Neufeld R.W.J. (ed.) *Psychological stress and psychopathology*, McGraw-Hill Book Company.

Shields S.A. (1986). *The body awareness questionnaire; reliability and validity.* (internal publication).

Silver R.L., Boon C. & Stones M.H. (1983). Searching for meaning in misfortune: making sense in incest. *Journal of Social Issues*, 39, 2, 81-102.

Simpson C.A. and Porter G.L. (1981). Self-mutilation in children and adolescents. *Bulletin of the Menninger Clinic*, 45(5), 428-438.

Slade P.D. & Bentall R.P. (1988). *Sensory deception: a scientific analysis of hallucination.* Croom Helm, London & Sydney.

Spiegel D. (1986a). Dissociating Damage, *Am.J. of Clin. Hypnosis*, 29, 2, 123-131.

Spiegel D. (1986b). Dissociation, Double Binds, and Post-traumatic Stress in Multiple personality Disorder. In: Braun B.G. (ed.) *Treatment of Multiple Personality Disorder, American Psychiatric Press,* inc. Washington, D.C.

Spiegel D., Detrick D. & Frischholz (1982). Hypnotizability and Psychopathology. *Am J Psychiatry*, 139-4, 431-437.

Spiegel D., Hunt T., & Dondershine J.D. (1988). Dissociation and hypnotizability in posttraumatic stress disorder. *Am J Psychiatry*, 145, 3, 301-305.

Spring B. & Coons H. (1982). Stress as a precursor of schizophrenic episodes, in: Neufeld R.W.J. (ed.) *Psychological stress and psychopathology*, McGraw-Hill Book Company.

Steinberg M., Rounsaville B. & Cicchetti D.V. (1990). The structured clinical interview for DSM-III-R Dissociative disorders: preliminary report on a new diagnostic Instrument. *Am J Psychiatry, 147*, 1, 76-82.

Stichting De Maan (1989). *Zie, De Maan schijnt..; meerjarenverslag 1986-1988*, Amsterdam, (internal publication).

Stolk van B. and Frenken J. (1986). Als kind met de kinderen; een netwerk van incestueuze en pedoseksuele verhoudingen, *Maandblad van de geestelijke Volksgezondheid*, 7, 8, 691-724.

Strauss M.A., Gelles R. & Steinmetz S. (1980). *Behind closed doors: violence in the American family*, Garden City, NY: Double Day.

Strauss J.S. & Bethesda (1969). Hallucinations and delusions as points on continua function. *Arch Gen Psychiatry*, 21, 581-587.

Summit R. & Kryso J. (1978). Sexual abuse of children; a clinical spectrum, *Amer.J. Orthopsychiatry.* 48 (2), 237-251.

Summit R.C. (1983). The child sexual abuse accommodation syndrome. *Child Abuse and Neglect*, 7, 177-193.

Thiel P. (1988) De behandeling van slachtoffers van verkrachting en incest. *Tijdschrift voor gedragstherapie,* 21, 4, 295-317.

Thigpen C.H., Cleckley H.M. (1957). *The three faces of Eve.* Secker & Warburg, London.

Vennix P. (1983). Seksueel misbruik van kinderen door volwassenen, in: Moors, J. and Wemekamp, H. (red.) *Handen thuis. Opstellen voor hulpverleners over geweld.* Deventer; Van Loghum Slaterus.

Vereniging Tegen Sexuele Kindermishandeling binnen het Gezin (1983). *De straf op zwijgen is levenslang.* Feministische Uitgeverij SARA, Amsterdam.

Verhoeff J. (1990). Voorwoord, in: Romme M.A.J.&Escher A.D.M.A.C. (Eds) *Stemmen horen accepteren,* vakgroep sociale psychiatry, Rijks Universiteit Limburg (internal publication).

Vries S. de (1990). *Verslag van een onderzoeksstage.* internal publication, vakgroep psychonomie, Department of psychology, University of Amsterdam, (doktoraal stage).

Vries S. de (1992). Stemmen horen. Department of psychology, University of Amsterdam, (doktoraal scriptie).

Walsh B.W. & Rosen P.M. (1988). *Self-mutilation; theory, research and treatment.* The Guilford Press, New York and London.

Wenstedt A.A., Wolken E.M. & van der Staak C.P.F. (1988). Spanning om te snijden. *Tijdschrift voor Psychiatrie,* June, 352-363.

West L.J. (1962). A general theory of hallucinations and dreams, in L.J.West (ed.) *Hallucinations.* Grune & Stratton, New York.

West L.J. (1975). A clinical and theoretical overview of hallucinatory phenomena, in R.K. Siegel & L.J. West (Eds.) *Hallucinations: behaviour, experience and theory.* Wiley, New York.

Wilkes K.V. (1988). *Real people; personality without thought experiments,* Clarendon Press Oxford.

Wing J.K., Cooper J.E. & Sartorius N. (1974). *Measurement and classification of psychiatric symptoms,* Cambridge University Press, Cambridge.

Wolters G. & van der Heijden A.H.C. (1989). Herinneren, in: van Leijden J. (ed.) *Psychologische functieleer,* Van Loghum Slaterus.

Wyatt G.L. & Peters S D. (1986). Issues in the definition of child sexual abuse in prevalence research. *Child Abuse and Neglect,* 10, 231-240.

Appendices

Appendix 2.1a : Contact persons cooperating in our study

Contact persons:

Tegen Haar Wil Amsterdam: Gonnie and Bernardette.

Vereniging Tegen Sexuele Kindermishandeling: Ineke Jonkers and Judith Rothen.

Stichting De Maan: Ingrid Foeken.

RIAGG's: Nelleke Nicolai, Ineke Faberij.

RIAGG-Gelderland: Margot van der Linden, Joke Groenenweg.

Therapist who advised during the initial interviews: Pasya Thiel.

Appendix 2.1b: Brochure 'Emotionele gevolgen van sexuele kindermishandeling'

Aan de subfaculteit Psychologie wordt in het kader van vrouwenstudies een onderzoek gedaan naar de emotionele verwerking en de gevolgen van ongewenste sexuele ervaringen in de jeugd. Sexueel misbruik is een probleem dat pas de laatste tijd bespreekbaar is geworden. Voor veel vrouwen die dit hebben meegemaakt is het moeilijk om erover te praten. Vaak schamen ze zich of zijn bang om erover te beginnen omdat ze al vroeg hebben geleerd om het geheim te houden. Soms hebben ze moeite om zich het gebeurde te herinneren en twijfelen ze aan hun herinneringen.

Sexueel misbruik kan erg pijnlijk zijn en het kan aanleiding geven tot langdurige problemen. Nog lange tijd nadat het misbruik is afgelopen kan men last blijven houden van nachtmerries en herinneringen die zich blijven opdringen. Ook andere problemen kunnen eruit voortkomen. Iemand vertelde ons dat zij een hele tijd niet gedacht had aan het misbruik. Door de televisie-uitzendingen over incest kwamen er bij haar allerlei beelden over het gebeurde naar boven. Ze begon er s' nachts over te dromen en ook overdag was ze er steeds vaker mee bezig. Ze werd er zich bewust van dat ze in situaties die leken op het misbruik vaak helemaal verstijfde. Ze had zich in die situaties altijd onprettig gevoeld, maar ze had nooit geweten waarom. Een andere vrouw vertelde ons dat ze rond haar twintigste haast helemaal zonder gevoel was. Ze voelde zich erg vervreemd van zichzelf en was nog vaak in de war. Later was dat over gegaan. Maar toen ze die programma's op TV zag, begon ze haar problemen in verband te brengen met de incest die ze vroeger had meegemaakt.

Wij Francine Albach en Bernardine Ensink, willen over dit ssort verschijnselen graag praten met vrouwen die als meisje sexueel benaderd zijn door familieleden, of door buren, onderwijzers, of andere mannen. Wij nodigen vooral vrouwen van 18 jaar en ouder uit omdat zij het meeste kunnen vertellen over hoe men op langere termijn met die problemen omgaat.

Het onderzoek is belangrijk voor vrouwen die sexueel misbruikt zijn en die hulp zoeken bij de verwerking daarvan. Op dit moment is er over de verwerking nog niet veel bekend. Daarom is het voor hulpverleners moeilijk om misbruikte vrouwen een goede begeleiding te geven. Wanneer er in de toekomst meer bekend zal zijn over de gevolgen van sexueel misbruik, zullen hulpverleners beter in staat zijn om te herkennen waar deze vrouwen last van hebben en zullen ze hen wellicht ook beter kunnen helpen.

Wij zijn van plan om ongeveer 100 vrouwen die als kind misbruikt zijn, diepgaand te interviewen. We vragen naar verschillende klachten en problemen waarvan de vrouwen de afgelopen jaren last hebben gehad, en naar de manier waarop ze met hun verleden zijn omgegaan.

Het interview bestaat uit een gesprek met een van ons: het gesprek zal ongeveer 2 a 3 uur duren. Het gesprek zal over het algemeen bij de vrouw thuis plaats vinden, maar als zij het op prijs stelt kan het ook op het Psychologisch Instituut. Wij vergoeden in dat geval de reiskosten. Wij garanderen de anonimiteit van de vrouw. Na het interview worden alle antwoorden gecodeerd. Dit doen we zo bij iedere vrouw en wanneer het laatste interview verricht is en gecodeerd is, worden de oorspronkelijke gegevens vernietigd.

Als U bereid bent om mee te doen en/of als u nog meer wil weten over de achtergrond van het onderzoek, kunt u met ons contact opnemen. Wij zijn bereikbaar via de secretaresse van de afdeling Klinische Psychologie van ons Instituut, (tel. no.020-5253666). Als u dit formulier bij uw therapeut hebt gekregen, kunt u ook uw naam en telefoonnummer aan uw therapeut doorgeven, of u kunt uw naam in het daarvoor bestemde bakje doen.

Francine Albach,

Bernardine Ensink.

Appendix 2.2: The Post traumatic stress list, reliving the trauma, pain feelings, depersonalization, depersonalization

The scales that are used to 'measure' these symptoms had a visual analog form. Subjects' scores on individual items are coded as actual distances in millimetres from the-left hand anchor point of the 100 mm line.

I. The PTSD questionnaire consisted of 8 questions; Items are summarised in order to construct a P.T.S.D.-score. The items concern:

- Intrusion of memories about unpleasant childhood incidents.

- Reliving an incident of the past.

- Repeatedly experiencing the same nightmare.

- Feeling numb, constricted.

- Being in a daze state.

- Being absorbed in one's own thoughts.
- Attacks of extreme anxiety.
- Attacks of extreme rage.

II. Reliving the trauma consisted of 4 items, three of them were also included in the P.T.S.D.-list. Items are summarised in order to construct a reliving the trauma-score. The items concern:
- Intrusion of memories about unpleasant childhood incidents.
- Reliving an incident of the past.
- Repeatedly experiencing the same nightmare.
- Being waked-up by others, because they saw you had a nightmare.

III Pain feelings consisted of two items. Items are summarised in order to construct a painfeeling-score. The items concern:
- Not feeling any pain the first hours after an injury.
- Being able to exclude pain from consciousness in situations that are supposed to be painful (surgical operation, dentist).

IV. Depersonalization (body) consisted of 7 items. Items are summarised in order to construct a depersonalization-score. The items concerned:
- Experiencing the body as becoming smaller and smaller.
- Experiencing the body as becoming larger and larger.
- Experiencing the body as scattering.
- Experiencing the body as disappearing.
- Experiencing out of body-feelings.
- Experiencing the body as being empty.
- Experiencing the body as consisting of some parts of the body only.

V Depersonalization- 'disturbances in self-reference'. Items are summarised in order to construct a 'disturbance in self-reference' score.
- Not recognising one's face when looking in the mirror
- Having the experience of looking at one self, being separated from 'one's self'.
- Being withdrawn behind a wall, not existing in reality.

VI. Derealization consisted of 4 items. Items are summarised in order to construct a derealization-score. These items concern:
- Experiencing the world as alien.
- Experiencing a well known place as alien.
- Experiencing the world as hidden in a fog.
- Being intruded by intense and extraordinary vivid perceptions.

Appendix 2.3: Criteria distinguishing disturbances in consciousness

Criteria differentiating forms of 'disturbances or alterations in consciousness':

1. The person has or has no consciousness of the environment. This criterion differentiates dissociative phenomena, like being in a daze, time-gaps or intense depersonalization feelings from derealization feelings etc.

2. The person can or can not describe any focus of attention. This differentiates time-gaps or depersonalization feelings from daydreaming, being absorbed in thoughts, events excluded from awareness because the focus of attention was on another event.

3. The person has or has no consciousness and voluntary control over complex behaviour (like speaking, reading, writing), normally guided by consciousness. This criterion differentiates extensive time-gaps from passive behaviour, like staring, sitting down and acts that are not normally selectively attended, like driving a car or cleaning the dishes.

4. Other (naive) people do or do not notice any difference in functioning of the person: This criterion differentiates 'extensive time-gaps, derealization, depersonalization feelings from immediately evident disturbances in consciousness, like coma, fainting, pseudo-epileptical attacks or more subtle changes in consciousness, like staring, daydreaming, sleep-walking etc.

Appendix 2.4: Pearson correlations of cumulative trauma-score and resp. D.E.S and T.D.I.S.[a]

	cumulative trauma-score
	Pearson corr.
D.E.S.	.39***
T.D.I.S.	.47****
Time-gaps D.E.S.	.48****
Time-gaps T.D.I.S.	.41****

* p<.05, **p<.01, ***p<.001,****p<.0001

[a] T.D.I.S.=the sum score of statements about various different disturbances in consciousness, like depersonalization, derealization, fugues, extensive daydreaming, acting automatically and time-gaps.

Appendix 4.1: Factor analysis (Orthotran/varimax factors, oblique solution): characteristics of child sexual abuse of main perpetrator

A principal component analysis was performed on characteristics of child sexual abuse by the main perpetrator included in this study. This analysis shows that 11 characteristics (age difference, age start, age end, sexual acts, 3 measures of coercion, pregnancy, ambivalence in attitude of the perpetrator, secrecy, and explicitness of resistance) are reduced to 6 factors explaining 70,8% in the variance.

Factor #	1	2	3	4	5	6
Age difference girl-perpetrator	-	-	-	-	-	.94
Age onset C.S.A [a]	-	-	.91	-	-	-
Age-end C.S.A	.61	-	.51	-	-	-
Intrusiveness sex.acts	.77	-	-	-	-	-
Coercion in period of C.S.A.	-	.82	-	-	-	-
Coercion during C.S.A	.31	.55	-	.30	-	-
Coercion after C.S.A.	-	.66	-	-	-	-
Pregnancy	.85	-	-	-	-	-
Ambivalence	-	-	-	-	.91	-
Secrecy	-	-	-	.79	-	-
Explicitness of resistance	-	-	-	.70	.33	-

[a] C.S.A. means child sexual abuse

Factor 1 concerns intrusiveness of sexual acts, fear of or actual pregnancy and the age at with the abuse had stopped.

Factor 2 concerns the severity of coercion applied during and around sexual abuse.

Factor 3 concerns age at which sexual abuse started and ended.

Factor 4 concerns secrecy and explicitness of resistance.

Factor 5 reflects ambivalences in the attitude of the perpetrator.

Factor 6 concerns age difference between girl and perpetrator.

The intercorrelations between those 6 factors are r=.14 or less.

Appendix 4.2: Multiple regression analysis, duration sexual abuse of father, relationship between father and girl preceding sexual abuse, with severity of coercion

N=65	severity of coercion				
	ß-Coeff.	partial F-value	Stand. Coeff.	t- value	p-value
Duration of C.S.A. [a]	.23		.31	2.6	.01
Aggression preceding C.S.A.	.33	8.65	.25	2.1	.04
Multiple R=.44	1.27	8.17	.21		.0004

[a] C.S.A. means child sexual abuse.

Appendix 4.3: Multiple regression analysis, emotional neglect by mother before 7 years of age, number of perpetrators and duration of sexual abuse

N=97	hiding sexual abuse from mother				
	ß-Coeff.	partial F-value	Stand. Coeff.	t- value	p-value
Emotional neglect by mother before 7 years of age	.78	30.49	.45	5.52	.0001
Number of perpetrators	.21	11.61	.28	3.41	.001
Duration of C.S.A.[a]	.19	7.55	.22	2.75	.007
Multiple R = .65	.16	22.93	.43		.0001

[a] C.S.A. means child sexual abuse

Appendix 4.4: Cumulative and subcumulative trauma-scores, descriptive statistics

N=97	sub (cumulative) trauma-scores		
	M	s.d.	min-max
Sexual Child Abuse (0-6y)	.53	.83	0-10
Physical Aggression Perpetrator (0-6y)	.29	.52	0-6
Other family Abuse (0-6y)	.41	.55	0-2
Sexual Child Abuse (7-12y)	2.35	2.06	0-10
Physical Aggression Perpetrator (7-12y)	1.14	1.36	0-6
Other family Abuse (7-12y)	.46	.56	0-2
Sexual Child Abuse (≥13y)	1.94	2.19	0-10
Physical Aggression Perpetrator (≥13y)	1.05	1.39	0-6
Other family Abuse (≥13y)	.49	.54	0-2
Cumulative trauma-score (C.T.S.)	6.23	5.38	0-30

Appendix 5.1: Review research on kind of trauma and dissociative disorders

Authors	Numb./types of subjects	Trauma	Statistical outcomes
Saltman and Solomon (1982)	125 publications about Multiple Personality	high occurrence of violent incest	
Putnam, Guroff et al. (1986)	100 Multiple Personality Disorder	incest (83%,) repeated physical (75%) combination physical/sexual abuse (68%)	
Ross, Norton, Wozney (1989)	262 Multiple Personality Disorder	incest (79.2%) physical abuse (74.9%) combination physical/sexual abuse (67,.1%)	
Ross, Miller et al. (1990)	102 Multiple Personality Disorder	incest 90.2%	
Brière and Runtz (1987)	152 female out-patients	incest 44%	Crisis Symp.Checklist (abused vs non-abused) derealization (p<.001), spacing out (p<.009)
Herman et al. (1989)	58 psychiatrics, 21 borderlines		cumul. traumascore x D.E.S. F=5.42, p=.02
Chu and Dill (1990)	103 female psychiatric.patients	incest (36%) combination physical/sexual abuse (24%)	child phys. abuse/no abuse (F=13.31, p<.001), child sex abuse/no abuse (F=6.75, p<.01) D.E.S.
Brière and Conte (1989)	468 female out-patients	all child sexual abuse history, 60% have been amnesic for sexual abuse.	Amnesia X age first abuse incident,(F=20.6,p<.0001) severity of physical injury (F12.1, p<.001) number of perpetr (F=9.12, p<.01).
Remell (1990)	52 female out-patients	incest (100%)	Mult. Regr. freq. abuse /abuse-supporting reaction env. x D.E.S. (resp. p<.07, p<. 03)

Appendix 5.2: Principal Component Analysis with the items of the D.E.S., the Orthogonal Varimax Rotation

N = 86	Factor 1	Factor 2	Factor 3	Factor 4	Factor 5
item 1 (43)*	-	-	.34	-	-
item 2 (35)	-	-	-	-	.76
item 3 (49)	-	-	-	.52	-
item 4 (50)	-	-	-	-	-
item 5 (51)	-	-	-	.83	-
item 6 (52)	.86	-	-	-	-
item 7 (28)	-	.72	-	-	-
item 8 (53)	.32	-	-	-	-
item 9 (54)	-	-	-	-	.81
item 10 (55)	.41	-	-	-	.54
item 11 (27)	-	.45	-	-	.32
item 12 (31)	-	.50	-	-	-
item 13 (10)	-	.75	-	-	-
item 14 (2)	-	-	.70	-	-
item 15 (38)	-	-	-	-	-
item 16 (32)	-	-	-	-	-
item 17 (37)	-	-	.78	-	-
item 18 (40)	-	-	-	-	-
item 19 (26)	-	-	.34	-	-
item 20 (41)	-	-	.43	-	.32
item 21 (7)	--	-	-	.39	-
item 22 (46)	.30	-	-	-	-
item 23 (47)	.34	-	-	-	-
item 24 (39)	-	-	-	-	-
item 25 (44)	-	-	-	-	-
item 26 (56)	-	-	-	-	-
item 27 (48)	.44	-	-	-	-
item 28 (33)	-	-	-	-	-

*The first number refers to the item number in the Bernstein and Putnam questionnaire, the
  second number to the item number in our questionnaire.

Factor #	6	7	8	9	10	11
item 1 (43)*	-	-	-	.36	-	.58
item 2 (35)	-	-	-	-	-	-
item 3 (49)	-	.30	-	.43	-	.44
item 4 (50)	.41	-	.50	-	-	.42
item 5 (51)	-	-	-	-	-	-
item 6 (52)	-	-	-	-	-	-
item 7 (28)	.31	-	-	-	-	-
item 8 (53)	-	.77	-	-	-	-
item 9 (54)	-	-	-	-	-	-
item 10 (55)	-	-	-	-	.32	.30
item 11 (27)	-	-	-	-	.48	-
item 12 (31)	-	-	.57	.37	-	-
item 13 (10)	-	-	-	-	-	-
item 14 (2)	-	-	-	.31	-	-
item 15 (38)	-	.79	-	-	-	-
item 16 (32)	-	-	-	-	.78	-
item 17 (37)	-	-	-	-	-	-
item 18 (40)	-	-	-	.80	-	-
item 19 (26)	.33	-	-	-	.6	.37
item 20 (41)	-	-	-	-	-	.49
item 21 (7)	.73	-	-	-	-	-
item 22 (46)	-	-	-	-	-	.72
item 23 (47)	.54	-	-	-	-	.37
item 24 (39)	-	.39	-	.51	-	-
item 25 (44)	-	-	-	.56	-	.39
item 26 (56)	.84	-	-	-	-	-
item 27 (48)	-	-	-	.30	-	.54
item 28 (33)	-	-	.83	-	-	-

Factor 1 (explaining 8% of the variance) loads highly on the items 6, 27, 10, 23, 22 and refers to time-gaps combined with identity disturbances [being approached by people whom you don't know, who call you and insist that they have met you before. (6), hearing voices in your head (27), being accused of lying, but not thinking that you lie (10), feeling that you change remarkably in level of performance (23), feeling as if you have two different personalities (22)].

Factor 2 (explaining 9% of the variance) loads highly on items 13, 7, 12, 11 and refers to depersonalization phenomena [you have the feeling your body does not belong to you (13), out of body experiences (7), objects in environment are not real (12), You do not recognise yourself while looking in the mirror (11)].

Factor 3 (explaining 9% of the variance) loads highly on items 17, 14, 20, 1, 19 and refers to a depth of absorption in images and flashbacks [being absorbed in a movie and shut off from the environment (28), intense flashbacks (14), staring, no time sense (20), driving a car automatically (1), ignoring feelings of pain (19)].

Factor 4 (explaining 7% of the variance) loads highly on items 5, 3, 21 and refers to time-gaps [You find new things among your belongings and don't know how they got there (5), you find yourself in some place and have no idea how you got there (3), you talk out loud when you are alone (21)].

Factor 5 (explaining 10% of the variance) loads highly on items 9, 2, 10, 11, 20, 24 and refers to psychoamnesia, (items are somewhat heterogeneous of contents) [you have no memories about important events (9), you have not heard stories just told (16), being accused of lying (10), not recognising oneself while looking in the mirror (11), staring, no time sense (20), do not remember if you have only thought about doing something or have really done it (24)].

Factor 6 (explaining 10% of the variance) loads highly on items 26, 21, 23, 4 and may be named as time-gaps 2 [Finding notes you've made but you don't remember (26), talking aloud when alone (21), changing level of performance (23), finding you have put on clothes you don't remember doing (4)].

Factor 7 (explains 8% of the variance) loads highly on item 8, 15, 24 and refers to a disturbance in reality-discrimination [you don't know if things happened in reality-or in dreams (8), you have been told you do not recognise your own family (15), you don't remember if you did something or only thought about doing it (24)].

Factor 8 (explains 8% of the variance) loads highly on item 28, 12, 4, and refers to derealization experiences. [seeing the world through a fog (28), the world seems to be unreal (12), you don't remember having put on these cloths (4)].

Factor 9 (explains 10% of the variance) loads highly on item 18, 25, 24, 3, 1, 12, 14 and 27. This factor seems to reflect again an absorption in internal mental processes combined with a disturbance in awareness. [absorbed in daydreaming (18), do things you don't remember (25), don't remember if you actually did things or only thought about it (24), finding yourself in a strange place (3), etc.]

Factor 10 (explains 9% of the variance) loads highly on item 16, 19, 11 and 10 and refers to a state of depersonalization and numbness [a known place is unreal (16), you don't feel bodily pain (19), you don't recognise yourselves when looking in mirror (11), you are accused of lying (10)].

Factor 11 (explains 12% of the variance) loads highly on item 22, 1, 27, 4, 2, 20 and 25 and refers to identity disturbances with attention deficits [feeling as if you have two different personalities (22), driving a car automatically (1), hearing voices (27), clothes you don't remember putting on (4), you realize you don't have heard other persons story, while you thought you were listening (2)].

Appendix 5.3: Median D.E.S.-scores in several studies

		N	M
Ensink 1991 The Netherlands	Adult women with a child sexual abuse history (this study)	N=97	M=24
van Otterloo 1987 The Netherlands	Psychology st >.22 yr with dummies	N=28	M=16
van Otterloo 1987 The Netherlands	Psychology st >.22 yr without dummies	N=11	M=23
Cohen 1990 The Netherlands	Jewish victims of the 2nd world war. 1th generation (younger than 12 in 1945 and older than 12 in 1945) and 2nd generation. Mean age= 45 years	N=38	first group M= 8 second group M=30 third group M=18
Ross et al. 1989 United States	College students, mean age= 24	N=345	M=8
Ross et al. 1989 United States	Adolescents, age 12-14	N=168	M=18
Putnam 1986 United States	Normal adults	N=18	M=11

Appendix 5.4: Multiple regression analysis of respondent characteristics and level of dissociation

N=86	level of dissociation				
	ß-Coeff.	partial F-value	Stand. Coeff.	t- value	p-value
Cumulative trauma-score	.08	6.96	.32	2.64	.01
Age start sexual abuse	.38	5.78	.26	2.40	.02
Assaults preceding C.S.A[a]	.60	5.70	.26	2.39	.02
unknown perpetrator	1.17	4.64	.23	2.15	.03
Multiple R=.52		7.37	.28		.0001

[a] C.S.A. means child sexual abuse

Appendix 6.1: Hallucinations in patients with a multiple personality disorder

	N patients with MPD	% auditory hall.	% visual hall.
Bliss, 1980	N=14	64%	36%
Coons & Milstein, 1986	N=?	60%	20%
Putnam et al., 1986	N=100	30%	28%
Kluft, 1987	N=30 (recovered MPD's)	50%	----
Ross, Norton et al., 1989	N= 236	72% voices arguing, 66% commenting hall.	----
Ross et al. (in press).	N=102	91%	----

Appendix 7.1: Child sexual abuse and self-injury

	N	Subjects	Results
Carroll, Schaffer et al., 1980	28	14 self-mutilating and 14 controls, from similar psychiatric population	Significant differences between mutilators and non mutilators in history of physical abuse (p.<.005) and major separations before age of 10. (p<.05), sexual abuse more present in mutilative group (N=small 3)
Adams-Tucker, 1982	22 girls, 6 boys	children of 3-15 years, recruited at psychiatric evaluation.	all sexually abused, chief complaints, self-destruction/suicidal behaviour
Carmen, Rieker & Mills, 1984	188	male and female psychiatric patients	43% sexual or physical abuse. 24% of abused females self-destructive vs 9% of the abused males. 20% of abused patients (males+ female) self-destructive vs 10% of non-abused.
Brière, 1984	153	females in walk-in community health centre	67 have history of child sexual abuse. 31% of abused group desired to hurt self vs 19% of non-abused (χ^2=3.3, p=.07)
Herman, Perry & van der Kolk, 1989	55	29 women, 26 males, ambulant mental health setting	24% sexual abuse, 51% physical abuse. frequent self-injury.
Goodwin, Cheeves & Connell, 1990	20	history of child sexual abuse with prior psychiatric hospitalization	35% self-cutting, 20% head or hand-banging
DeYoung, 1982	45	father-daughter incest, recruited by advertising	57% had been engaged in self-injurious behaviour
Shapiro, 1987	17	father-daughter incest, patients in ambulantory psychotherapy	55% are engaged in self-injurious behaviour
Simpson & Porter, 1981	20	self-mutilating psychiatric patients	50% of the females had a history of child sexual abuse and 65% had a history of physical abuse.

| Favazza & Conterio, 1989 | 240 | female habitual self-mutilators, recruited by advertisement | 29% child sexual and physical abuse, 17% sexual abuse and 16% physical abuse, total 69% with a history of child abuse. |
| Draijer, 1988 | 1054 | sample female community population age 20-40 years | 16% child sexual abuse by family members, self-injury in 4% of the women without child sexual abuse and 9% self-injury with child sexual abuse, p<.01 |

Appendix 7.2: Multiple regression of characteristics child sexual abuse and frequency of self-injury

N=90	frequency of self-injury			
	ß-Coeff.	Std Coeff	t-value	p-value
Physical Aggression Perpetrator (0-6 years)	.78	.30	2.98	.003
Explic. of resistance	-.34	-.29	3.12	.003
Age difference girl-perpetrator	-.84	-.22	2.4	.02
Severity of coercion 3rd perpetrator	.40	.23	2.41	.02
Stepfather	.78	.18	1.99	.04
Age start sex. abuse	.23	.17	1.65	.09
Multiple R=.55		.31		.0001

Appendix 8.1: Childhood trauma and suicidality

	<u>N</u>	Subjects	Results
Brière &Runtz (1987) United States	152	sample of women at crisis counseling department of local health centre	child sexual abuse history 44%, history of suicide attempts in abused group 51%, difference with non-abused group χ^2=4.5, p=.03
Bryer et al., 1987 United States	66	consecutive series of female patients in a private psychiatric clinic	59% child sexual/physical abuse history, suicidality (suicidal ideation/ attempts) in abused group 3,13 x more frequent than in non-abused group, p=.03
Cavaiola & Schiff, 1988 United States	500	adolescent participating in a chemical dependency program	30% child sexual/physical abuse history, 46% suicide attempts in abused group, non-abused group 23%.suicide attempts
Egmond & Jonker, 1988 The Netherlands	158	cohort of female patients admitted in a medical hospital after a suicide attempt	53% child sexual abuse. One suicide attempt 11% child sexual abuse, more than one suicide attempt 34% child sexual abuse, χ^2=10.4, p<.002.
Egmond et al., 1990 The Netherlands	129	follow-up study of patients who made a suicide attempt one year later	repeated suicide attempt within one year, difference child sexual abuse history vs non abuse history, χ^2=4.05, p<.05
Draijer, 1990 The Netherlands	1054	sample female population age 20-40 years	16% child sexual abuse by family members, suicide attempts by women with a child sexual abuse history 14%, non-abused group 4%

Appendix 8.2: Multiple regression of characteristics of child sexual abuse and severity of suicidality

N=90	severity of suicidality			
	ß-Coeff.	Std Coeff.	t-value	p-value
Spouse-beatings	.27	.21	2.18	.03
Age end sexual abuse 1th Perpetrator	.16	.19	1.91	.06
Visual hallucination (sum)	.15	.19	1.89	.06
Intrusiveness of sexual acts	.20	.17	1.69	.09
Multiple R=.45		.21		.0004